# TROUBLED MASCULINITIES: REIMAGINING URBAN MEN

In the contemporary urban environment, the once-dominant concept of a 'masculine' identity is being replaced by alternative ideas of what it means to be a man. *Troubled Masculinities* explores and theorizes the ways in which men who experience marginalization in urban settings reimagine and reconstruct their identities as males.

Through personal narratives and assessments of artistic expression, the contributors present critical and inventive views of masculinity and how it is performed and interpreted in urban space. Set against the backdrop of Toronto, the essays engage with the global and trans-national processes that affect identity and consider how the social hybridity of large cities allows individuals to work against fundamentalist and essentialist attitudes toward gender.

The contributors represent diverse backgrounds, races, ethnicities, sexualities, and gender orientations and they offer unique perspectives on conforming to and breaking away from traditional interpretations of masculinity. The essays in this volume explore the effect of race on one's own understanding of gender identity, the role of performance and visual art – from screen printing to drag king shows – in challenging hegemonic masculinities, and the impact of space – from bubble tea houses to punk rock clubs – on expressions of masculinity.

*Troubled Masculinities* is an important contribution to the growing field of masculinity studies and a valuable assessment of the nature of gender in a modern Canadian urban setting. The collected essays will appeal to a wide audience, from social scientists and artists to activists and general readers.

KEN MOFFATT is an associate professor in the School of Social Work at Ryerson University.

EDITED BY KEN MOFFATT

# Troubled Masculinities

## Reimagining Urban Men

UNIVERSITY OF TORONTO PRESS
Toronto  Buffalo  London

© University of Toronto Press 2012
Toronto Buffalo London
www.utppublishing.com
Printed in Canada

ISBN 978-0-8020-9823-8 (cloth)
ISBN 978-1-4426-1274-7 (paper)

Printed on acid-free, 100% post-consumer recycled paper with vegetable-based inks.

---

**Library and Archives Canada Cataloguing in Publication**

Troubled masculinities : reimagining urban men / edited by Ken Moffatt.

Includes bibliographical references.
ISBN 978-0-8020-9823-8 (bound).   ISBN 978-1-4426-1274-7 (pbk.)

1. Masculinity.   2. Masculinity – Ontario – Toronto.   3. Men – Identity.
4. Men – Psychology.   I. Moffatt, Kenneth James, 1952–

BF692.5.T76 2012      155.3'3209713541      C2011-905603-8

---

University of Toronto Press acknowledges the financial assistance to its
publishing program of the Canada Council for the Arts and the Ontario Arts
Council.

 Canada Council   Conseil des Arts
for the Arts   du Canada

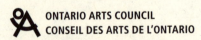 ONTARIO ARTS COUNCIL
CONSEIL DES ARTS DE L'ONTARIO

University of Toronto Press acknowledges the financial support of the
Government of Canada through the Canada Book Fund for its publishing
activities.

*This book is dedicated to Will Munro*

# Contents

# Illustrations

# Acknowledgments

I wish to thank Gil Adamson and Kevin Connolly for their careful review of this manuscript. I would also like to acknowledge George Rallis for manuscript preparation. Many friends supported me along the way, while Jennifer Prest, R.M. Vaughan, Sandra Friesen, Carol Anne Obrien, Jakub Dolejš, Lisa Barnoff, and Sarah Todd have been particularly supportive of this book. They intervened at key points with both concrete advice and emotional support so that the project stayed alive. I would also like to acknowledge the Office of the Dean, Faculty of Community Services, Ryerson University, and the School of Social Work, Ryerson University, for their financial support of the publication.

The authors of Chapter 2 would like to acknowledge financial support for their study from the Senate Committee of Teaching and Learning grant, York University.

Chapter 5 is based in part on research for the PhD dissertation, 'Anti Racism Education in the Cosmopolis: Reflections by Chinese Canadian Elites about Race and Racism,' graduate program in Language, Culture, and Teaching, York University.

Chapter 6 is based in part on research for the Master's thesis, 'Keeping It Real: Drama, Masculinity, and Performance,' graduate program in Education, Ontario Institute for Studies in Education/University of Toronto.

Chapter 7 was originally published in slightly modified form as 'Dancing without a Floor: The Artists' Politic of Queer Club Space,' in *Canadian Online Journal of Queer Studies in Education* 2, no. 1.

Chapter 8 was originally published in a slightly modified form as a chapter in Bobby Noble's *Sons of the Movement: FtMs Risking Incoherence in Post Queer Cultural Landscape* (Toronto: Women's Press, 2006).

Ken Moffat

# Contributing Authors

**Allan Irving**, born in Vancouver, received his PhD from the University of Toronto. He is Professor Emeritus in the School of Social Work at King's University College, University of Western Ontario. He also served as coordinator of the College's Centre for Creativity for five years. Earlier in his career he taught for sixteen ambiguous years at the University of Toronto. A major scholarly interest is how the arts and humanities can be deployed to disrupt the baneful influence of the eighteenth-century Enlightment on social work practice. His publications include *Brock Chisholm: Doctor to the World* (Fitzhenry and Whiteside, 1998) and he is co-editor (with Adrienne Chambon and Laura Epstein) of the Columbia University Press imprint, *Reading Foucault for Social Work* (1999). He enjoys drinking Ontario wine, listening to jazz, and reading Nietzsche and Foucault.

**Carl E. James** is Director of the Centre for Education and Community and Professor in the Faculty of Education at York University, Toronto. He teaches in the Undergraduate Program in Education, as well as in the Graduate Programs in Education, Sociology, and Social Work. His research interests include identification in relation to race, ethnicity, class, gender, and immigrant status; educational access and equity for marginalized youth; the complementary and contradictory nature of sports in the schooling and educational attainments of racialized students; and practices and implications of multiculturalism as a state policy in addressing racism and discrimination. His publications include *Seeing Ourselves: Exploring Race, Ethnicity and Culture* (Thompson Educational, 2010) and *Race in Play: The Sociocultural Worlds of Student Athletes* (Canadian Scholars Press, 2005). Born in the Caribbean, James, a former youth worker, holds a PhD in Sociology and an Honorary Doctorate from Uppsala University, Sweden, where he has been a visiting lecturer in the Teacher Training Department for more than fifteen years.

**Philip Lortie**, born in Chicago, began a career as an actor shortly after graduating from the University of Chicago with a major in English. He co-wrote, directed, and performed in numerous shows with Cardiff Giant Theatre Company, a group he co-founded. For a decade, he worked with several other companies in Chicago and toured with a Shakespearean troupe. Arriving in Toronto in 1996, Philip continued in the theatre, while also pursuing a long-standing interest in education. He has worked as a teaching artist with Learning through the Arts, and taught Drama in the pre-service teaching program at OISE/ University of Toronto. Broadly stated, Philip's research interests are drama and the social. More specifically, his focus is on how the metaphoric performance of drama affects social positioning and opens up new ways of thinking about culture, sexuality, and identity. He is also currently developing projects that, for want of a better term, could be called performance ethnography. He received a BEd degree from OISE/University of Toronto, and completed his MA in Education at OISE/University of Toronto.

**Sean Martin** began his social work career in child welfare and then moved into children's mental health, focusing primarily on children and teens impacted by Attention Deficit Hyperactivity Disorder. He is a Children's Mental Health Therapist at the Scarborough Hospital in Toronto. He is also a Counsellor in the Health and Counselling Centre, University of Toronto, where he provides individual and group therapy to students with mental health concerns. In addition to his private clinical practice, he is a part-time faculty member in the School of Social Work, York University. Born in Kingston, Jamaica, Sean currently lives in Toronto, Canada with his same-sex partner and their four-year-old son.

**Ken Moffatt,** born in Windsor, Ontario, is Associate Professor in the School of Social Work at Ryerson University. He has taught at Kings College, University of Western Ontario, London; Atkinson College, York University, Toronto; Autonomous University of Santo Domingo, Dominican Republic; and Smith College, Northampton, USA. He is former Graduate Program Director at the Ryerson School of Social

Work and the York University School of Social Work. His research interests include identity construction particularly with respect to masculinity; poststructural theory and social intervention; the arts, and symbol creation; and how global processes affect knowledge construction, and contemporary pedagogy. He is the author of *A Poetics of Social Work: Personal Agency and Social Transformation in Canada, 1920–1930* (University of Toronto Press, 2001) and co-author of *Promoting Community Change* (Nelson Press, 2010). He received his PhD from the University of Toronto.

**Bobby Noble** is a FtM transgender person, and an Associate Professor of English, Gender, and Sexuality Studies cross-appointed to the Sexuality Studies Program, School of Women's Studies, and Department of English at York University. Dr Noble's publications include *Sons of the Movement: FtMs Risking Incoherence in a Post-Queer Cultural Landscape* (Women's Press/Canadian Scholars Press, 2006); *Masculinities without Men?* (University of British Columbia Press, 2004), listed as a Choice Outstanding Title, 2004; and the co-edited collection, *The Drag King Anthology* (Harrington Park Press/Haworth Press, 2003), a 2004 Lambda Literary Finalist. Bobby Noble received his PhD from York University, and hails most recently from the West Coast of Canada.

**Henry Parada** is Associate Professor and Graduate Program Director at the School of Social Work, Ryerson University. He is Visiting Professor at the Autonomous University of Santo Domingo, Dominican Republic; National Autonomous University of Nicaragua-Esteli Campus, Nicaragua; and University of La Plata, Buenos Aires, Argentina. His pedagogical and research interests include working with children, family, and communities both in Canada and Latin America. He is the coauthor of *Promoting Community Change* (Nelson Press, 2010). Dr Parada completed his BSW at York University, MSW at the University of Toronto, and PhD in Sociology and Equity Studies at OISE, University of Toronto. He was born in Latin America as Salvadoran, and was transformed textually and culturally into a Latino when he immigrated to North America.

**Gordon Pon**, born in Ottawa, is Associate Professor at the School of Social Work, Ryerson University. His research and teaching interests include anti-racism, anti-oppression, child welfare, and the Toisan Chinese in the diaspora. He completed his BA at the University of

Ottawa, MSW at Carleton University, and PhD in Language, Culture, and Teaching at York University.

**Steven Ruhinda,** born in Uganda, is Counsellor and Professor in the Continuing Education Department at Centennial College, Toronto. His research and teaching interests include global citizenship and social justice education, as well as community development. He completed his BA Honours at the University of Lethbridge, Alberta, and BSW and MSW at York University.

**Frank Sirotich**, born in Hamilton, Ontario, is Director of Community Support Services with the Canadian Mental Health Association – Toronto Branch. Dr Sirotich's research interests include the construction of masculine subjectivities, the psychology and social ecology of crime and violence among persons with serious mental illness, and the efficacy of diversion mechanisms for persons involved in the criminal justice system. Recent publications include 'The Criminal Justice Outcomes of Jail Diversion Programs for Persons with Mental Illness: A Review of the Evidence,' *Journal of the American Academy of Psychiatry and the Law* 37: 461–72; 'Correlates of Crime and Violence among Persons with Mental Disorder: An Evidence-Based Review,' *Brief Treatment and Crisis Intervention* 8: 171–94. He completed his BSW and MSW at York University, and his PhD at the University of Toronto in 2009.

**Joseph Vaz**, born on a ship in the Indian Ocean, is a clinical therapist working with families, couples, and individuals at Durham Region. He has taught at the School of Social Work, Ryerson University. For the past seventeen years he has specialized in working with both victims and perpetrators of domestic violence as well as with men who are in conflict with the law. In addition to his private practice, he facilitates groups that deal with domestic violence for men at the John Howard Society. He has completed BA, Honours (Sociology), BSW, and MSW degrees at York University.

# Contributing Artists

**Michael Comeau,** born in Barrie, Ontario, is a member of the Punchclock Workers Art Collective in Toronto, where he provides culture to the masses in the form of printing, publishing, performance, and parties. He has been an advocate and exhibitor in the Toronto street scene for the past twelve years. He has conceived and created art work for Toronto's well-known events such as Vazaleen, Hump Day Bump, and Kung Fu Fridays. He has shown his art across Canada, the United States, and Europe. (See comeaumichael. blogspot.com.)

**Will Munro,** born in Sydney, Australia (1975–2010), was a visual artist, cultural activist, and community organizer. He graduated from the Ontario College of Art and Design, Toronto, in 2000. He had an interest in performance and creation of spaces that allowed for the expression of a mixture of genders and sexualities. He had shows at Paul Petro Gallery, Mercer Union, and Zsa Zsa Gallery as well as Art in General, New York. A posthumous show of his work entitled Will Munro: Total Eclipse was shown at the Art Gallery of Ontario in 2010. He was nominated for the Sobey Art Prize in 2005.

**Eugenio Salas,** born in Mexico, lives and works in Toronto. His practice is based in digging and testing potential cracks in borders for transgressing social identities. He engages in collaboration and interventions through installation, publishing, and performance. Salas's work has been presented at the New York Art Book Fair, Art Gallery of York University, University of Toronto Art Centre, Mercer Union, and Toronto Free Gallery. His videos have been screened in a number of festivals in Canada, United States, Mexico, Spain, and Italy. (See www.eugeniosalas.org.)

**Vincent and Feria** are an artists' collaborative based in Paris, France. **Françoise Vincent,** born in France, and **Eloy Feria,** born in Venezuela, have been known on the international art circuit since the late 1990s. Vincent is Maître de Conférences Université Rennes 2, Arts Plastiques. Feria is Maître de Conférences Associé Université Paris 8. They represented Venezuela at the Venice Bienniale in 2007 with 'Re-Situation Multipolar.' Vincent and Feria's first Toronto art performance, 'All under the Poncho,' was staged in April 2008 at the School of Social Work, Ryerson University. They have published *Zones de Recherche, Perspective Antarctique 2003–2041* (Paris: Hallaca Press, 2007) and *Post, Post Antartica, Situations Performatives* (Hallaca Press, 2010). Their art practices and research interests include new forms of art work and environmental mobilizations; alterity; interventions in urban settings; and interventions in institutions. (See www.vincent-feria.com.)

**Daryl Vocat,** born in Regina, Saskatchewan, is a visual artist, author, and educator based in Toronto. He completed his BFA at the University of Regina in Saskatchewan and his MFA at York University, Toronto. He has received grants from the Toronto Arts Council, the Ontario Arts Council, and the Canada Council. His main focus is printmaking, specifically screen printing. His work has been acquired by the National Gallery of Canada Library and Archives, the Morris and Helen Belkin Gallery permanent collection, the Saskatchewan Arts Board permanent collection, the City of Toronto Fine Art collection, and the Robert Blackburn Printmaking Workshop collection in New York City. He has had solo exhibitions at Toronto's Thrush Holmes Empire, Open Studio, and York Quay Gallery; SNAP Gallery and Latitude 53 Gallery, Edmonton; Eastern Edge Gallery, St John's; Wilfrid Laurier University Gallery, Waterloo; Artist Proof Gallery, Calgary; Malaspina Printmakers' Gallery, Vancouver; Definitely Superior, Thunder Bay; and Artspace, Peterborough. He has shown in curated shows at the International Print Center, New York, as well as the Robert Blackburn Printmaking Workshop, New York. He received the Robert Blackburn Purchase Award in 2009. (See http://www.darylvocat.com.)

TROUBLED MASCULINITIES:
REIMAGINING URBAN MEN

# Introduction

Within the context of globalization, contradictory social processes are at play. On the one hand, these processes standardize and normalize dominant identities such as masculinity, and on the other, they challenge overarching definitions of these same identities. Even as culturally dominant claims to the proper nature of male and female are reinforced, the very notion that there could be a fundamental and authentic expression of human identity has been brought into question.[1] Within complex urban environments such as Toronto, London, or New York, global dialogue has become the social reality. In these cosmopolitan settings, some women and men are engaged in an escape from the confines of a mainstream expression of culture that has been reified historically both in thought and practice. Artistic and cultural expressions have morphed into a 'plurality of local oppositions' working inside and against the context of social and economic standardization imposed by globalization.[2] Any epistemological exercise that attempts to define a sole expression of what it is to be male is challenged through local cultural practice.[3] These new approaches to identity run counter to the dangers associated with fundamentalism, nationalism, consumerism, and global mass culture, all of which, in their own ways, support the status quo.

This book is focused on a variety of social expressions of masculinity in the global urban environment. The authors and artists represented here are engaged in documenting, imagining, and reimagining local cultural practice. Together their investigations enrich our understanding of masculinity by inquiring about specific local practice of gender in the context of global influence, be it performance, art, education, or dialogue. The male-identified authors and artists collected here write about and engage in local resistance in a plethora of ways to conventional views of masculinity to the point where homosocial cultures and identities come to be seen as syncretic, fragmented, and ambiguous. Those local realities are understood in the context of multiple layers of social influence, including broad forces such as capitalism, racism, and homophobia. A central premise here is that masculinity is a contradictory concept best understood as dangerous, but also revelatory at times. These essays also discuss the liberating processes of modes of masculinity which stand in tension with dominant forms while remaining aware of the ever-confining social constructs that repress alternatives.

With social heterogeneity and global dialogue as starting points for our understanding of globalized urban settings, social practice such as gender is best understood from the viewpoint of migration, exodus, and diaspora.[4] Displacement has become a central metaphor for understanding current social and cultural realities. The dislocation of identity has its roots in the movement of people through physical dispersal,[5] as well as through hybridity caused by exposure to and mixing with other cultures and pluralistic forms of cultural belonging.[6] These processes cause us to become dislocated conceptually from conventional mainstream gendered social practice and thought. Cultural expression has become akin to works of art that 'unravel themselves along receding lines of perspective, the course they follow eclipsing the static forms through which they originally manifest themselves.'[7]

In Canadian urban settings such as Toronto, the notion of a singular definition of maleness has been broadly challenged. The social hybridity of such large cities, with their complex interplay of social relations defined by race, ethnicity, gender, class, and sexuality, has instead led to a multitude of specific masculinities. A number of the authors here theorize about the social construction of masculinity, showing how a person's gender identity is widely affected by social relations.[8] Nicolas Bourriaud, the French writer, theorist, and curator, has coined the term *altermodern* to define a contemporary sociocultural reality marked by plurality. According to Bourriaud, social norms, rules, and expectations in contemporary multicultural urban nodes are defined by their constituents' desire to escape from such reified notions of nation and identity. As a result, it is a mistake to assume that cultural change is predetermined by a single line of sociohistorical change leading to a singular expression of the masculine. Instead each cultural expression is defined through its own historical reference and spatial framework.[9] Bourriaud maintains 'there are no longer cultural roots to sustain forms, no exact cultural base to serve as a benchmark for variations, no nucleus, no boundaries for artistic language.'[10] The many local plural expressions of masculinity develop their own signs and symbols for understanding social reality. Social imaginings within global urban areas are contingent in nature, so much so that they involve 'a positive experience of disorientation through an art-form exploring all dimensions of the present, tracing lines in all directions of time and space.' [11]

This book is distinguished by the range of men who have chosen to participate as authors, artists, or subjects. The contributors and their subjects are diverse in terms of race, cultural heritage, sexuality, and age, and have all crossed boundaries prescribed by normative concepts of masculinity. All of the contributors feel they have had to address dominant male disciplinary codes and paradigms in order to express their own subjectivity. This book presents a central contradiction: while addressing the broad category of identity, the masculine, the authors also illustrate the tenuous, fluid nature of this form of identity. It is for this reason the book is entitled *Troubled Masculinities* – rather than solely documenting dominant male identity, the book discusses the subjectivities of men whose masculinity has been troubled by that dominance. 'Troubled,' in this case, is not meant to express an inherent difficulty in the men's identities in the book. Rather, 'troubled' can be viewed as a productive expression of subversive subjectivities that itself problematizes the discourse of dominance. At the same time, the word suggests an admission among most contributors that their masculine identity is unsettled; unsettled because it is incomplete in some cases while in others it is difficult to express.

The social-institutional relations that are revealed in this book are those of a Canadian urban setting. Our purpose is not to suggest the environment is the root cause of the multiplicity of expressions, but rather to map the terrain of masculinity in an urban area manifestly marked by global forces. By locating masculinity in a particular place – Toronto – the authors reveal some of the local conditions of masculinity while discussing the global and transnational processes that influence the specific construction of masculinity proper. The authors deconstruct historical manifestations of the masculine in Toronto so that the notion of universal rules or structures that fully constrain human relations is brought into question.[12]

A range of cultural practice is explored in an effort to better understand the network of symbols and discourse that contribute to the expression of local masculinities. It is within this discourse that men come to understand themselves. The importance of cultural studies for understanding the masculine comes alive in these studies, whether it be through poetry (Chapters 5 and 9), performance (Chapters 6, 7, and 8), visual art (Chapters 1, 3, 7, and 9), music (Chapters 7, 8, and 9), fiction (Chapter 6 and 9), or narrative (Chapters 1, 2, and 5). Since the widespread visual images of men in media act as formative discourse that contributes to the constitution of our male subjectivities (Chapters 3, 4, and 5), figures are included alongside the text. The art in *Troubled Masculinities* not only helps us to question images of and discourse about the nature of maleness: they are meant to help give us pause to reconsider ideas of masculinity that are often taken for granted. The figures also document particular historical attempts to creatively deal with male expression. At the same time, as is the case in a text with so much diversity of expression, the notions of culture are necessarily challenged.

The authors in *Troubled Masculinities* insert themselves into the text through methodologies such as narrative, auto-ethnography, photography, and poetry. This disruption of the distant, objective authorial voice works against what Julia Kristeva has characterized as the 'pure and clean' body of the male that needs to be protected against incursion and change.[13] When men insert themselves into the text they open themselves up to a 'politics of messiness' and can no longer hide behind the façade of certitude. When men critically reveal themselves as social actors they also run the risk of being subjected to the negative social characterizations attributed to women, such as the shameful, the grotesque, and the abject.[14] By becoming speaking subjects, the authors claim an embodied masculinity based in social relations rather than one defined by events, discourse, and social actions that attempt to lie outside of historical influence.[15] In doing so the authors implicitly or explicitly suggest that their masculinities are open to reflection and re-articulation. By engaging in and being present in their texts, the authors are put in the position of reworking their own subjectivity. They also implicitly agree it is necessary to situate oneself in the narrative, in the social practice that constructs a man, and to declare oneself as a man open to reflection if we are to deal with troubling social issues such as racism, misogyny, and homophobia.

Masculinity is constructed not just through social expectations tied to gender, but also through our attitudes about sexuality, class, race, and ability.[16] While the dominant forms of understanding of the male remain powerful, masculinity is now regularly expressed without an overarching principle. The hope inherent in this interplay of social factors is that the nature of masculine identity is left open to re-signification, allowing the possibility of alternative and/or subversive expressions of maleness. The 'evidence' supplied by this book is that we are in a historical moment, however fleeting it may prove to be, that at times adopts a positive attitude toward complexity and even chaos when it comes to gender.

## Themes and Interconnections

### Hegemonic Masculinity

In spite of the notion that multiple masculinities are not only possible but perhaps even preferable, one troubling legacy of masculinity is its tendency to be socially constructed as a singular, irrefutable, and unchangeable entity. Certain forms of masculinity are always more valued than others. The political purpose of expressing masculinity as if it were a singular entity is to create a dichotomous relationship to the feminine, which in turn maintains gender dominance. A model of masculinity is constructed against which men are expected to measure themselves. The hegemonic image is constructed and understood through its relationship to subordinated masculinities and, most importantly, to women.[17] Men are defined as much by who they are not as who they are; the male identity is defined by the domination of women and of men who are marginalized according to race, sexuality, ethnicity, age, and able-bodiedness.[18]

The definition of dominant social constructions of masculinity can be characterized as a form of hegemony. Derived from an analysis of class relations, hegemony is that sociocultural dynamic through which a dominant group maintains a privileged social position. Hegemonic masculinity is a system of social practice that supports patriarchal legitimacy and guarantees the dominance of men over women and other gender-defined marginal groups. The success of hegemony has as much to do with an implied violence as it does with a claim to social authority. One of the strategies of dominant social constructs of masculinity is a process of overdetermining the nature of men even if they differ according to race, class, or sexuality.[19] The political consequences include social marginalization and oppression.[20]

The concept of the hegemonic male has been a useful way to orga-
nize thought since it deals with unequal social relations associated
with gender while allowing for a multiplicity of masculine subjectivities both in the dominant and subjugated groups. Hegemonic masculinity cannot be reified as a fixed entity to the point where it is present
in all situations at all times. Instead, men adopt a position that varies
according to patterns of social relations. A person can be in a hegemonic social position in one circumstance but not in another, and in this
way hegemony is contestable.[21] While dominance is as varied as
male expression, some aspects of the normative male expressed
through male symbolism have been transmitted across national borders
with the advent of global communication. Certain gendered forms,
such as the athlete or the warrior, continue to be favoured, their attendant desires and subjectivities considered superior to other male
expressions.[22]

Hegemony is also maintained through epistemological constructs.
One such combines concepts associated with identity – 'authenticity,
objectivity, universalism and essentialism' – to construct a hegemonic
male identity. This epistemology serves a strategy of power that pro-
tects the sphere of male dominance, in particular that of white and
middle-class men.[23] Since these four concepts, in conjunction, construct
a form of masculinity that lies outside the play of historical social relations,[24] they rely on a faulty logic to create their concept of the masculine. Since masculinity is assumed to be static, it is also assumed to be
immutable. The male-identified person simply need withdraw from the
politics of the discussion of his own identity.[25] But essentialist definitions of masculinity and unitary forms of masculine practice are not relevant to lived experience. At best, the idealized coherence implied by
this paradigm of masculinity merely addresses conundrums in a sim-
plified fashion. At worst, they obscure troubling social relations based
in gender.[26] While the essentialist approach has served to subjugate
women and other marginalized groups, it has also created constraints
on how men can express their masculinity.[27] It is this limiting of male
expression that we hope to challenge in this book.

Another epistemological construct that serves social dominance is
the idea of the rational man,[28] which characterizes men as reasonable
via an instrumental/emotional dichotomy set up between men and
women. Rational man is associated with technology and science, as
well as the foundation of social progress, each assumed to be a male
enterprise. In the context of advanced capitalism, rationalization,

efficiency, and technique are highly valued, with efficiency becoming a value, both as a means and an end.[29] In Canada, modernity has been particularly amenable to male dominance by certain groups. The modern experiment sought to define social change with respect to progress based on rational interventions that included the management and exploitation of marginalized people. Modern social development, with its technocratic vision of the world, highly values the character traits of self-control, reason, and expertise.[30] By assuming that such traits were masculine, men were able to take control of leading professional roles and public positions, creating social spheres designed to reward those who manifest these traits. The circular logic held that men were best suited to positions of governance, leadership, and control since they had the qualities that were needed for modern leadership. The modern technical rational paradigm has also been used to justify inequality in gender roles. In the context of global capitalism this form of modernism is accomplished by increasing the status of occupations that require technical expertise. The rise of knowledge-based occupations has resulted in a greater stress on credentials, a demand for expertise, and technical skill all based on rational paradigms.[31]

Chris Dummitt argues that in the historical narratives of modernism and development, male identity has been so absent it almost seems as if men are non-gendered beings. This absence of gender has allowed for the domination and exploitation of others. Dummitt further argues that men need to lose their façade of universality and generalization if they are to understand human affairs.[32] When masculinity is perceived as both immutable and beyond reproach, there is an assumption that identity can persist regardless of social influence. But too often, states Dummitt, men are discussed as if they existed outside the relations of gender altogether. This type of separation of men as given and therefore not worthy of reflective consideration occurs both in academic settings and in popular culture.[33] Maurice Hamington and William Cowling similarly argue that 'to be powerful is to be unproblematic.'[34] They add, 'to be white, able-bodied male in western civilization has rendered such bodies unproblematic to the point of invisibility.' This lack of presence of men in the social and cultural domains because of their assumed primacy has made it difficult to discuss masculine identity as a political category. Too often masculinity is a topic that needs no discussion. Male bodies, when not problematized or discussed as subjects of reflection, are assumed to exist as normative while female bodies become the 'wholly other.'[35] The invisibility of masculinity serves the political purpose of conferring privilege on one group: this same process occurs at the intersection of race and gender, such that privilege is conferred upon a certain race, most often white. White men enjoy the freedom of not having to think about either their patriarchal dividends or their racial privilege.[36] They become the 'control' while every other identity is the variation.

As a result of this hegemonic discourse of manliness, certain men are seen as intelligible while others are left out of the discussion. Judith Butler refers to this cultural matrix of power, practice, and thought as the *heterosexual matrix*:

> I use the term heterosexual matrix to designate that grid of cultural intelligibility through which bodies, genders and desires are naturalized . . . a hegemonic discursive/epistemic model of gender intelligibility that assumes that for bodies to cohere and make sense there must be a stable sex expressed through a stable gender that is oppositionally and hierarchically defined through the compulsory practice of heterosexuality.[37]

Máirtín Mac an Ghaill and Chris Haywood agree, suggesting that the matrix uses dyadic representation of sexuality not just to make the heterosexual authentic but, just as importantly, to support gender relations. They argue that the binary construction of male versus female or masculine versus feminine allows for the continuing definition of men as separate from women. This in turn both serves the purposes of domination and limits the expression of both genders.[38]

The authors in this book are involved in the political project of problematizing the notions of the male as well as challenging hegemonic understandings of masculinity. While the book is based on the premise that there is no one thing that can encompass the entity of masculinity,[39] for each of the authors the idea of the hegemonic male identity is real. It exists both as an imaginary concept and as a social construct with material consequences. The hegemony of masculinity is most often associated with the dominant group of men defined as white, middle-class, and heterosexual. The hegemonic male is, in the words of Michel Foucault, an 'episteme,' that is, a general way of knowing that is taken for granted as common sense.[40] This 'general way of knowing' is received through discourse or language tied to relations of power (Chapters 1, 2, and 4), and through symbols and visual imagery that are widely available in the culture (Chapters 3, 5, and 8). The hegemonic male is also constructed through beliefs and values that have become expectations for all men (Chapters 2 and 4). The cultural expectations associated with this definition of the male include the values of productive citizenship, individualism, competition, and progress (Chapters 1 through 4).

The hegemonic male is enacted through a series of social expectations meant to define the proper social roles of minority men such as the Black mentor in Chapter 4, the model minority in Chapter 5, and the productive citizen in Chapters 1 and 2. Unfortunately the logic of these social expectations for good citizenship also perpetuates derogatory social roles and stereotypes such as the aggressive Latino discussed in Chapter 1, the desexualized Asian man in Chapter 5, or the dangerous and immoral Black youth discussed in Chapter 4. These social constructs, taken together, create social mythologies that suggest minority men are in need of correction to engage in citizenship. More importantly, these minority men are also seen as dangerous, abject, and in need of discipline. So, the hegemonic male model is experienced not just as a set of disciplinary practices and environments by minority men, it is also experienced as corrective, since the restrictive range of expressions of masculinity is experienced as disciplinary (Chapters 7 through 9).

Does the hegemonic male exist as a concept prior to such social practice of masculinity? Reading the chapters of this book, I contend that, for minority men, the question of what is a priori is a luxury they do not have, since they constantly have to be on the alert for potential discipline and domination. For example, in Chapter 7 the club space is defined as an elusive space so as not to allow for ossification of the practice and roles of the dominant male within that space. The hegemonic male is also alluded to in the performances within the club, both on stage and among participants in both Chapters 7 and 8. It is in the realm of imagination that the hegemonic male is played with, at times serving as the object of satire while at others reinvented. The performance of the imaginary hegemonic male takes back the power of the real, felt hegemony outside the club.

The hegemonic male position also has social repercussions so dire that one needs to be attentive at all times. In Chapter 4 the masculine expectations of Black youth to conform to the social expectations of the dominant middle-class white male have real consequences concerning their sense of belonging as well as their sense of worth and accomplishment within educational institutions. Similarly, the expectation of the Black male as role model is defined within a white masculine hegemony that refuses to address the social structures of prejudice in defining identity or to make transparent the complicity of the dominant white male group in creating such structures of prejudice.

How are we to make sense of a hegemonic male who is present conceptually, in the imaginary realm, and whose relations of power have real social consequences for men from marginal groups? How do we make sense of it when it is enacted in differing ways among different groups? How does this book enrich our understanding of the hegemonic male and male power? Perhaps social practice is best understood as the act of masculinity in the moment – as Butler explains, the practice makes the man.[41] But there is a network of understanding and social roles present in the consciousness of the minority male as he enacts his range of masculine practice that is associated with the hegemonic male. The practice serves both as an agent of masculine expression and as a construction of each man. At the same time, the social practice of masculinity for minority men represents either a reaction against dominance or a subversive strategy designed to address that dominance.

The hegemonic male is also present in the personal consciousness of the struggle of the man who feels marginalized. Henry Parada (Chapter 1) consciously locates himself within a male milieu that includes violence but has made a political choice to work counter to it. The men in Chapter 2 speak of their struggles within the social expectations of modernist notions of academic careerism while acknowledging that the impulse to belong socially as men continues to drive them to participate in this competitive sphere. In these cases the hegemonic male is seen not as an absolute other, external to the men themselves, but as integral to their social network and their sense of self. So the practice of masculinity that creates the possibility of the man is also imbued at times with a consciousness among minority men of the limits and problems with that practice.

## Gender as Social Practice

Power is very real in gendered relations, and the current social organization of power ensures that women, and some less privileged men, are dominated both in the private and public spheres. Our understanding of male domination can be enriched by taking into consideration specific sociocultural realities, since relations of power are multi-faceted and enacted differently according to social and historical relations.[42] When considered in a global urban context, masculinities are better understood from the point of view of a number of subjects co-existing within a specific historical framework. By looking at what specifically constitutes masculinity, one can account for the variety of forms of knowledge about manliness, the range of discourse that defines the parameters of its expression, as well as the practice and objects that influence that expression.[43] Through specific documentation of a variety of masculinities the authors here try to avoid claims of neutrality, rationality, and objectivity which only serve the purposes of male dominance. The dynamics of gender are best understood 'without having to make reference to a subject which is either transcendental in relation to the field of events or lies in its empty sameness throughout the course of history.'[44]

At times men are involved in a self-conscious exercise of working against universalizing the values, images, and cultural artefacts associated with globalization. In particular, men who have experienced marginalization draw upon that new awareness of power relations to reconsider and restate their identities rather than simply naively taking on socially prescribed masculinities.[45] In this way the local is not overdetermined by global imagery or social expectations, rather the two concepts are mutually constitutive and related and men need not assume that global relations are simply inserted into a person's subjectivities.[46] While global hegemonic gender relations undoubtedly affect the subjectivities of marginalized men through regulation, global processes also offer the possibility of transgression.[47]

How do we capture the troubling power relations of masculinity while respecting multiple expressions of it, especially those that seek to subvert hegemonic forms of the masculine? According to R.W. Connell, gender is both a site of social practice and a way in which social practice is ordered. Gender is both constitutive (constructing the limit of what it is to be male) and productive (creating practice for the production of masculinity) and is enacted through daily expectations and everyday activities.[48] The binary system of male and female, while important to understanding the process of masculine domination, is complicated by practice based on multiple subjectivities that can be both troubling and emancipatory. We can now better acknowledge that the experience of masculinity can be fragmented, contradictory, and subversive in nature.[49] Gender is a social terrain defined by competing images, cultural and social practices that construct both femininities and masculinities. By looking at gender as practice one can analyse a variety of forms of social behaviour, including personal interaction and institutional and governing relations. Gender as practice also allows us to challenge taken-for-granted constructs of the male based on reified, prescriptive symbolism. Gender, while influenced by global sociocultural patterns, is always defined in specific contexts.[50]

Butler explains that 'there is not gender identification behind the expression of gender . . . identity is performatively constituted by the very expressions that are said to be its results.'[51] Drawing upon Nietzsche's notion that there is 'no subject behind the deed,' Butler questions essentialist notions of gender in her influential book *Gender Trouble*. Here she argues that the very act of naming constructs the person as gendered; for Butler, gender is a political act at its moment of constitution, through the act of naming. Rather than imagining that there is a doer either underlying or behind the deed (or act), 'the doer is constituted in and through the deed.'[52] The consequences of the ontological presuppositions of gender are different depending on the individual, as those suppositions are also open to re-articulation. Central to the concept of what is real or true is the interplay of knowledge and power. The way with which both men and women are known, Butler argues, occurs at the point 'acceptable' gender is instituted through the orchestration of power – through naming or act.[53]

Butler argues that the discourse that links power, knowledge, and practice is so powerful that some gendered persons are not represented at all in terms of normative understanding and legitimization. Gendered persons live with received notions of reality and 'with implicit accounts of ontology, which determine what kinds of bodies and sexualities will be considered real and true and which kind will not.'[54] The expression of multiple sexualities/genders is a matter of making present (and therefore intelligible) masculine scripts and norms that have not previously been visible. The politics of this practice are tied to issues of survival; those who understand their gender as non-normative are involved in a struggle to overcome their own sense of unreality, and working toward living without the threat of violence.[55] As Butler says, 'the thought of possible life is only an indulgence for those who already know themselves to be possible. For those who are still looking to become possible, possibility is a necessity.'[56]

Having agreed on the political necessity to question universal notions of gender that promote strategies of power for men, the authors of this book move on to disrupt notions of masculinity from the inside. The philosophical practice of this book, drawing upon the philosophies of Kristeva, Deleuze, Guattari, Foucault, and Butler, is not intended to reflect and document the nature of life for all men, but rather to disrupt the fixed idea of masculinity and make room for new possibilities for its political practice. Rather than summarize abstract models or rigid conceptual frames defining a fixed essence of masculinity – an exercise Kristeva points out has mostly benefited men[57] – this book instead is about thinking differently and trying to reframe our masculine selves entirely.[58] On the one hand, we acknowledge the limits structurally defined positions place on our expressions of masculinity. On the other, those social structural conditions are rejected as determinate, and the idea that a uniform teleological foundation for masculinity exists is rejected outright. Men do not act solely according to general rules of social law; rather they are plural subjects in diffuse relations of power.[59] By refusing to be constrained by preexisting structures, one can start to imagine productive possibilities of masculine expression and to help men claim identities that have been previously hidden, oppressed, misrepresented, or unacknowledged.[60]

The mechanisms of masculinity and male performance discussed by these authors are not easily understood, nor are they always expressed in a simple manner. A major theme running through the book is an interest in making masculinities visible that have been underreported in the historical record as well as in social theory. In this sense, the authors are making such multiple masculinities intelligible so that they are involved in the discourse of gender and so that they can be dealt with through critical reflection rather than rarefied notions of male innocence or distance.

In fact, the nature of masculinity here is sometimes difficult to understand, while at other times it is merely elusive. Some forms of masculinity are barely intelligible simply because they do not have a long history of public expression, and because they have been so actively repressed that they have not been allowed to be present in discourse (Chapters 7, 8, and 9). Some have been barely intelligible because of their pervasive dominance by others (Chapters 4 and 5). At the same time, the authors of the essays in this book reject popular male notions of certitude by discussing the ambiguous, the fractured, the elusive, and the poorly understood. This refusal to come to definitive conclusions about what is masculine in Toronto not only accurately reflects the current pluralistic reality of the city, it also is a political method meant to work against the closed, knowing stance so often associated with masculinity (Chapters 2, 7, and 9). For others, the full performance of the male is withheld, consciously awaiting the proper adjustment of social relations that allows full engagement of men from minority positions (Chapter 1).

## Outline of the Book

Henry Parada (Chapter 1) illustrates how he has been constructed as an immigrant, that is, as a person who does not conform to a proper, normative image of masculinity, and is therefore treated as if not authentic in his male identity. He points out that the stereotype of a macho Latino man varies according to location, whether that location is a social grouping or a nation state. Using standpoint theory he challenges demands on the immigrant male to reveal the suffering that must be endured to be accepted as authentic, and questions whether the confessional mode is merely one more way of disciplining men with minority status. He argues instead for parrhesia or plain talk as a way for Salvadoran men to speak about and construct their masculinity.

In Chapter 2, authors Frank Sirotich, Sean Martin, Steven Ruhinda, Joseph Vaz, and Ken Moffatt, a diverse grouping in terms of race and sexuality, challenge the notion of a singular male identity. The authors argue that through a series of strategies interrelated with power and knowledge, men are able to construct a wide variety of male identities. The authors focus on silence as one such mode of masculinity. Rather than considering the singular silence that defines a stereotypical male, the authors discuss the many silences that can be seen to construct masculinity. There is a contradictory nature to silence, valued for the social protection it offers while also allowing for feelings of liberation when the silence is broken. As with so many concepts addressed in this book, silence here is a fluid concept; it 'bleeds.' Implicit within this definition of silence is the concomitant yearning to break through the silence and speak.

In Chapter 3, Ken Moffatt interprets the art of Daryl Vocat to discuss masculinity as network of difference. A subversive side of Vocat's work is seen in the manner with which he uses universal symbolic imagery associated with homosocial bonding. By reinventing the images of popular culture and the Boy Scout movement he reveals desires that are often either hidden or poorly understood. Moffatt discusses how Vocat pays tribute to that which is masculine, while also bringing it into question, often in a playful manner. He suggests Vocat's work shows how the masculine is tied to a realm of desire that is not as easily inscribed or coded as one might believe, and is best understood as a network of connections with ambivalent relationships.

Carl James (Chapter 4) reveals the interconnection between gender and race in his discussion of Black youth. More specifically, he argues that the call for Black role models to guide Black youth is a manifestation of a new racism. Blaming the social alienation of Black male youth on the community's lack of fathers, disintegrated families, and on Black culture in general allows the enduring problem of racism to remain obscured. It is, in effect, a convenient way of maintaining a social order that privileges whites. If we see Black youth's problems as situated entirely within the Black community, then structural racism and white dominance need not be addressed. The terrible reality, James argues, is that Black mentors become corrective agents and role models within their community, encouraging Black youth to adjust to the dominant standards of white, middle-class men. He argues for a new form of mentorship that includes a critical awareness of the social demands on Black men as well as the prejudicial treatment of Black male youth.

Gordon Pon (Chapter 5) takes up the decades-old debate in Chinese North American communities around Asian masculinities. He disrupts cultural-nationalist responses to racist portrayals of Asian men, and instead promotes David Eng's queer theory for understanding racial formation processes in Canada. This lens reveals that Asian masculinities are constituted transnationally and globally, and are never allowed to exist outside of racialized, gendered, sexualized, and classed discourse. Drawing on interviews with Chinese Canadian youth living in Toronto, Pon helps us to understand how the youths' subjective masculinities are imbued with class privilege, double-consciousness, ambivalence, and rage. Yet, while they express critical understandings of power and domination, the Asian youth remain pro-capitalist. The author concludes that grappling with how Asian masculinities are implicated in global capitalism and culture can offer important windows into anti-oppression perspectives and consciousness-raising.

In Chapter 6, Philip Lortie, an actor, playwright, and educator, takes the construction of masculinity to the level of the imaginary. By reconstructing real historical moments as fictional dramas he challenges the notion of masculine voice as reportage. Lortie uses drama with students as he unveils how men and boys trap themselves in the construction of male identity. The importance for the man to perform for others, most often other men, becomes clear through this dramatized ethnography.

In Chapter 7, Ken Moffatt explores a queer social event called *Vazaleen*, organized by Toronto community activist and artist Will Munro. The author explores this space where the ontological foundations of being are refused. Based on honouring specific sensuous relationships, the club space contributes positively to queer transformative politics and cultures of diversity through the reconstitution of gender. The gender relations within that space are both real and acted out as fictions. Munro's *Vazaleen* is seen as an example of a social event in which a man is given a chance to experience his masculinity anew in the presence of other genders.

Bobby Noble (Chapter 8) documents three waves, or historical moments, of drag king performance in Toronto. He shows how the first wave is lesbian-identified, how the second integrates gay male and transgendered masculinity, and how the third wave – 'boys to the power of three' – challenges the intelligibility of gender as it exists now, with the performance of the male defined by ambivalent paradox and contradiction. The manner in which the current wave of drag kings renders gender identifications incoherent does not create chaos, but rather offers a plethora of gender identities that are productive while being incoherent. And each wave of drag king performance shares with the others a proximity to masculine discourse. Both those performers who identify as masculine and those who dis-identify challenge the larger problematic cultural scripts of gender.

In Chapter 9, Allan Irving has written a discourse about growing up male in Toronto in the 1950s and 1960s. At the same time, his chapter is a narrative about his intense cross-dressing urges and practice, and desires to be a woman. This story draws on Nietzsche, Bataille, Foucault, Beckett, and Butler as well as the personal journals of his parents. Rather than being a modernist tale that provides explanations through cause and effect, the narrative speaks to various moods, desires, and life experiences that have arced through his mind and body to create a life. It is about the beating of his heart toward the end and darkness.

## The Elusive Quality of Desire

Masculinity is a conceptual terrain rife with disruption. In these essays, we have hoped to engage in what Jacques Derrida has called a strategy of 'exploiting the target against itself,' the masculine used as 'the basis of an operation directed against it.' It is hoped that within the concepts of the masculine discussed here there can be a strategy that seeks the 'cryptic reserve of something utterly different.'[61] This might be best illustrated in the art discussed in Chapter 3, where a universalized reductive style of imagery is used to express secrets within the homosocial environment of the Boy Scouts. The attempt to confine gender within a categorical reference point can now be challenged from within the category itself. In this context, the act of revealing and discussing multiple constructions of the masculine becomes a subversive act.[62] The appeal of this kind of subversion lies in the thought that 'shattering the law might be less groundbreaking than forcing the same law to recognize subjects that it had tried to reject.'[63]

This strategy of subversion also yields some surprising insights into such things as the elusive quality of productivity and desire. Arguably, every chapter speaks to desire whether implied or explicit while refusing an ontological foundation for that desire. There seems to be a desire to belong that exists prior to coding and social norms, whether it is the yearning for acceptance described by the men in Chapter 2 or the desire to be a woman described by Irving in Chapter 9. To be a man, as it turns out, is not simply about social constraint or dominance. This elusive male desire might best be looked at as something not easily defined by discourse and codification. And it may best be known through practice that seems to have no purpose (because it is not intelligible) or is ambiguous (because the code for it either does not exist or is for the moment poorly understood). Marginal men must practise their masculinity at times as if it were unknown or creative: 'The only way to confront omnipresent power is to repeat its signifiers disobediently, thereby engaging in discourse-based acts of subversion.'[64] The assumptions of normalized gender roles, practice, and behaviour must sometimes be dealt with through protest and rejection of those expectations.[65]

The promise of places such as Toronto in the current historical moment includes the promise of reconstituting identities, in this case masculine identities. It is also the possibility of imagining power as diffuse. The authors in *Troubled Masculinities* speak from specific, embodied male social locations to disrupt prescribed and prevailing notions of masculinity. They speak as embodied male voices involved in connective global relations. As speaking subjects, they choose to articulate the masculine as contingent, incomplete, and ambiguous. For the authors of this book, crossing the borders of masculinity is both a personal and social crossing, whether it's through emotions, gender, body, or geography. This form of border crossing at times has no final destination; it continues daily in the present.

While dominance is acknowledged throughout the book, the authors collected here are more interested in how masculinity can be created and co-created in enclaves, social spaces, and through specific acts in spite of, and at times in resistance to, that dominance. The promise implied in each author's point of view is a refusal to accept the troubling dominant discourse of male identity, especially when it has been associated with power that has been concentrated in troubling ways. In a sense, each author shares a dual consciousness; on the one hand understanding that male dominance exists, while on the other, experimenting with masculinity associated with subversion and resistance. Through aesthetics and identity reconstruction new citizenships and subjectivities are made possible.[66] *Troubled Masculinities* sets the groundwork for collapsing male identities and points to the possibility of breaking down the ontological certainty of masculinity. It is through such deconstruction and reconstitution that I suspect we may begin to find points of commonality and of alliance with women and with other men.

# 1 The Mestizo Refuses to Confess: Masculinity from the Standpoint of a Latin American Man in Toronto

HENRY PARADA

> It happens that I get tired to be a man navigating in the water of the beginning and the ashes
>
> *Pablo Neruda*

> A discourse of trauma came to displace political discourses about pacifism and anti-imperialism
>
> *Charles Taylor*

> The obligation to confess is now relayed through so many different points, is so deeply ingrained in us, that we no longer perceive it as the effect of a power that constrains us
>
> *Michel Foucault*

## Introduction

I am writing this chapter experiencing an internal tension. One side of the tension involves my commitment to autobiography, history, and ethnography based on feminist ideologies that encourage me to speak from my own voice and locate myself within its discourse. This process of 'reconstructive self-disclosure' encourages those who have been silenced to challenge and deconstruct discourse. The other side of the tension is a kind of strategic self-protection, my resistance to disclosure, and to confessional practice commonly used to provide legitimacy to my statements.

Such resistance to disclosure is a form of self-protection from both real and imagined experiences that have affected how I interact with others. I am trying to be more definitive in my approach to autobiography, coming from a clear and/or politically sound point of view, but the tension remains. It is difficult to write neatly about life, it being so messy, and that messiness enters the self-reflective process when I write my own narrative.

In this chapter, I write an autoethnography of my masculinity as a man of Latin American origin who immigrated to Toronto in the early 1980s. I draw upon my personal experience including my immigration process, my settlement, development of my transnational identity, as well as my engagement with the Salvadoran community. I also draw upon my experience as a professional social worker including work in the fields of child protection, sexual abuse, family reunification, and family counselling. Finally I draw upon my research on international immigration within the Latin American context. Taking into consideration the social construct of myself as an immigrant man, I think through the manner with which I engage in speech acts in the context of Toronto. When I was invited to contribute to this book, I admit to being puzzled as to what I should write about. Similar to the way in which the discourse of whiteness makes itself invisible by asserting its normalcy,[1] the manner in which the discourse of masculinity has shaped my identity has largely been invisible to me.

In fact, I have largely exercised the 'privilege of ignorance,' under which my masculinity has been, as Shannon Sullivan and Nancy Tuana write, 'a form of ignorance that is produced and sustained and play[s] a role in knowledge practices.'[2] Lorraine Code has argued that simply '[acknowledging that such ignorance is culturally produced or] socially-culturally pervasive neither excuses nor exculpates its particular, individual episodes, even though it may offer a partial explanation and open new sites of analysis.'[3] All three authors discuss the epistemologies of ignorance with respect to race and gender. I have used this approach to knowledge-construction to challenge my own assumptions about maleness. The struggle to disclose my masculine self is evident throughout the chapter as I challenge my 'privilege of ignorance.' At the same time, I take a posture of refusing to confess as an immigrant male from El Salvador in a manner that allows me to be reconstructed by others.

This is not to say that I am unaware of the social construction of gender and male privilege, nor of my own privilege as a male in certain contexts. At the same time, I have come to see the embodiment of my particular form of masculinity, that is, of a 'Latin' man living in

Toronto. My understanding is that specific social relations have (re) constructed me into a 'masculine brown body,' so that others have assumed my embodiment to be an expression of 'machismo.' This reconstruction has intersected with my experience as a racialized immigrant from El Salvador.

I will also bring into focus some forms of oppression that racialized bodies may face in Toronto through discussing how I have experienced it personally. I do not write this from what Nietzsche calls the *vulgarity of mind*, the assumption that personal accounts must be full of suffering as evidence of truth. Nor do I construct my politicized identity on the foundations of victimhood or trauma discourse.[4] Rather I offer my auto-ethnographic account of masculinity from the point of view of parrhesia, which Foucault discusses at length in *The Hermeneutics of the Subject*. Parrhesia for Foucault is 'the act of telling all,' through plain speaking, and speaking openly.[5] It is a speech act compelling us to say what has to be said and/or what ought to be said. While confession has a passive quality and puts the confessional speaker in a position of dependence, parrhesia entails a more direct and active voice. While confession is laden with psychological freight, parrhesia conveys a more social and political imperative. Although there were different ways of practising parrhesia in the ancient Greek world, Foucault preferred the strain that included the defying of conventions and encouraged agonistic debate.[6] In this chapter I use plain speak and parrhesia interchangeably.

## Masculinity from the Racialized Standpoint

I begin my analysis from the standpoint of a racialized man living in Toronto, a city largely dominated politically, socially, and culturally by discourse on whiteness. Following Dorothy Smith,[7] I use this position as a point of departure toward an exploration of the process of textual transformation, and of shifting identities assigned to me in my everyday experience. I also draw on Fairin Herising's understanding of the 'politics of location' whereby the subject uses 'means of interrupting and accounting for the formulations and constructions of one's social political locations.'[8] Critical reflexivity has helped me to understand the politics of location of a Latin American man within the context of Toronto, Canada. This provides a means to interrogate the complex meanings of 'Latin' masculine discourse. The self-reflexive process also allows me to speak about the multiple forms of power relations that co-construct me as a man.[9] In particular, I speak about Salvadoran experience due to the experience of social cultural disruption I have experienced both in El Salvador and in Toronto.

Nicholas Holt describes autoethnography as 'a genre of writing and research . . . in which authors use their own experiences in a culture reflexively to look more deeply at self-other interactions.'[10] My sense of masculinity has been influenced through my continued contact with the Latin American diaspora, and my many trips to Central and South America as a Canadian researcher. I am one of the group of immigrants who experience 'transnationalism from below,' one of those 'ordinary people, whose macro and micro activities generate . . . multiple and counter-hegemonic forces . . . whose daily life . . . [involved] the development of cultural hybridity, multi positional identities.' These male hybrid identities intersect with other forms (race, sexual orientation, ability, class) and are disconnected from the essential notion of belonging to a particular nation or particular space.[11]

Judith Butler's concept of how subjectivity is performatively constituted is helpful in exploring how behaviours, ideas, and expressions that are considered acceptable[12] in the South (in my case, El Salvador, Mexico, and Dominican Republic) are considered dubious, and looked upon with suspicion in the north (in my case Toronto) and vice versa. The construction of my masculine identity is a hybrid of that found both in the Latin American diaspora and in Toronto. I find my identity as a Salvadoran has been transformed into that of a 'Latin macho man' through my immigration to North America. And that 'macho-ness' is a social construction of my identity that is created performatively, through both my own self-conscious acts and the acts of others in interaction with me. I offer this narrative to help us reconsider troubling social relations that allow the social construction of macho-ness to further marginalize immigrant men.

## The Diaspora: Negotiating Identity in a Fragmented Community

The Latin American community in Canada is relatively small. Daniel Schugurensky and Jorge Gininiewicz note that in 2001 the census showed that at the time there were more than 220,000 people of Hispanic origin living in Canada. Although Latin American immigrants, including Salvadorans, are a relatively new group, we have become the third largest minority group in Canada.[13] The settlement process of

Latin Americans has been challenging because of lack of meaningful employment and downward social mobility due to unemployment rates that are higher than other visible minority groups.[14] Latin American youth experience a 46 per cent dropout rate from Canadian schools.[15]

Luisa Veronis argues there are differing forms of transnationalism among different immigrant groups. Salvadorans in Canada fall into the 'new transnationalism' including: 1) strong family and emotional affiliations with the country of origin; 2) use of cheap technology – Skype, fax, and phone contracts; 3) close awareness of the different political, immigration, and security aspects affecting our country of origin; and 4) the high scale of remittances benefiting family and friends in the country of origin.[16] In fact 18 per cent of the national Gross Domestic Product in El Salvador comes from remittances.[17] In addition Salvadorans have created a number of hometown associations; 295 in the United States and 14 in Canada were reported in 2007.[18] In addition we bring personal legacies from our countries of origin. We are not a self-sustaining community, and rely heavily on the 'mainstream' society for survival. My experience is typical of many Spanish-speaking people who maintain strong attachments to their country of origin; many Latin American immigrants are transnational, travelling back and forth between Canada and Central and South America regularly.[19]

Although much has been written about the transnationalism of Latin Americans in the United States, little has been written on the subject in Canada.[20] Luin Goldring separates Canadian literature dealing with the Latin American diaspora into three categories: 1) early work on refugees; 2) census data about Latin Americans focused on employment, occupational mobility, and income; 3) recent immigrants to Canada no longer limited to refugees.[21] Latin Americans in Toronto are building a new narrative that allows us to understand ourselves in the context of our new Canadian home. Torontonian/Latin American academics such as Mirna Carranza and Judith Bernhard[22] have begun to research and write that narrative. Since Latin Americans are a relatively small immigrant group within Toronto, and Salvadorans a fraction of the total Spanish-speaking population, our Canadian/Salvadoran identities have largely been reshaped within white Canadian society. This reshaping has been written about by Carranza.[23] Authors such as Carranza, Bernhard, Patricia Landolt, and I are in process of considering the tone, purpose, and value of the narrative, especially when spoken in a context where further marginalization may occur due to contact with 'mainstream' North American culture.[24] I hope to contribute to my colleagues' work in imagining how to speak so that the cultural, social, and political are all present in the narrative.

I, as an embodied man, am also an immigrant who has been reconstructed in different textual institutional realities and so I experience a fluid intersection of my masculinity (my position in gender relations) with my race and ethnicity.[25] My interactions with others in Toronto also concern how the discourse and practice of whiteness affect my racialized body. Firstly, I must deal with expectations placed on me by men within the hegemonic white masculinity.[26] At the same time, I must interact within a circumscribed space of immigrant men. As a racialized man it is also incumbent upon me to present myself as capable and productive. When I interact with white people in Toronto I am conscious of the expectation that I must be seen to be effective and to 'function properly' if I am going to be considered a good citizen of the city. How I negotiate spaces defined by people perceived by me to be more powerful is key to the understanding of my masculinity.

When living and travelling in South America I am met with an entirely different set of interactions, and thus my social identity is constructed in a different manner. While in the Caribbean and South America, class and gender are the most dominant categories in my social interactions with others. In those spaces I embody a hegemonic masculinity through which class is reproduced both consciously and unconsciously. Furthermore, the personal and political dynamics of my masculine self are influenced by *Canadianization*, in this case, the influence of living in Toronto as a dynamic space where ideas of gender and masculinity have evolved differently from those in El Salvador and Mexico. And I work to politically engage in the discourse that implies a criticism of hegemonic masculinity in both Canada and Latin America. In this manner, I am neither completely a Latin man nor am I completely a Torontonian man. I have an amorphous, hybrid, indefinite self in Toronto, and am a mestizo[27] in both the Latin American and Toronto contexts.

Mestizaje and indigenismo are discursive forms used to address the problematic issue of neocolonialism and racism. On the one hand, these terms refer to the inclusion of indigenous people with white people within the racial practices of Latin nations. On the other hand, they exclude those indigenous elements from active participation in this nation building. Mestizaje discourse was introduced to the official languages of Latin America (particularly in Mexico, Central America,

Bolivia, and Peru) as a way to determine citizenship. Mestizaje discourse sought to correct the brutal forms of racism against indigenous people that prevailed at the end of the nineteenth century. But mestizaje and indigenismo were concepts used to construct Latin American nations in a manner that acknowledged the presence of 'Indians' but continued to exclude them in all forms of benefits defined for citizens.[28]

The above nation-building discourse in Latin America is codified in national constitutions that determine the way nations deal with indigenous people. Thus a contradiction exists in Latin America. Although indigenous people seem to have disappeared into the official discourse, they are visible as a group who appear to passively accept these new nations. The last two decades have seen a challenge to this discourse of passivity through the actions of mestizo people.[29] This is one reason that the passive concept of confession is impossible to accept for an indigenous Salvadoran such as myself but rather I need to engage in a form of citizenship marked by plain talk or parrhesia.

In this case, I use mestizo, one who belongs, and does not belong, as an identity on the frontier of hybridity in both the south, as represented by El Salvador and Mexico, and in the north, as represented by Toronto. In the case of Toronto, mestizaje is the experience of not being white while claiming a rich subjective contextualized reality of otherness. The historical Latin American experience of exclusion and an assumed passivity makes one consciously mestizo in Toronto to avoid the obliteration of identity. I have included the imagery of the artists Vincent and Feria from France and Venezuela, whose work represented Venezuela at the Venice Biennial in 2007 with the image entitled *Mestizo*. I include this piece, which I saw in person, because the artists play on the plurality of location in the fluorescent construction.

By speaking to the many identities of mestizo, the artists announce the presence of the transnational Latin diaspora to which I belong, and the mestizo identity which I share. While both constructing and expressing the hybrid identity of the mestizo, the artists, one of whom also self-identifies as a part of the Latino diaspora, make visible the identity through plain talk in the Spanish language.

## So You are Latin, eh? From El Salvador to Toronto: The Making of a 'Latin' Body

In Toronto, I have experienced my masculinity reconstructed as something different from the one I assumed I had upon my arrival from

Figure 1: Vincent and Feria, *Mestizo* (Mestizo, I am coming from Black, Indian, Spanish, and Arab) (1998–2007). Courtesy of the artists.

Central America. My identity has been a site of struggle and contestation, not an essence but a fluid positioning.[30] It is also a process that is never complete, but is in constant state of becoming.[31] My masculinity continues to be a process of hybridity, the result of occupying several social and geographical spaces, each calling for a particular form of masculinity. I have culturally translated my masculinity through my relations with others in the same way Homi Bhabha talks about how marginalized persons translate their racial identities through relations with others.[32]

I left El Salvador in the early 1980s while the country was embroiled in a bitter civil war. The brutality of that war alone was enough to disrupt my sense of identity as a mestizo Salvadoran, and the masculine identity I embodied during the first twenty-five years of my life. While in El Salvador, I adopted the identity of a proud university-educated man, but upon landing in Toronto, I was immediately seen as an immigrant, refugee, and worker. Repeatedly, in my interactions with others,

I was confronted with the assumption that I was an uneducated Latino. Often my behaviours and expressions were labelled with the pejorative adjective macho. Given the tendency of white Torontonians to essentialize my 'self' as the macho Latin American, it now strikes me as surprising that I never questioned my sense of masculinity. Instead, I questioned my racialized immigrant self. Richard Connell defines masculinity as the 'configuration of gender practice[s] which embody the currently accepted answer to the problem of the legitimacy of patriarchy, which guarantees the dominant position of men.'[33] In this light, my masculinity has been a position of relative power, regardless of how the 'brownness' of my body, my accent, or my status as an immigrant might construct me as *other*. I have unconsciously done what Sherene Razack describes as running to the margins, that is, occupying a place on the margins of social groupings while negotiating my sense of self in my new city.[34] Furthermore, I chose to negotiate and trouble my sense of self as an immigrant and racialized person while imagining that my masculinity had remained intact. It seems I was protecting my epistemology of ignorance, as defined at the beginning of this chapter, with respect to gender. At times I was implicated in a troubling type of search for personal innocence by reflecting on my marginality through race and immigrant status while reflecting little on my dominance through masculinity. I clung to the power that I could strategize socially.

Since my arrival in Toronto twenty-five years ago, I have engaged in a continual process of developing a reflexive version of my new self. Through the writing of this chapter I seek to do what I have not done in the past, that is, to look at my masculinity, to consider the nexus of how my identity is dominant as a male, university-educated professor while living the context where my Latino masculinity is constantly being interrogated by others. I see this autoethnography of my masculinity as a further step in this self reflexive project.[35] This is not to say that I have completely lost track of my 'old self' from El Salvador, but rather that I have had to undertake the task of developing a new narrative for that self in a new context.

I have also had to renegotiate aspects of my identity that I had formerly viewed as solely related to my status as a racialized immigrant or 'Latino.' Over time, I have had to come to terms with my *Canadianization*, since my academic career has repeatedly taken me back to Central and South America. How do I understand the problem of negotiating masculinity in Toronto, having now spent half of my life in El Salvador, Mexico, and the Dominican Republic, and the other half in Toronto? How do I, as a Latin American man living in Toronto, embody a notion of masculinity? And do I embody the hegemonic masculinity of Latin America or am I a representative of masculinity in the diaspora?

As a transnational man who does not belong in any one space, I am a combination of both global and multiple local realities. A masculine body can be understood as a process. That is, a 'body-reflexive practice ... bodies that can be seen to be located in a complex circuit as simultaneously both objects and subjects of social practice.'[36] Moya Lloyd uses Julia Kristeva's notion of *subject in process* to capture the idea that 'subjectivity is constituted by language, power, discourses [that are] inessential and thus perpetually open to transformation.'[37]

Máirtín Mac an Ghaill and Chris Haywood also argue that economic, social, and political global processes are not neutral, and that they have an impact on what it means to be a man or woman at both the local and global levels. Globalization and localization should be understood as phenomena that produce identities and differences, including within masculinity.[38] As a Latin American man living in the diaspora, but actively challenging the forces of globalization through my work in Central and South America, I have experienced global, social, and cultural transformations that have involved fragmentation, dislocation, and mobility. In other words, though my work I also am experiencing the effects of globalizing forces on my own sense of self, one result being a fragmented masculinity.

As an aspect of identity, masculinity is developed in dynamic relationship with others within a particular space. The embodiments of various socially constructed discourses may be understood as sites upon which there are differing epistemological interpretations enabling social categories and through which fragmentation of politics is played out. Such a definition allows me to talk about the fluidity of masculinity both in different contexts and within the relations of power that function inside each particular context. This definition of masculinity allows me to politically engage in epistemological disputes of my identity by experimenting with how I speak to it.

Butler describes the construction of a gendered subjectivity as arising through the practice of performativity.[39] Butler and Edie Sedgwick have investigated performativity in feminist, gay, lesbian, and queer studies in order to theorize about sexuality and gender.[40] I draw upon their work to discuss masculinity and the construction of a Latin man. For Butler gender is not an identity shared by either men or women as there is no fundamental essence to describe a man or woman. Instead, she argues gender is based on social and cultural production. Gender is not latent but enacted, defined through political and cultural cooperation rather than through any inherent biological difference.[41]

Butler has argued that in the process of naming we engage in the process of freezing relations. When brown bodies from Latin America are quickly defined as macho Latin men, this naming 'tends to fix, to freeze . . . singular kinds of being and this name carries within itself the movement of a history that it arrests.'[42] David McInnes uses the naming of a child as a *sissy boy* as an example of this process. This analysis can be useful to understand the process reconstructing the notion of Latin masculinity as machismo. By drawing upon Butler's theory I can better understand how other people construct me as a macho Latino. I can also help us to reconsider the word macho so that we can take pause in the service of wondering about Salvadoran masculinity in Toronto.

The key question in the construction of Latin male identity in the diaspora is how a Latin man becomes macho. McInnis argues such a transformation happens through processes of 'recognition and witness,'[43] relying on social structures and the discourse of gender and race. Through complex social processes, an acceptable masculinity is constructed that is in opposition to the perceived deviant Latin masculinity which needs to be controlled and placed under surveillance. To enable such social control I have been repeatedly assigned a label – *macho man,* a deviant one, and a socially constructed *other.* I hope to reveal one manner with which macho is a construction in my attempt to engage in the reconstruction of new masculinities. *Latin man* is *othered* based on so-called acceptable forms of masculinity – white masculinity. *Latin man* is conceptualized as a problematic masculinity that is potentially dangerous and violent. *Latin man* needs to be under constant surveillance due to his brownness, his loudness, and his refusal to talk about himself.[44] Studies done in Latin America regarding masculinity have questioned this approach of conflating Latino masculinity with machismo. In Latin countries the notion of masculinity is in process of reconstruction. For example, Rafael Montesinos argues that the traditional model of Latin American masculinity is in a process of diminishing without finding an alternative model. Latino men seek new forms of identity in order to enable us to recognize ourselves as being part of new groups with intersections of class, race, and sexual orientation. In addition, this seeking of new forms of masculinity also allows Latino men to distinguish themselves from the *other*, that is, the otherness of women, based on features that are not strictly biological.[45]

In the context of Toronto, I am aware that aspects of my Latin American identity construct me in a manner that is different from other men. At times, this difference has been used to silence me. At other times my difference has been used to promote my 'expert' knowledge on issues that I am presumed to understand from my position as a racialized immigrant, a Latino, and a refugee. Manuel Salas and Alvaro Campos describe the 'dominant masculinity' as a social strategy by which certain men recognize and respect other men.[46] It is an implicit alliance in which most men participate consciously or unconsciously. Depending on which space I occupy, I am either part of this alliance, located on the margins, or excluded from it altogether. Over time I have learned to identify the aspects of my difference in Toronto as my Latino self – a hybrid identity of a Canadianized Salvadoran man – the mestizo. As a mestizo I am a man who at the extremes finds himself either allied with male dominance or excluded from it. To deal with these contradictions I must understand my identity as mestizo not only in terms of race or citizenship but also mestizo in terms of interpersonal social power relations. In the following I outline two examples of performativity – the reactions to my accent as well as to my expressions of intensity – that have contributed to the construction of myself as *other* in the some contexts in Toronto.

**Sounding Latino**

One of the personal qualities that sets me apart in Toronto is my Spanish accent. My strong accent has been a 'problem' that has identified me as an outsider for the many years I have lived in Toronto. During an interview with an immigration officer upon landing in Toronto, I indicated that I wanted to teach. His response was to say, 'You have to get rid of the accent, because I wouldn't like my children learning to speak as you do.' Thus began the process of my reconstruction as a mestizo in Toronto. I had never considered my accent before. Since my goal was to teach at the university level, the most striking element in the immigration officer's comment was the assumption that I would be teaching children. Shortly after the incident with the immigration officer, a well-meaning white friend suggested that if I did not want to have problems getting a job I needed to go to a speech pathologist to rid myself of my accent. This problematization of my accent continues today in my role as a university professor. At the university where I teach there is a program that encourages those professors who speak English as second language to improve their accents. In this program professors learn how to vocalize words with correct English intonation. Students have complained many times that my accent impedes their understanding of what I am saying. One student expressed it by saying, he is a nice person but 'his teaching is shit, I cannot understand what he says.' In this manner, the focus of others on my accent becomes a social practice that creates my identity through reiteration, that is, performativity.

## Expressions of Intensity

Growing up in El Salvador and Mexico, I was socialized to value certain traits, some of which are considered stereotypes of Latin American men. Ideas, expressions, and behaviours that I understood as positive cultural attributes in El Salvador and Mexico have been recast negatively in Toronto. Perhaps the most common characteristics valued by Latin men are those associated with macho aggressiveness. In many Toronto contexts, male assertiveness associated with enthusiastic engagement is seen instead as aggressiveness. In addition, I am perceived to be overly aggressive in my communication. This has led to conflict with others. I speak loudly, with emotion, with strong body language, and I have a tendency to stand closer to my listener than he/she may feel comfortable with. All of the above characteristics are consistent with my upbringing in Latin America. My characterization as an aggressive macho man (who may be dangerous) is accentuated by my Spanish accent. Furthermore, my desire for respect and recognition by others, when coupled with my assertiveness, has led to my being characterized as ambitious in the context of Toronto.[47] This is often characterized as a negative trait of me as a Latin American immigrant male although ambition is a highly valued trait in capitalist culture.

I have found that when friends and colleagues want to silence me, they tell me that I am 'behaving macho' or tell me that there is 'no need to act macho and raise your voice.' Patriarchal discourse as an expression of male dominance contributes to serious social problems in Latin American countries. This discourse contributes to violence against women and children. Ironically, much of my work in Central and South America directly confronts the practice and beliefs that are founded on patriarchal principles and are culturally repressive to women. My understanding of machismo goes well beyond recognizing an expressive style of speaking or strong body language.

I share with women and some other men a deep belief in the troubling nature of men's dominance over women. I have been striving to disengage from concepts and practice associated with machismo through years of education in Toronto as well as through new experiences, both personal and professional. For all men elements of troubling male superiority are present in their interactions with women. The category of the macho as a useful political conception begins to slip when it is used to create a stereotypical Latin man. As noted previously, the categorical significance of macho-ness shifts when it is used by outsiders to describe Latin men in a manner that does not make sense to the experiences of men from Latin cultures.[48] At the same time, it is useful to question machismo and patriarchy and men's collusion in this discursive practice.

Having lived in patriarchal societies in both Canada and Latin America, I feel the need to take responsibility for any form of violence that men have perpetrated on women and children. The principal focus of my academic research has been to work to ensure the eradication of those male attitudes and practice that perpetuate violence. It is my hope that my research contributes to the end of the worst and most destructive forms of male expression. I take responsibility to be constantly vigilant of behaviours and actions that may be a reflection of hegemonic masculinity whether constructed in Latin cultures or in the hybrid culture of Toronto. An irony prevails in my life in Toronto: as I work to deconstruct patriarchal culture, others reconstruct my repertoire of expressions and behaviours into a troubling macho identity.

I take responsibility for the troubling aspects of the patriarchy, and know that macho cultures defined in patriarchal social structures are harmful. I resist, however, the constant reconstruction of myself as a macho man simply because I am embodied as a brown man. Butler defines the performative as repetitive acts that function as a form of authoritative speech invoking power. Repetition, such as naming Latin masculinity as macho, is part of a network of shaming and disciplining, as well as a network of authorizing dominance. The repeated act of naming me as macho contributes to constructing my Latin brown maleness in a manner congruent with shaming and abjection.[49] Therefore I refuse to accept being called macho when it is used to define me as deviant within mainstream masculine Canadian culture.

The efficacy of repetition as a form of regulation is in the associations that are made to other acts. Through repetition, one repeats the norms of the gendered subject. Gender is an obligatory practice defined through repetitive acts that become powerful in their persistence.[50] Butler argues that 'an act is itself a repetition, a sedimentation, and congealment of the past which is precisely foreclosed in its act-like status.'[51] The singular act of naming refers to the many acts of a community based in prejudice; the performative can also be used to understand the nature of race relations and hegemonic masculinities. My experience of the naming by white Canadian males of my brown body as loud, posturing, intense, and 'high maintenance' recreates me as a macho Latin man who is deviant and deserving of abjection.

## Refusing to Confess

One of the elements of 'confessional discourses' is the need to confess an 'inner existence.'[52] Foucault argues that the confessional is used in a wide variety of relationships including patients and helping professionals, delinquents, and experts, as well as educators and students. The confession has multiple effects, one of the most powerful of which is the reconstruction of self through interrogation. The confessional constructs the subject as a passive participant engaged in the examination of hidden aspects of his or her self in order to change his or her self.[53] There is some usefulness to these forms of expression, but to reduce most experiences to a need to talk and to be heard is reductive, and at times counterproductive. In my line of work, progressive social work practice, there is a tendency to value voice and narrative from minority and marginalized people. Although I highly value the social work field of study, especially its commitment to anti-oppressive practice that includes political, social, cultural influences in helping,[54] I am concerned that the necessity to speak to emotional past experience may have unintended consequences for Salvadoran men. The need to talk about past traumas for Salvadoran women and men contravenes two treasured modes of self-protection outlined below: 'no pensar' and the veil of distrust.

It is my experience that immigrants such as me, from war-torn countries, who are racialized in the Canadian context are regularly encouraged to express ourselves, to talk to others, and to share. In addition to my accent and my expressions of intensity, my refusal to participate in confessional practice has resulted in my construction as macho. In some of the literature of the helping professions emotional inexpressiveness is understood to be a serious problem for men. Not only is it considered unhealthy, but a lack of expression is also perceived as a means for men to maintain their power and their position of privilege.[55]

In fact Salvadorans in Canada, myself included, may be engaged in 'no pensar,' that is, the act of 'not thinking about' the past.[56] While often refusing to be confessional on an individual level, Salvadorans are in fact proud of their own stories of resistance. But parents also teach their children that political resistance can bring about serious consequences, including death. Stories are told in the safety and privacy of the home. According to Carranza, 'no pensar' is a social mechanism used by Salvadorans to avoid thinking about difficult events experienced in the past. Both individual and collective forms of oppression are kept out of the mind through this process.[57]

Furthermore, Carranza describes Salvadoran Canadian people as affected by the *veil of distrust* as a response to 'social polarization spread throughout all sectors of Salvadoran society during the civil war beginning in the mid-1980's.' She writes, 'individual [and collective] survival in social interactions demanded a group self identification; that is, "are you one of us" or "are you one of them" . . . Salvadorans have carried these specific features of their history of oppression across contexts.'[58] Carranza states that when Salvadorans experience racism and discrimination, they respond in ways that have been useful in the past, by engaging in *no pensar* and constructing a *veil of distrust*. A Latin man who has been educated to adopt these attitudes is not simply acting macho and using his power to control others. In spite of the well-meaning misinterpretations of those who would encourage us to talk about our experiences, the confessional can also potentially destroy the safety of self-protection.

Considering that the experiences most of us had before coming to Toronto have often been extremely difficult, why are we compelled by others to talk about them? Why must we confess to experiences that are painful? What if our choice of silence and privacy of thought is a form of self-protection? What if dealing quietly with painful memories is for us in fact a healthy way to cope in a new setting or environment? Why are we encouraged to pathologize or reconstruct our experiences

as a mental health issue? Against the background of the marginalization of racialized immigrant men and the specific cultural modes of
protecting oneself for Salvadoran men, the field of social work needs
to theorize further the usefulness of narrative as a healing technique.

## The Refusal of the Psychologization of Everyday Living:
## The Politicized Mestizo

The mental health label is perhaps one of the most powerful tools
used by confessional discourse and helping professions.[59] Putting
everyday experiences in North America under the lens of psychology
has encouraged a belief that common elements of life damage people's
emotions.[60] Frank Furedi argues that failure to engage in confessional
professional discourse might be misrecognized as a sign of emotional
immaturity that requires help in itself.[61]

When a Latin man refuses to confess, he may be considered to be
flawed. If the refusal to participate in therapeutic narratives is made
abnormal then the Salvadoran might be considered to possess a 'weak
psyche' that requires intervention. Forms of self-protection and instru-
mentalism such as *no pensar* and *veil of distrust* associated with the process of settling in a new place, in my case Canada and Toronto, may
be reinterpreted as acts of denial, or an inability to be in touch with
one's feelings. It is my experience that when I refuse to accept this
notion of emotional deficit my self-protective practice is reinterpreted
as a mental health issue. I am concerned how this mental health discourse might contribute to the means of managing the subjectivity of
the other as in the case of the Latin man.

As a Latin man who has experienced both real and imagined threats
to my safety prior to coming to Canada, I do not believe that the discourse of trauma and vulnerability is the best way to interpret my experiences. To my mind, trauma and vulnerability discourse removes
or weakens the sense of agency and control required for me to settle
comfortably in Toronto. I worry that political activism at times is interpreted as a form of trauma. Having endured difficult events does not
necessarily mean one has a 'damaged or traumatized' psyche replete
with emotional issues. The Salvadorans' resistance to political oppression has been intense; reinterpreting those experiences as macho at
best and mentally unwell at worst involves an erasure of historical
memory. Such reinterpretations of the immigrant brown body also
mitigate the collective responsibility of those oppressors in El

Salvador who used the army, government, and paramilitary organizations to massacre people and eliminate political opposition, and to impose imperialistic ideologies.

When I came to Toronto I experienced sadness, loneliness, and vulnerability. Perhaps the most difficult time for immigrant men such as me comes shortly after the arrival to this new safe place. A sense of safety is not easy to accept and it takes time. Sadness is an appropriate reaction to difficult experiences. Loneliness and vulnerability are appropriate reactions to social isolation. I have refused since my arrival to accept a culture of therapy that is tied to a confessional and to having to reconstruct myself due to pathology. I have been vulnerable. I continue to be vulnerable. Vulnerability has always been the experience of the mestizo and will continue to define that experience. I need to be careful how I tell my story.

In fact speech acts have import for Salvadorans in Canada. Perhaps, a manner to characterize health-inducing speech acts is to see them as performative acts which are a 'discursive act of subversion.'[62] Through the performative, subjugated voices can repeat 'the reactionary in order to effect a subversive reterritorialization.'[63] Marginalized persons can create knowledge about themselves by subversively reclaiming the dominant signifiers. Queer people, the mentally ill, and the macho Latin man can all be similarly reconstituted. The subject takes pejorative signifiers and transforms them. According to Janell Watson, this re-signification process follows a series of steps: 'Your name brings me, as subject, into being, performatively, since you create me, the subject, by naming me; however, I can repeat that name, subversively, thereby performatively altering your act of performativity.'[64]

To me and to other Salvadoran men living under the veil of distrust, the confession is understood to be a social technique used to make way for new mischaracterization, pathological interpretation, and domination of the Latin male. Yet the discursive exchange between Salvadoran community members as well as with those outside the community can be useful as long as it includes re-signification and plain talk. Plain talk or parrhesia involves a particular kind of truth telling that combines challenging criticism with a declaration to be telling the truth. Truth in this context does not refer to some universal, absolute truth. Instead truth refers to definite views of the way things ought to be spoken on a public stage. Parrhesia as outspokenness was often risky behaviour since, in opposing popular views and dominant regimes of truth, it often meant a confrontation with those in authority and prevailing power structures.[65] I engage in a form of parrhesia in this chapter; I consider it to be a possible means for immigrant men to talk about their experience. Parrhesia might be a means for racialized immigrant men to create alliances with each other and possibly with those persons in hegemonic male positions.

## Conclusion

Writing about masculinity is a privilege mostly available only to those who are living in countries of the north. I am pleased to use my privilege as a professor in the north to contribute to masculinity studies to blossom in the plurality of a city like Toronto. Toronto offers us the possibility of making this kind of hybrid reality in the everyday living of men. The city provides the possibility of creating new forms of the mestizo male but also all the dangers of introducing dangerous processes of mestizaje we cannot yet imagine. It is time to move away from unexamined dominant identity discourse and toward the development of a Torontonian sociology of masculinities. I hope to see masculinity develop in combination with critical race studies to the point that it can take on the discourse of whiteness and how it has affected those of us who refuse to conform to dominant white hegemonic notions of the masculine. We need to study the consequences of racism in the identity formation of racialized boys and men in Toronto over the last three decades. Only then can we understand the forms of mental health stressors associated with oppression experienced by racialized boys and men, and how those stressors are reflected in practice in everyday life.

This new understanding of men might include new directions for helping immigrant men based in alternative forms of masculinities. This practice of helping through narrative and speech comes with possible double binds or contradictory tensions for an immigrant man such as me. For example, many of us want to engage in reconstruction of the Latino from troubling patriarchal macho culture yet we must refuse to change those aspects of ourselves that characterize us as macho through performative acts that marginalize us. Another tension involves making the decision when to engage in speech acts to promote both personal and social change. For example, my refusal to engage in reconstruction of the self is mitigated by the strong stories of resistance spoken by Salvadorans. I need to speak but the manner of my speaking comes with the risk of being further characterized as macho.

I offer up from this ethnographic account a manner to listen to immigrant men from El Salvador. Rather than helping through imagining reconstruction of the self through confession to a become a better person, it is best to listen to these boys and men as if we are listening to one engaged in plain speaking or parrhesia. Now I am left with the tension resulting from the expression of my Salvadoran maleness in my home, Toronto. I continue to refuse the confession of my maleness in the face of dominating discourse, particularly whiteness. I refuse to participate in discourse that too easily allows others to construct me solely as 'suffering immigrant.' As a Salvadoran man I continue to be cloaked in a *veil of distrust* that results in *no pensar*.

I long to tell our story. I wish to bear witness to experiences in El Salvador and the dangers of racialization in Toronto. So I suggest we listen attentively to stories of pain and discomfort due to past experience as well as experiences in Toronto. Just as importantly we listen to the stories of Salvadoran men as a form of parrhesia – the talk might be surprising and uncomfortable but allows for a narrative that is contextually and socially relevant and politically placed. The social background for this type of story-telling in Toronto as well as in Latin America is one where the stereotype of the 'Latin American macho' could disappear through the process of cultural change. As a result of cultural globalizing changes that allow the exchange of new symbols, that macho figure could disappear as a form of marginalization. This does not imply that a new object of stigma will be avoided without some careful vigilance. The deconstruction of the ideological construct of Latino masculinity – a simple macho man – is important in order to re-signify Salvadoran men.

As a sociologist interested in dynamic forms of oppression within institutions and as a social worker interested in transformative practice, I would like to better understand how masculinities intersect with factors like race and sexual orientation. I am also interested in how masculinities affect and are affected by education, professional knowledge, and academia. I am curious to know how masculinity affects our construction of knowledge. We transform as we move forward toward the construction of politicized identities, rather than on the basis of victimhood. With my accented English, my assertiveness, my intensities, and my enthusiasm, I hope for a new vision of masculinity in Toronto.

New hybrid forms of masculinity, still poorly understood, have developed in Toronto for those who have immigrated here. I suspect that there are many forms of masculinities for racialized men that go beyond the typical association of violence with male immigrant identity. I believe the cross-cultural experience in Toronto continues to reconstruct and rehabilitate male identity. I am certain that in Toronto there are specific African-Toronto or Latin-Canadian or Arab-Canadian masculine identities in our midst. In Toronto we have the opportunity at this historical moment to talk about transnational masculinity. After all, I see myself as a *Torontonian Latin man*.

# 2 Yearning to Break Silence: Reflections on the Functions of Male Silence

FRANK SIROTICH, SEAN MARTIN, STEVEN RUHINDA, JOSEPH VAZ, AND KEN MOFFATT

> You never achieve it and there's no way out because you'll just replace it with something else, the essence of that yearning
>
> *Sean Martin*

> When I have used silence for survival there is an uncomfortable part
>
> *Steven Ruhinda*

## Introduction

Silence has historically been associated with the archetype of the western male. Popular images of men, such as movie stars Gary Cooper and Clint Eastwood, have represented silence as a singular, stoic attribute, indicating strength. Silence has also been associated with an idealized image of masculinity: the 'strong, silent type.' In fact, there are many kinds of masculinity and silence just as the links between them are many. In this chapter, the authors use a reflective process to bring some relationships between silence and masculinity out into the open, showing how silence is used as a technique for self-formation and also as a strategy of power and resistance.

Following upon Michel Foucault's analysis of subject formation through specific technologies,[1] the authors have revisited their experience of silence as males from diverse backgrounds. Based on findings from our discussion we consider how different aspects of silence relate to masculine identities. In the process, the authors discuss a palpable but somewhat nebulous yearning that underlies each of their experiences of masculine silences.

The authors met in 1998 in York University's Master of Social Work part-time program in Toronto. York University was originally built as a large suburban campus in Toronto but the city of Toronto has grown to the point that a campus that was once considered to be remote is now surrounded by the city. The group consisted of eight men diverse with respect to race, ethnicity, religion, and sexual orientation. Following the completion of a formal course in social work, the group of men discovered, over the course of our conversations, an interest in discussing expressions of masculinity within the context of a 'cross-cultural' classroom. Our group created a space, free from evaluation, to think about our relationship to each other. We also reflected on how masculinity is socially constructed, deconstructing the education of males who have felt marginalized in the classroom due to race, ethnicity, socio-economic class, or sexual orientation. We identified ongoing challenges implicit in cross-cultural communication among males, including the relationship between reflexivity and cross-cultural learning and teaching; the multiple definitions of masculinity; the risk of stereotyping in the classroom; and the replication of male privilege. The results of this study were presented at the International Association of Schools of Social Work Annual Meeting in Montreal. As a result of these discussions, we came to see a connection between silence and expressions of masculinity. This realization prompted further research to explore how silence informs masculinities.[2]

This chapter is based on the inquiry of a smaller group of five men who were members of the original research group. The five men have co-authored this chapter and have continued to meet both formally and informally for ten years (see Figure 2). Our group is diverse in the following ways: three men identify as straight and two identify as gay; two men self-identify as black, one as South Asian and two as white; two of the participants are fathers. The participants' countries of origin include India (Goa), Uganda, Jamaica, and Canada. At the time of this research, the men ranged from age thirty to fifty.

Taking responsibility for our masculinities, each of us spoke of our experiences of marginalization and privilege. The reflective process was used as a way to turn the research gaze upon ourselves and in effect to become the subjects our study,[3] intentionally inserting ourselves into various narratives of masculinity. Each of us reflected on our own experience of silence as it relates to masculinity. In so doing, we have embraced the position of Bob Pease, who argues it is

Figure 2: Eugenio Salas. Photo of Frank Sirotich, Steven Ruhinda, Ken Moffatt, Joseph Vaz, and Sean Martin (front) (2009). Courtesy of the artist.

important that men avoid hiding behind the veil of objectivity and distance in research.[4]

During this study, we shared narratives that placed the self within a broader social and cultural context.[5] The use of autoethnography allowed the subjects to unpack, or unveil, hidden narratives,[6] and allowed them to challenge and deconstruct their assumptions about cultural and historical expressions of masculinity.[7] In this way, method, as much as theory, contributed to the possibilities of cultural interpretation.[8] Each member of the study group worked from his personal history, intertwining ideas and lived experience.[9] The use of autoethnography helped the authors to investigate structures of masculinity and silence, unveiling concealed experience obscured by those conceptual structures.[10]

Each participant in our group shared his own personal stories relevant to the subjects of silence and masculinity; each person also worked from his distinct social location, choosing to express specific aspects of his identity. While there are overarching themes running through the narratives, we assume that those themes do not apply to all participants. The disruption of the concept of a universal masculinity was welcomed by all in the group.[11] We avoided creating 'perfect wholes but instead sought to reveal those cracks in the smooth surface of our conceptual world that may suggest new interpretations.'[12] By reflecting on silence as a concept, we found we could break the silences, often for the first time publicly.

## Technologies of Masculine Silence

It is our contention that concepts such as discourse, technologies of power, and technologies of self are useful in understanding the relationship between silence and masculinity, and in the process we discovered yearning was key to understanding men's complicity in their own silences.

Part of Foucault's philosophy entails identifying and exploring the construction of the contemporary self, and the modes that constitute this self.[13] In 'The Subject and Power,' Foucault wrote, 'My objective has been to create a history of the different modes by which, in our culture, human beings are made subjects.'[14] For Foucault, the self is not an essence, a unified entity of consciousness apparent to itself; rather it is contingent and historical, the product of discursive and institutional operations, of relations of power and of individual agency.[15] In exploring the mechanisms which serve to constitute the contemporary self, Foucault articulated four types of 'technologies,' or modalities: 1) 'technologies of production,' which enable individuals to produce, convert, and control things; 2) 'technologies of sign systems,' which permit signification and communication; 3) 'technologies of power,' which concern the way in which the conduct of individuals is influenced, and how states of domination are established and maintained; 4) 'technologies of self,' which concern the way in which human beings achieve a sense of themselves as subjects, and turn themselves into subjects.[16] Though making distinctions among the four modalities, Foucault notes that these technologies frequently function simultaneously.

The concept of technologies of sign systems is related to the production of the linguistic forms or discourse we use to shape our reality. How we name, characterize, and explain things shapes our reality.[17] Foucault suggests that it is through discourse that our view of reality is created and sustained,[18] that is, our language and our modes of communication do not reflect reality, they create it. Foucault's notion of discourse is salient to our study of silence. Since each gives significance to the other, silence and discourse are irrevocably woven together. Speech is born from silence, and silence is given meaning through speech. For example, splinters of silence juxtaposed with series of vowels and consonants contribute to the creation and utterance of language.[19] Much like language, silence can be instrumental in the creation of social realities. Moreover, as in discourse, silence can be used to convey meaning. Consequently, silence becomes a type of 'positivity' that can be studied, not simply an absence but a 'positive' or present impact on the world.[20]

'Technologies of power' also have a direct application in studying the interaction between silence and masculinities. This term refers to the application of instruments, techniques, and procedures used to control the conduct of individuals. 'Technologies of power' also include strategies of power that affect our discourse and subjectivity. Silence may be studied as a possible strategy in power relations, as the effects of specific strategies or techniques of power or, conversely, as a strategy of resistance in relations of power. For example, silence can be used as a form of aggression by men, conveying contempt, derision, and disapproval for the purpose of controlling the behaviour of others, especially women and children. Alternatively, it can be part of a strategy of defiance and survival in a situation where one feels threatened by domineering institutionalized political structures.

Foucault's notion of 'technologies of self' is also used during this investigation to understand the role of silence in the self-formation of the subject. Social identities or subjectivities are made available for individuals to assume through discourse.[21] It is within this discourse that we take up subject positions, such as what it means to be a man or woman.[22] One acquires a sense of self as 'belonging to the world in certain ways and thus sees the world from the perspective of one so positioned.'[23] Each individual may be labelled and assume a plurality of subject positions, and each may have a multiple sense of self.[24] For example, characteristics such as age, class, ethnicity, race, religion, and sexual orientation are socially constructed through 'technologies of self' and converge in a variety of ways to influence the identities of specific men. One's sense of self is constituted and reconstituted, through changing discursive practice and material circumstances. But the availability of multiple subject positions can lead to an individual being composed of a collection of contradictory positions or subjectivities. The individual chooses which positions to occupy and in which contexts he wishes to occupy them. Thus, masculine subjectivity can be seen as something that we create within the limitations of available discursive subject positions. In this chapter, we open our masculinities to inquiry in order to unveil some of the 'technologies of the self' associated with manhood.

Foucault's notion of technologies of self is relevant in many ways to how individuals use silence to turn themselves into subjects. Given the discursive foundations of the self, self-formation may be understood as the purposeful interplay of the presence and absence of possible subject locations. That is, an individual may give voice to certain subject positions and concomitantly silence other such positions. Making such choices implicates us within broader discursive patterns and strategies of power associated with masculinity.

Recognizing masculinity as a discourse also allows us to question the social presumptions in definitions of the masculine.[25] A study of masculinity as a socially constructed malleable concept can lead to the social transformation of its definition.[26] In what follows the authors examine some of the key topics discussed during our self-reflective sessions, and we excavate technologies of masculine silence. We begin by exploring the interplay between masculinity and silence within the context of academia.

## Male Silence within Academia

The following section concerns silence that is created as a result of the relationship between masculinity and prescribed notions of work. In our discussions, the authors found that in academia, 'technologies of production' are so influential that they have a disciplinary effect on us. Thus silence here is constructed by the desire to engage in productive work that is socially valued. The academic workplace, defined by technical proficiency, competency, and symbol creation,[27] acts to obscure other aspects of masculine knowledge and identity. The discipline-based competitive nature of academia allows for a limited repertoire for the expression of the masculine self. Collectively, the group members attended or taught at one or more of three universities in the city of Toronto – Ryerson University, University of Toronto, and York University – as well as Centennial College. In the following exchange Ken Moffatt, a professor of social work, Frank Sirotich, a social worker in forensic mental health and doctoral candidate, and Sean Martin, a social worker in child welfare and lecturer at York University, talk about the construction of academic productivity as experienced at the graduate level of education:

KEN: I have spent most of my life trying to prove that I was a competent, intelligent male, and I think that is tied to my masculinity. I have to be competent, I have to be on top of things . . . I think it is tied to how I was told to be a male as I grew up, and you know you are a male if you know how to do things, as opposed to expressing yourself . . . and I really feel that it takes me away from who I am, and kind of obscures those struggles I had with silence as a kid.

FRANK: I can relate to that. I can relate to that in terms of what you're saying when you're still buying into external criteria and standards of success or competency. You lose a sense of who you are . . . why you are doing it? Why you want to be an academic or why you want to pursue a set of procedures . . . it is an end in itself, and you lose a sense of who you are. You ultimately wanted . . . acceptance, and the way to get acceptance is very narrow and burdensome because it is always an external standard. It's an external standard in the context of competition and not only competing against other males, but trying to prove to yourself . . . The struggle itself has defined me, so who I am outside of this would be difficult to articulate.

SEAN: There is another hurdle right after the last one, another hope.

A vague yearning tied to social acceptance pervades the nature of the work environment for some men. This yearning is tied to the fact that the academic setting is experienced as a disciplinary environment where men are constructed through procedures and social expectations as singular, competitive persons. The disciplinary effect is further heightened by the demand for competency both in social performance and in rigorous mastery of a field of study. The disciplinary effect of the academic setting is so encompassing that it is difficult to imagine the self outside of academic procedures. Work performance creates a series of meanings and rewards that are congruent with an internal desire for recognition, belonging, and acceptance. This is particularly troubling for men since we reconstruct ourselves according to an abstract discourse of productivity that has served to marginalize women.

Competitive social relations focused on technical competence have the effect of silencing male expressions of vulnerability, uncertainty, ambivalence, and fragility as they relate to social relations. We may struggle to conceal emotional engagement by disguising it as a form of technological competence. Ultimately, this process often leads to a silencing of the self, because of the pervasive and rigorous expectations surrounding what it means to be a male. The yearning in our discussions creates a form of personal complicity within the unattainable search for the proper social expression of being male.[28]

In the following exchange, Sean, Frank, and Joseph are recent graduates from the York University graduate program, and Ken is their former instructor for one of the graduate courses. We continue to discuss the nature of the discourse in academia as well as the elusive, unattainable quality of achievement:

SEAN: So that's the question. What would happen if you chose not to do that game, be in that game? So then what what's left, what does that look like, like what's left?

FRANK: You would still have that appetite, or that hunger for recognition and approval. So, if you gave it up I think it would manifest itself in some other way. Unless you are addressing that need for recognition and acceptance umm, at its core you'll find, I think, an alternative, external standard to measure yourself by.

JOSEPH: What happens when you achieve it? Or do you ever think you achieve it?

FRANK: That's my point. You never do.

SEAN: You never achieve it, and there's no way out because you'll just replace it with something else, the essence of that yearning. Maybe inherent in this is that you just can't opt out. You have to always participate in it.

KEN: Yeah, yeah, even if it feels forced.

SEAN: Even if it feels like it is not you.

The exchange above demonstrates how academic discourse can constrain the practice of being male. At the same time, even though the practice is experienced as unpleasant, each individual man is complicit. In this respect, silence operates as a 'technology of self.' The male subject silences certain aspects of the self, while expressing others, with the goal of reaching a state of self-acceptance, happiness, or satisfaction. Consciously or unconsciously the individual silences aspects of the self to fit within a specific masculine mould that affords privilege through acceptance, but in the process, a sense of alienation from self is created because of a desire to attain an elusive endpoint. The horizon of significance of being male is poorly defined here, constructed as a promise 'to arrive' through competent, individual, competitive achievement.

Of course, a similar struggle is likely to exist for women within the academic context. In fact the experience of silencing and sense of alienation is likely to be even more profound. It is a limitation of this study that we do not discuss how these processes of silencing work for women. What is unique to the male experience is that this yearning not to be defined by technologies of production operates within a historical context of privilege afforded by these same technological regimens; regimens which have underpinned and institutionalized the prevalent male power structures. With the men being aware of these structures the sense of complicity for men carries with it a responsibility to make visible these technologies and their influence. In the next section silence and alienation are further complicated by the social expectations tied to discourse associated with race, gender, and sexual orientation.

### Silence at the Interface of Race, Gender, and Sexual Orientation

In this section we discuss how silence can be created as a result of the interplay of race, gender, and sexual orientation. According to Foucault, men are constantly incited to speak as a product of western culture.[29] Anne Gere suggests that 'silence provides protection from as well as shelter for power.'[30] That is, silence can serve the purpose of shielding portions of one's life from public view.[31] The individual tends to choose the optimum subject location for each social context. At times, such expression of the self comes at the expense of feeling that other aspects of the self are silenced as a result. Men therefore develop strategies to reveal different aspects of their identity depending on the social location or circumstance in which they find themselves. In the course of our discussions we came to realize that we all adjusted our masculinities to match the shifting power relations in which we find ourselves; in other words, we engaged in the 'technology of the self.'

For example, Sean Martin, who identifies as both gay and black, often finds aspects of his masculinity silenced. On one hand, with widespread homophobia in the black community, he has been ostracized, and also accused of abandoning his culture/race simply by virtue of being gay. On the other hand, racism within the gay community has left him with no guaranteed place of safety there either. This silencing of his identity in different circumstances is deliberate. Sean explains:

There is always this sort of yearning, I've always had this yearning for that place that would feel like home, like I could bring everything [sexuality and race]. There is stuff about umm West Caribbean culture, Jamaican culture that I could not bring. My gayness was at the top of that list. That was not accepted anywhere in my home, or what I thought was my home, or whatever. That sort of really stands out for me. The strategy, the power, and that sort of network and of strategies and ah . . . I've been trying to make sense of that, to locate myself in that, and I guess in a very non-vocal way trying to break down some of the silences within those networks. The network that exists right now, it's just different, and actually I've just been trying to understand it. I think a lot of the choices that I make today though have to do with my experiences, both in my family and in my coming out process. You know, sexuality, sexual identity, I think is rooted in my cultural experience. I just think that by definition that's where I came from, everything that happened has to do with my culture.

Even though Sean immigrated to Canada as a young child, prevailing ideas about masculine and feminine displays and behaviours were entrenched at an early age. For most of his adolescence, Sean's sexual identity was securely packed away 'in the closet.' Meanwhile the cultural and ethnic script regarding masculinity was well rehearsed and played out daily, though most of the time unconvincingly. By his early twenties, Sean was excited to seek out a community of gay men, some of whom shared his Caribbean background. His isolation was broken and his story was understood at a deeper level for the first time. It was at this point in Sean's life that 'coming out' seemed to be the only way to be fully alive.

One question lingered for Sean: 'How would my parents respond?' Over the next several months, he encountered two very different responses. His mother was histrionic, openly tormented him about what family, friends, and the church community would say and think. Conversely, his father had almost no response at first. Then, eventually, he came around to expressing a sense of unconditional love and acceptance. Sean recalls 'the pride he continued to show when introducing me to new friends, the way he reached out to my friends, and eventually to my partner, and never asking that I act different were some of the ways that my father demonstrated his acceptance of the whole me.' The example provided by Sean's father led to a cultural redefining, at least within this family, of masculinity. The batty boy was one recognizable expression of masculinity but so was the accepting Jamaican-born father. His father had always moved among Jamaican men, but now he chose to break his silence about his son's masculinity and his relationship to it.

Men find identity, belonging, love, and emotional well-being in groups; however, silence is often required in exchange for that membership. Men learn early in life to master socially acceptable roles and act them out accordingly. Once again, a type of yearning is expressed by Sean. It is a yearning for a place that would 'feel like home,' a place where sexuality and race would be fully present and accepted, and be considered a welcome expression of masculinity.

At times, Sean is 'complicit' in his silence, even though he experiences it as unpleasant. In other words silence is used by Sean as a technique of self-formation. In certain contexts, aspects of Sean's identity are made manifest just as other aspects are suppressed. These decisions about what is manifest and what is silenced are what construct Sean as man. Yet, strategies of breaking those silences come into play with both father and son, who together represent a type of recasting of the Jamaican/Canadian male. Still, the marginalized man's self is incongruent with his external expression of self when there is a necessary silence for safety, or when there is still no 'home' in which to be free of either racism or homophobia in Toronto.

## Silence as Survival Strategy in Idi Amin's Uganda

In the following discussion, silence is described as a strategy of power and resistance, and is associated with survival. In this instance silence has multiple meanings. It is the result of political oppression, but it is also a form of resistance, a strategy for survival, and an expression of political meaning. Steven Ruhinda grew up under the Ugandan dictatorial government headed by Idi Amin (1971–9). During Amin's reign of terror, the constitution of Uganda was abolished, and human rights violations ran rampant. As a child Steven witnessed the suppression of human rights through the imposition of martial law, and the regular meting out of arbitrary and heavy-handed punishment. Oppression was usually worst when applied to suspected opposition members including Steven's family. He himself witnessed abductions and firing squads. Steven lived through two wars, and a guerrilla insurgency. The violence in Uganda kept his family apart for close to ten years. Steven recalls,

I remember one of our uncles saying 'You guys ought to be careful, you know. You've already lost the family name but you better stop disturbing the government.' We never hid our distrust of the government. So that kind of silence was really, really, very hard because you don't know whom to trust. There is no way you can share what you are going through in life and you don't know whether you're going to survive. So you use silence as a survival tool. We were just quiet.

In the context of Steven's narrative, silence serves as a moral choice, a choice to pursue a vision, however ill-defined, that stands in resistance to dominant power relations. He explains,

I already had a little resilience, you know, to survive. It couldn't be worse, that was the way I looked at it . . . I kept on being quiet a little bit. Growing up if you said something you were killed. I mean there were no rewards there – [but] there were rewards to silence . . . So, maybe I hung onto silence as the only way I was not going to be punished . . . There was a passive resistance. You are helping, you are hiding people, you are providing shelter . . . I thought there should be a third way [other than dictatorship and armed struggle].

A type of yearning is invoked as a result of Steven's use of silence as a strategy of survival and resistance, a yearning to express his thoughts, opinions and feelings:

When I have used silence for survival there is an uncomfortable part. In other words, you keep quiet and you survive, but it doesn't discount that you know there is help out there. There is someone who knows. So silence is always trying to knock down the door. It cannot be a permanent state. It can carry you through . . . but I think it is the discomfort that you always have that you know what you didn't say . . . maybe I should just say it.

This yearning to speak, to know who else is available, makes this kind of silence an ambivalent experience. Though necessary for survival, the silence also brings out a desire to express one's story and to find someone with whom you can speak freely. In the same way that masculinity is an ambivalent state with blurred boundaries, so too is the silence that constructs the male identity. But both also carry with them the hope that there might yet be connection beyond the silences.

## Group Response to the Ugandan Narrative

In response to Steven's story about Uganda, other group members talked at length about their own families, the discussions including stories of social upheaval, war, and immigration. We especially talked about the silences associated with the histories of our fathers. Steven explains that his father's silence revolved around two deeply, and perhaps conflicting, values: the value of family, and the value of self-determination. Steven's father had lost his own father (Steven's grandfather) in a war at a young age. Moreover, Steven's father had been separated from his mother (Steven's grandmother) and his sole brother (Steven's uncle) from an early age until his adolescence. As a result, he craved a large, united family, and created one with his own children. Steven's birth family was his father's universe and his sanctuary.

Steven told us his father was an educator who believed in education as the means to guarantee social mobility and success for his children. His father also believed education could improve the well-being of colonized peoples. He made financial sacrifices himself to ensure that his children, including Steven, completed post-secondary education.

Steven's father was close to achieving his dream of educating his family, when the military gained power and suspended the democratic rights of Ugandan citizens. The struggle that ensued ruptured the family in catastrophic ways. Older brothers opted for armed resistance to the Amin regime. The military, especially the guerrillas, responded with unprecedented assaults on the educated classes. Steven remembers as a young boy overhearing an armed soldier taunting his father: 'Let your education degrees save you now.' While Steven's father supported the resistance he maintained his silence. Those who spoke out against Amin's regime faced death by firing squad.

Soldiers regularly searched the family's house, and ransacked the property as they hunted for Steven's missing brothers. Steven remembers that whenever the soldiers left the home, his father would attempt to soothe family members, sometimes with a Bible verse or a religious song. At the same time Steven's father never uttered a word of complaint about the actions of Steven's older brothers. He believes now, upon reflection, that his father's silence was tied to feelings of pain and struggle. He kept his silence out of a desire for self-determination and freedom, and to protect the family.

Steven's discussion of Uganda prompted Joseph to discuss how Amin had also displaced his family of South Asian descent from

Uganda. Joseph's father was born in 1929 in Calcutta to a prosperous family in the hotel business. But he lost his business in India, and travelled in search of work. Joseph's father joined the British army, where he learned a highly skilled trade in the textile industry. After moving to Kenya to seek employment he met Joseph's mother. Since Joseph's father was compelled to travel to find work, each of Joseph's five brothers was born in a different country: Kenya, Uganda, Zambia, Angola, and Rhodesia. Joseph himself was born on a boat in the Indian Ocean. Through our group discussion, Joseph was better able to understand the role of Amin and the silent resistance of Ugandans. His own family had moved to Kenya from Uganda before moving to Canada in 1970. The family immigrated to Brandon, Manitoba, moved to Cambridge, Ontario, and finally settled in St Catharines, Ontario, where Joseph's father died in 1982.

Frank talked at length about his father's time in the military during the Second World War, an experience that involved two warring camps, the Italian Army and the Partisans in Croatia. At the time, young men were often randomly forced from their homes and pressed into military service. Both the Italian army and the Partisans, the organized resistance to fascist occupation of Yugoslavia, went door to door in villages looking for boys and men to conscript. It was not uncommon for families to have one member pressed into military service with one group and another pressed into service with the rival faction. In Frank's case his father was taken for service by the Italian army while his younger brother was taken by the Partisans. Suspicion and distrust were the order of the day since there was ongoing concern about what might happen if a military faction learned that members of the family had taken up arms with their rivals. Consequently, silence became a necessary survival strategy. The necessity of silence as a survival strategy was further reinforced for Frank's father in the post-war period when he was arrested and held in a prison camp after attempting to flee the country. He had been turned in by government informants. Central to Frank's father's story were his memories of not being able to trust anyone, or to speak about what was happening to him.

Ken's father was forced from rural Ontario during the Great Depression to take employment in a dairy in Hamilton. There he renewed an acquaintance with Ken's mother, who had also been forced to Hamilton from a farm to work in a munitions plant. The couple got married and moved to Windsor, Ontario, where Ken's father found work as a skilled labourer in the automotive industry. Although called to serve in the army during the Second World War, his father was deemed unfit to serve for health reasons when he showed up for duty at the London, Ontario, armouries. Ken feels the weight of many silences in his father's personal history arising from his need to move away from home to find employment and from the shame he felt at being unable to serve during war.

Finally, Sean's father immigrated to Canada in 1969. He was the first of an extended family who came to Canada to find employment so that he could sponsor relatives to bring them here. He worked as a photographer, ultimately saving enough money for his wife, mother-in-law, and his two sons to join him. The family lived in Toronto on Melrose Avenue until the parents separated. Sean's father then moved to the United States to pursue his career, and Sean's memories of his father are tied up with the summer vacations when Sean and his brother would join their father in the United States.

In all of these families, a type of silence was involved in all discussions of the various fathers. In each case, group members reported that their fathers found it difficult to speak to their sons about atrocities they had witnessed, life disruptions, and, perhaps, feelings of personal shame. These stories belie prevailing notions of cultural continuity and linear intergenerational development within families. Instead these stories, tied either to the employment of our fathers or to the legacies of violent conflict, are defined by disruption and dislocation. They are also defined by wonderment due to lack of knowing the personal history and the identity of our fathers. For each of us a strategy of silence by the father was reworked to reconstruct our self and our current strategies of silence. Instead of a linear development of the narrative of family, it makes more sense to patch together a series of silences.

By volunteering to talk about silence Steven was able to make sense of his experience in Uganda, his childhood of victimization, and to reach out to other Ugandans who might recognize and understand that silence. One of the ironies inherent in male silence is that when stories and emotional affinity are exposed, their telling is more soothing than the original silence.

In the following exchange, we talk about the importance of the conscious creation of space and time to imagine a possibility of new 'technologies of the self' associated with masculinity. It is in the contravening of some aspects of discourse, we decide, that new narratives are shared.

JOSEPH: These people (group members and their families) have lived through all this and have dealt with silence as a sort of subverted protest. They see its benefits from what they have come through and consider it this way. It is interesting.

STEVEN: But family-wise we talk now about things. We talk about what we went through. But sometimes there are those uncomfortable silences. Those who came here have a different view. Those that remained [in Uganda] have a very, very different view, you know, yeah.

KEN: Did I hear you correctly that you said this is the first time that you have told this story through?

STEVEN: Yes. Nobody knows what I went through. And in [university] class I never used personal examples . . . the thing with this group . . . part of my 'coming out' for lack of a better word . . . slowly we started with the group, with shared experiences, and then you feel a bit more comfortable. You feel safe, when in most instances you do not have that safe ground. You are busy working to deal with 'the real world.' You just keep quiet and move on. But this kind of group . . . is a safety net . . . it would be difficult for me to know how I would start. So, I appreciate all of you.

KEN: Yeah, I was thinking earlier I did not say . . . that you need to take time with each other. Do you know what I mean? If we did not bother to make the choice to meet as a group we would not hear Steven's story. So without the group my impression of Steven would be very superficial – a nice guy who was in the [social work] class and moved on.

STEVEN: Yeah.

KEN: There is something about taking time to get to know each other.

FRANK: I was thinking how our stories will trigger things with one another. Sometimes it is conscious but other times it is more of a feeling, like a feeling of affinity. There is probably an underlying experience, or if not the exact experience, the same feelings were invoked in us, even though we are coming from different backgrounds and different situations . . . like it was the same on the emotional level, stemming from differing experiences.

JOSEPH: Having heard the experience and the risk in people sharing their stories . . . it is ironic what we are talking about is the theme of silence but we are risking not to be silent in some way.

KEN: Another thing that occurred to me is the notion of choice. It seems to me, Steven, you chose not take a male violent role even though you had this overwhelming circumstance . . . you made a choice in moralistic terms but almost a redeeming choice. You chose a third way or knew a third way even before you knew it.

STEVEN: Yes.

Silence is directly linked to anticipated support, and only broken outside the competitive relations of work and education, where production is the *measure of the man*. In the absence of support, or a supportive environment intended to help members break their silences, those silences persist. Sometimes group members felt they needed permission from others to talk about silence. Steven explains that he kept his silence, even while living in Toronto, maintaining it out of a need for emotional survival rather than fear of physical retribution. But breaking silence involves risks. Steven still wonders if it will provide people new weapons with which to judge him, or will it change the way he has been perceived? Emotionally, he, and other group members, expressed the view that they felt less vulnerable as long as they kept silent.

Self-reflection in the presence of a supportive and diverse group of men helped us to begin to explore violent family histories, or painful social circumstances. It also helped us to understand how we construct and present our selves through discourse. But silences continue to exist between us. Silence can serve as a soothing balm, sealing old wounds and protecting us from dealing with new unfamiliar ones. In this sense silence continues to operate as a strategy in relations of power even after it has been broken.

Silence is tied to complex historical, familial, and social realities that construct our present-day masculinity. Our current use of silence is linked to the memory of those practices that went before. The *safe space* of our group meetings allowed for fuller expression based on careful negotiation of silence and discourse between us. It existed as a formalized meeting of men but this safe group also is filled with the disruptions of distrust tied to past narratives and to practice among ourselves – many, many silences based in distrust prevail among us. Taking time together by the group runs counter to an idea of individualized, competent, competitive males who are directed to an elusive horizon of significance that is tied to their becoming whole in the future. Because a conscious decision by group members was made to form a group in the present, men from diverse backgrounds met in formal but intimate discussion and created a *third space* within the hybrid culture of Toronto – a space troubled by distrust even as it makes possible the discussion of secrets.

### Silences and Masculine Yearnings

The use of Foucauldian analysis had been useful in helping us to understand the multiplicity of silences associated with masculinity.

We found that there was not a single silence associated with masculinity, but rather many, an idea which runs counter to the stereotype of the rigid, silent, unchangeable male.[32] Male silence is perhaps best understood as fluid, changeable, and permeable. And each form has a boundary waiting to be broken.

By understanding that it has multiple manifestations, each of us can deploy silence for his own personal reasons based on aesthetic, political, or moral judgments. We came to understand that silence worked differently for each of us, even as we recognized thematic commonalties. Through reflection we determined that silence, at times, can be a social strategy so that power and silence are interrelated in the same way power and knowledge are. In the same way power engenders knowledge, and knowledge reinforces power relations, power also engenders silence, and silence reinforces relations of power. Silence may also function as a mechanism of self-formation. We construct our social identities as men through discourse that includes silence. We therefore construct our subjectivity to fit the social groupings with which we are engaged. The act of silencing our own subjectivity so that we can be congruent with the messages we receive socially can be so powerful that we can even become confused about who we are.

We also found that the strategic use of silence had consequences for us. As men, we are constantly negotiating a balance between self-worth, social acceptance, and belonging which entails self-regulation and self-censorship. A yearning experienced by men is tied to a desire for social membership, often experienced as *lack* cloaked in silence. Male yearning also does not seem to be separated from social relations and social history.[33] Networks of social relations and technological systems influence silence and male yearning.[34]

There seemed to be a tension between group acceptance, self-expression, and silence. At times, silence seems to be the mechanism used to achieve acceptance or to feel safe at the price of the aesthetics of the self; silence at times is a central mechanism in constructing a technology of the masculine self that is constrained. Silence may serve to reinforce relations of power in which dominant, masculine subjectivities and scripts are privileged, and concomitantly, elements of alternative subjectivities are marginalized or excluded. In the end, silence seems to be a strategy employed to address a yearning for acceptance, or to ensure survival, but its adoption, ironically, often leads to alienation. Beyond silence there remains a further yearning; a yearning to express oneself through alternative masculine subjectivities.

This study of silence and masculinity encourages us to study silence as a positivity, as it contributes to the construction of the masculine self. Further exploration could be done about the interpolations of silences across generations, and across cultural and racial divides. Perhaps this exploration is best done in an environment of difference and diversity, such as what is offered in an urban culture such as Toronto.

We propose that our process of reflection may unveil patterns of self-formation and interaction in the context of social relations of which men may not be fully aware. Certainly, the experience of our group members was that telling our stories changed us. Silence is part of how we construct our selves, and when it is treated differently we experience our selves differently. Utterance has a power that helps to achieve some mastery over a complex problem or unresolved issue. At times our utterance invokes a flood of empathic response. At the same time, the dynamic plurality of silences in social relations creates and informs our social realities and subjectivities. In conclusion these silences reconstructed in creative combination appear to have the power to reconstitute the troubling nature of our masculinity and reveal the underlying assumptions of the social relations that constrain it.

# 3 Instruction in the Art of the Masculine: The Art of Daryl Vocat

KEN MOFFATT

## Introduction

Large cosmopolitan centres such as Toronto are saturated with commercial global media in both the private and public spheres. Images of men and women are in constant competition for our attention. In spite of this cacophony demanding our attention, many of the images are sadly banal and reductive in nature. The images suggest no more exists to the man than the two-dimensional beauty we see on video screens and signage. At the same time, urban centres such as Toronto have become cultural hubs that attract both national and international artists. In Toronto, contemporary artists such as Moynan King, Andrew Harwood, R.M. Vaughan, Roy Mitchell, Will Munro, Patrick Decoste, Lex Vaughan, and Peter Kingstone all address gender in a manner that is both playful and provocative. Daryl Vocat is another member of this community of artists who question gendered social expectations. Vocat exposes fields of desire and difference that may be under-represented in commercial imagery. In this chapter I argue that Vocat's art enriches the cultural conversation about masculinity by exposing messages within dominant cultural symbols. He helps us to consider that desire and difference lie within and prior to the dominant social codes of masculinity in a manner that helps us to imagine creative ways of being boys and men.

Born in Regina, Saskatchewan, Vocat moved to Toronto to complete a Master of Fine Arts degree at York University, where he created a body of work focused on the Boy Scouts. He has been an educator teaching printmaking at Open Studio Toronto and Seneca College.[1] Most recently, he has been a participant in refereed group shows in

New York City at the International Print Centre as well as the legendary Robert Blackburn Workshop, where he won the Purchase Award in 2009. Vocat creates art in a variety of media, including printmaking, photography, and fabric work.

## Propaganda

Much of Daryl Vocat's art is based on the premise that each of us experiences a saturation of images so intense and pervasive that it is difficult to create meaning outside these images. Since these pervasive dominant images construct one's worldview, they also have a political purpose. According to Vocat, many publicly available images tell us how to construct our identities, most notably in the imperative that we be consumers. The public construction of the male as consumer, he argues, ensures an ongoing concentration of wealth in the hands of certain individuals and corporate entities.[2]

Vocat works against this instruction we are given through commercial imagery by creating his own propaganda, recasting many of the pop images one encounters on a daily basis.[3] Based in the subculture of punk, this propaganda is both intentionally provocative and easily accessible.[4] As a reaction to the commercial profusion of images in Toronto, Vocat has purposively decided to create his propagandist art so that it makes its way into people's everyday lives.[5] This accessibility is ensured by creating art works that are both easily replicable and affordable so that they can be widely distributed and shared. Vocat's art invades popular culture through the media of clothing, patches, quilts, and photography. These art works are spread throughout the city in an effort to create tension and dissonance with respect to the ubiquitous commercial imagery, and to provide a different form of instruction in public spaces.[6]

The universalized nature of commercial imagery in western capitalism has been characterized as a coding of productive relations that serve a regulatory purpose.[7] According to Gilles Deleuze and Felix Guattari, to make social relations possible there must be a way to code human flows such as productivity and desire. Desire, in particular, is coded so that subjects take on social functions and roles. A key goal of coding in the contemporary context is to consolidate capitalism as a system. Capitalism involves complex processes freeing desire from some forms of coding – often local norms – so that the capitalist social order can re-situate desire as a reductive commodity.[8] Commercial codes of human productivity, such as the ones that Vocat addresses, are reconstructed in a banal form so that desire is linked to consumption: the acquisition of property and goods. These codes can be seen in, but are not restricted to, the images present on video billboards and television, and in movies.[9]

In this way, commercial imagery has created a dissonance for Vocat, whose own understanding of desire is not contained by such profit-oriented symbols, including the images of people as they are depicted in advertising and pop culture. Vocat sees commercial images not simply as a form of entertainment freely taken up by the viewer but also acting as propaganda, a form of regulation that controls a person's acts, language, and gender through repetition.[10] As he describes the problem: 'after seeing or hearing something so often and with such regularity, I find it difficult to think outside of the patterns unless I actively seek alternatives.'[11] The individual's desires are coded as objects ready for manipulation within a chain of signifiers.[12] He bases his work on his own desires and hopes, exactly because they are not present in the symbolism of popular culture. In fact, his artistic strategy is 'to reach out, to invade popular culture, to spread dissent and to have fun along the way.'[13]

One of the ways Vocat infiltrates popular culture is to couple statements and aphorisms – 'Live to Craft, Craft to Live,' 'Sissy,' 'Quentin Crisp Has a Posse – 5 foot eight inches, 124 Pounds,' and 'Riot = Life' – with borrowed but reconstructed images printed on fabric patches that can be sewn to clothing, handbags, and computer bags. While he starts with images that already exist in the public sphere, he appropriates them for his own purposes and reinvents them. These re-imagined images create a dialogue with the profit-oriented images that exist in the public sphere that have been unresponsive to our reactions in the past. The re-imagined image creates this dialogue so that previously unheard narratives within the commercial imagery of masculinity can be considered.[14] The image *Out of the Closets* in Figure 3 is typical of the series of fabric patches, particularly in the simplicity of the image.[15] Vocat introduces *Out of the Closets* by suggesting that we 'grab our cultural studies readers and "dive in." '[16]

The phrase 'out of the closet and into the libraries' reminds the viewer that both gender and sexuality are constructed, and reproduced through social and cultural productions. The concept of the 'closet,' borrowed from gay culture, refers to the idea that some aspect of one's identity needs to be hidden. Coming out of the closet becomes

Figure 3: Daryl Vocat, *Out of the Closets* (2005). Courtesy of the artist.

a form of passage to personal acceptance as well as a challenge to social relations that have previously been based in prejudice. By keeping the meaning of his phrase open-ended, Vocat widens the passage to acceptance beyond gay male identity to include anyone who has felt the need to hide a gender orientation. By suggesting people head to the library, the passage becomes not only about sexuality, but also about a socio-cultural re-imagining and re-interpretation of both the self and social relations.

Other patches in the series, such as *Sissy* and *Quentin Crisp Has a Posse*, are direct challenges to conventional manifestations of masculinity and the North American male social norm. Vocat's propaganda disrupts gender constructs based on political cooperation enacted through cultural interpretation.[17] A person wearing these patches challenges conventional interpretations of their gender and becomes a participant in gender reconstruction. Crisp, for example, becomes part of the visual landscape and a historical reference point in contemporary pop culture through the spread of his image. The patch suggests even Crisp, an outspoken, effeminate, gay British author with a slight physique, can have a posse, the most masculine of social groupings. Furthermore, Vocat challenges the assumption of an essential or fundamental nature of gender as well as the inherent value of macho masculinity by proudly creating works with word 'sissy' stitched into them. This word is spread as an 'infestation' of cultural networks, through its repetition in public spaces stitched onto people's clothing and backpacks.

Another series of Vocat's images is focused upon male-defined professions. This series of self-portraits, entitled *What my parents want me to be when I grow up, A to Z*, deals with assumed expectations of the male. As with his propaganda, the artist borrows widely available images of masculinity and re-imagines them. He uses the imagery of mass media to create his digital collages, overlaying his face on a series of stereotypical masculine images, such as the cowboy, the fireman, and the golfer. The series explores parental expectations of a boy, along with the boy's idealized views of the male adult world. Through the play of images, such as the golfer in Figure 4, he creates new caricatures of masculinity.

While each is distinct, in the repetition of idealized images the performative nature of the symbols and the occupations they represent – including policeman, sailor, basketball player, and scientist – are brought into question. As with Vocat's other forms of propaganda, the power of the imagery lies in how easily it can be replicated. In the same manner that assumed codes of masculinity gain power through their repetition,[18] the questioning of those codes becomes powerful by presenting the photographs as a series and offering the images for free in a downloadable format. Vocat's propaganda first disrupts patterns and networks of commercial imagery, but through its repetition it also re-invents and re-iterates images in such a way as to allow for the easy spread of new meanings.

Vocat describes this series of male images as 'representations which point to their own reductive qualities.'[19] Although humorous, they take on a serious aspect as they unveil the anxieties associated with re-defining masculinity through questioning its social construction.[20] The A-Z series not only brings into question gender signification, it also offers up a complex affective discourse on the subject. In the same manner, American photographer Cindy Sherman reconstructs herself in her photographic self-portraits as the tipsy fashion model on a

Figure 4: Daryl Vocat, *Golfer*, from the series, *What my parents want me to be when I grow up, A–Z* (2001). Courtesy of the artist.

patio or the mature patron of the arts sitting in her library. Sherman also deals with the reductive nature of these images while suggesting that deeper anxieties associated with gender lie below the surface. Both Vocat and Sherman use their own images as tableaux to recode gender. 'Since the images are archetypal and extreme in their depiction of stereotypes,' says Vocat, 'they point to the artificiality of the original construct.'[21] We laugh at the absurdity while knowing we are caught it its web.

The surreal and at times absurd nature of masculine expectations is further highlighted when Vocat includes unusual professional symbols of the masculine such as the ventriloquist, the 'rough and sexy worker,' and the magician.[22] The social expectations that define the nature of the professional male are disrupted by the inclusion of non-traditional professions. As Vocat explains,[23] 'No parent would aspire for their child to be in a profession such as the ventriloquist.' But by including images of masculine professions that are seldom considered, Vocat points to the complexity of identity and the impossibility of configuring masculinity solely in conventional imagery.

The unexpected nature of Vocat's images creates an opening within the reiteration of gender. Through his folio *A Boy's Will*, he takes up the question of masculine coding and productive desire in a different format. Looking through this folio we are asked to re-think the universalizing imagery of the Boy Scouts and Cub Scouts to become aware of how desire exists within presumably conventional social institutions.

## Cubs and Instruction in Masculinity

The Scout movement, and the ideals represented through its illustrations, have had a tremendous impact upon generations of Canadian boys for whom Scout meetings were a regular occurrence. Perhaps because it was so pervasive at one time, Scout imagery has become a thematic inquiry Vocat has returned to throughout his career. While at the University of Regina he created a project based on images from the *The Cub Book*. Vocat uses these images to reconsider the structure of the learning environment within the Scout organization.[24] He addresses this homosocial environment through a series of screen prints such as *A Boy's Will*. The style of *The Cub Book* is used to portray the behaviour of boys.[25] Vocat reconsiders Cub imagery to think about the 'story that wasn't told or the story kind of beyond the appearance.'[26]

As was the case for many Canadian boys, Vocat was part of the Scout movement for twelve years. He appreciates how the readily available images in *The Cub Book* have a universal appeal that represents a masculine ideal of citizenship. At the same time, Vocat enjoys the sense of nostalgia associated with these images.[27] Instruction in good citizenship is provided to boys through text and images created mostly in the 1940s and 1950s. Perhaps most appealing is the naïve quality of imagery and content; repeatedly boys are instructed that if one engages in simple acts of citizenship then the world will be a better place.[28] As Vocat explains, the images 'come from these handbooks which are basically tools of instruction . . . this is how we do things. Everything's laid out fairly clearly: this is what you are supposed to do to be a good citizen and these are our rules.'[29] Vocat is not interested in simply critiquing the institution of the Scouts, rather he is interested in working within the logic and strengths of the imagery and the social ideals they represent. He merely reconstitutes the Scout images with affection and appreciation of the possibilities for kind instruction that this homosocial environment created for him as a boy.

Cub illustrations were meant to be transnational, universal images. The abstract creation of codes, in this case the sanitized image of the Cub, functions as a technical re-definition of productivity and desire. The images are abstract, oversimplified, and reductive measures of men, since they do not reflect diversity of race, ethnicity, or desire. While ambivalent at times, these abstract images do not represent human worth and well-being in all their radical differences.[30] The oversimplified images instead act as codes because they become measures of masculinity by controlling externalities and reducing the range of interpretations for human behaviour.[31] They also allow the observer to project his own desires onto the image of a boy or man. But a dissonance exists between the coding of desire and identity and how men and boys actually identify and behave in groups. The illustrations therefore do not reflect the real, lived experience of the Cub troop. For example, Vocat contends that the images in *The Cub Book* fail to show the aggression and conflict that occur in male-defined environments.[32]

Furthermore, the simplicity of the Cub images allows some boys to identify with the image without being burdened by a great deal of interpretation. In some cases boys are able to say, 'Yeah, that is me' or 'that's us.'[33] But of course, not all young men can identify with these images. For those who have felt marginalized, it may in fact be impossible to identify with Cub illustrations since the behaviour portrayed is alien to one's own experience. Vocat laments that 'a lot of it was feeling like I was not represented by those images . . . I wish there was an image . . . that said, "It's okay that you're not having the same experience" or . . . "that your experience does not have to be totally sanitized" . . . or "you don't have to feel guilty about not having the same life as that is in all these books." '[34]

The Scout movement could readily be critiqued as a homosocial organization that instructed boys in dominant hegemonic masculinity. The explicit series of instructions about masculine behaviour associated with the images and text of *The Cub Book* function as a version of the performative, part of a series of obligatory practices defined through repetitive acts that become powerful through their persistence.[35] In practice, many of those instructions are refinements of themes of aggression and domination. Within the intricate structure of

Scout training, troop members are awarded patches or stars to put on their uniforms (which give them status) if they accomplish a series of actions leading toward an overall purpose. For example, the image of a boy hitting a punching bag is part of a series of requirements necessary to achieve a Tawny Star. The overall purpose of the Tawny Star is for the Cub to use his 'imagination and creative skills.'[36] In order to be awarded his badge, the boy must meet a series of six requirements and complete two projects to be chosen from a list. The image of the punching bag, part of the thirteenth Tawny Star requirement, is situated within a series of instructions on how to create equipment for boys' games. In this manner creativity is tied to strength, male violence, and aggression, and ironically, actually becomes a prescriptive mode of masculine expression. Similarly, the Black Star with its stated purpose to 'find out about the natural world'[37] also includes an instruction on the proper use of herbicides on a lawn. This passage is accompanied by an image of a boy being instructed by an older man, presumably his father, on how to spray chemicals from a tank on his back.[38] Such domination of the natural world is an instruction one might expect in a homosocial organization, such as the Scout movement, and the boy's practice in the proper use of chemicals is beyond question an act of masculinity. As part of the Black Star requirements, the boy is expected to learn from a mentor about the use of chemicals to kill weeds; domination of the natural world through science thus becomes a taken-for-granted lesson in maleness.

In spite of this critique, Vocat still characterizes the Scout troop as a complex learning environment. His experience of the educational and performative expectations of the Scouts includes a form of ambivalence that invites a nuanced reading of masculine expectations. Although he is well aware of the limits of Cub representations, Vocat is not interested in posing a simple opposition to or a dogmatic message about dominant forms of masculine social expression. Vocat's re-interpretation of Scout images is meant both to pay tribute to the Scouts and to challenge the gender lessons taught to its members.[39]

One of the central characteristics of the Scout experience for Vocat was the dissonance between instruction by rote through a manual and the lived experience of the Cub pack. Vocat is interested in 'the kind of rift between what was taught and how we acted and how people perceived us. So, all of these things were very different, one from the other. The outside perception of any Cub group typically tends to be one of reverence and, you know, "these are good boys, they're doing good things, they're very noble" . . . and then there's the sort of milita-ristic ideas that come along with that, like in terms of regimentation and discipline.'[40]

For Vocat, the oversimplification of the Cub troop as either a group of ideal citizens or a militaristic enterprise is not consistent with the teaching style of his own Cub leaders. Rather than enact the regula-tions of the Scout movement in a dogmatic manner or restrict the range of masculine performance, the members of his Cub pack were held accountable, but he says 'never in a punitive way.' On the con-trary, Vocat feels that leaders gave the Cubs a great deal of autonomy, putting them in the position of making their own moral decisions. The boys were also allowed to make decisions that led to mistakes, then deal with the consequences of those decisions on their own.[41]

Vocat feels at times that Cub instruction and imagery in fact do rep-resent honourable thought and intention. Based on the logic that good acts create good citizens and therefore a good world, many of the les-sons were based in altruism and selflessness. For example, the idea of doing good deeds for people and performing those deeds daily is de-picted as a form of masculine performance with positive social conno-tations. These good deeds were often expected to be acts of kindness with no expectation of personal reward. Vocat sees such sentiments of the Scout movement as laudable.[42] Furthermore, when the boys are left to make their own moral decisions based on altruism and idealism some of their choices can also be surprising. For example, a boy might decide good citizenship involves challenging capitalist notions of aggression and competition. It is possible that such ideas can take root in homosocial environments based on systems of learning that elevate principles like honour.

In light of Vocat's observations, one is encouraged to revisit the *The Cub Book* to find ambivalent characterizations of the masculine. For example, the handbook devotes an entire section to acting and perfor-mance. As with other images in the handbook, the instruction to act is not just an instruction about acting technique, but also touches on the possible expressions of maleness. One illustration concerning acting outlines a range of emotional states such as joy, fear, and innocence that can be acted out. The implication is that emotions which may be in other circumstances defined as being outside the normal range of masculine emotions can be legitimated within the context of the Scouts. In fact, much of the training through illustration and text in

*The Cub Book* concerns people in relationship to each other. In spite of the North American preoccupation with the male as a solitary individual, the Cub imagery regularly illustrates boys cooperatively engaged with one another. For example, an image of a boy feeding a blindfolded boy from a spoon clearly lies outside strictly normative masculine definitions of the male as a solitary, competitive being.

### New Instructions in Masculinity

Vocat builds upon elements of the Scout organization, such as the sense of autonomy afforded the boys and the sense of cooperation between boys, to create his own set of instructions about how to be a man. In the process he also stays true to the design, tone and style of *The Cub Book* by creating elegant, accessible, and simple prints. He re-creates the imagery in a manner that makes us reconsider the instructions about manhood associated with the Scout movement. In the process he also urges us to reconsider gender and desire by building on the potential strengths, such as idealism and kindness, even in the homosocial environment of the Scouts.

As Deleuze was interested in the elusive quality of desire, Vocat is interested not only in masculine regulation and performative possibility, but in the elusive desires and drives of human beings. At times, those desires stand outside the socially constructed prescription of social norms,[43] and Vocat's images enrich the discussion by suggesting that something lies 'beneath the stable world of identities . . . [There is] a world of difference that at once produces those identities and shows them to be little more than froth of what there is.'[44]

Vocat elaborates his ideas of masculinity by layering images – conflicting messages overlap one another within a single frame. Vocat's art can be partially understood as a challenge to masculine social codes, but it also reveals secrets, to 'talk about the idea of the secret' by constructing a new narrative.[45] The power of Vocat's art work lies partially in the secret desire suggested by the image, a secret desire not readily observable nor readily represented in art. In this case, desire exists on the plane of immanence and is seen as continuous.[46] By creating dissonant imagery, Vocat not only represents desires that are easily discernible but suggests desires not yet imagined or coded. The desire articulated in the art is purposely not easily understood. It alludes to qualities that lie beneath and/or outside social convention, and dissonance is created when one image tells a story while the image behind it may be relating quite a differing narrative.[47]

In Vocat's work desire becomes the productive expression of an infinite number of differences. There is also a suggestion that desire may exist prior to coding, not just tied to sexuality but multifarious. In fact, to suggest that the desire expressed by Vocat's images is sexual at all is to jump to the coding of psychoanalytic theory. If desire is seen as elusive no singular act brings about a man and a woman.[48] In Vocat's re-imagining of images, and by implication the coding of desire and productivity, he reminds us of the importance of understanding the discourse of masculinity as a kind of constraint, as suggested by Michel Foucault,[49] constructed through social practices such as those discussed by Judith Butler.[50] Yet the artist expands on these ideas by suggesting that the ambivalent nature of the masculine is by definition difficult to constrain. Whether it is boys exchanging blood, as in Figure 5, or creating anti-war posters as in Figure 7, Vocat's art unsettles by using universalized recognizable images to illustrate difference.

The impact of Vocat's work is made greater by his use of existing scripts and discourse, both in his propaganda and his art, to express desire that hides within the logic of the original images. By using the same style as *The Cub Book*, he suggests that states of desire and secrets of productivity exist within the homosocial context of the Scouts, rather than locating difference as something outside that social environment; Vocat does not construct his understanding from a position of victimhood or from an outsider position. At the same time, he acknowledges both his pleasure and his alienation within this male society,[51] reinterpreting masculine performance and practices to include alienation while admitting to a certain pleasure in his own experience of homosocial environments.

Vocat entitles one of his Scout folios *A Boy's Will*, suggesting that beyond the social constraint of the homosocial is desire and intent. The will of the Cubs is not easily contained within coded imagery: anything is possible when desire is seen as creative and experimental in nature.[52] This difference can also be constructed within an environment that allows for error, has ambivalent leadership, and allows for agency and self-determination. The subversive quality inherent in the image is that a boy might combine the elements of his social environment to become a peace activist or someone who uses a slingshot to hit an SUV (Figure 6) as easily as he would to become a boxer or a chemical engineer. The Blood Brothers image (Figure 5) is especially

Figure 5: Daryl Vocat, *Blood Brothers*, from the limited edition folio, *A Boy's Will* (2006). Courtesy of the artist.

powerful because it documents a common, and dangerous, social ritual among young boys while making it difficult to imagine what desire could lead to such an exchange of blood.

Repetition through a series is another important principle in Vocat's art. Through his use of series his art anticipates and reinvents the 'regulated process of repetition that both conceals itself and enforces its rules through the production of substantializing [*sic*] effects'[53] that makes certain genders possible. Vocat, however, is careful not to use repetition to construct an overarching image or a generalized paradigm of masculinity. Although there is similarity of technique in his image construction, the content of the image is not intended to create a similitude. Quite the contrary, repetition in Vocat's work is best understood in the spirit of Deleuze, who values each image as a singularity even as it is repeated. According to Deleuze, repetition is important for the manner in which it unveils the expression of difference

Figure 6: Daryl Vocat, *Untitled*, from the limited edition folio, *A Boy's Will* (2006). Courtesy of the artist.

rather than as a means to seek out similarity through repeated patterns.[54]

Repetition in a series serves an additional purpose for Vocat, who has no interest in being adversarial no matter how unsettling the image. According to Vocat, 'I think the relationship between having serial work is a more rich one, where the work kind of develops its own conversation, rather than having a more adversarial relationship with the viewer when you know you're just seeing one work.'[55] An individual art work makes a statement that ends once it is presented to the viewer, while in a series images can have a conversation with each other, not simply with the viewer. The richness of the series is in its ability to find connections between individual works and allow for narratives to exist among the individual images. The series suggests a plane of immanence, a place where connectivity occurs between difference. Rather than implying an external or transcendent definition

Figure 7: Daryl Vocat, *Repeat this process until you reach your objective* (2005). Courtesy of the artist.

of the social, the plane of immanence is an affirmative place where intensity becomes manifest in all its difference in this context. It is less important to know the source of difference than to honour the expression.[56] The expression of male desire does not anticipate an audience; rather it has an a priori existence. It is as well understood in relation to networks as it is in the binary of the observer and the observed.

In a sense, Vocat is claiming a space between and beyond the symbols he is using. Surely this type of interpretation is best done by men who have not been able to fully identify with male codes. Even as Vocat exposes secrets, he intimates that there are other secrets not yet known. His images offer an instruction that suggests there are many possible ways to live as a man or a boy, that male identity is filled with creative possibilities.[57] His Cub prints represent a series of realities, however poorly understood, that exist side by side, as well as alongside the illustrations of *The Cub Book*.[58] The images include boys in relation to each other, and the images as a whole are presented in relation to each other. This connective web of singular representations of masculinity makes revolutionary forms of interaction possible whether they be within the singularity in the space between the boys or the images. This, in turn, allows for a new flow of desire to be expressed.[59]

Of course, an irony exists in having Vocat as an instructor. He does not direct us to the practice of the masculine; rather he alludes to possibilities that are poorly documented, and perhaps even not yet known. In this manner, Vocat directs a form of rhizomatic change when it comes to masculinity. His images ask us to question whether intensities or desire pre-exist the visual coding of men. The activities depicted by Vocat suggest a series of behaviours and activities within the Cub troop without imposing hierarchy either through a moral code or through the original source. Since there are no hierarchical classification systems here, the Cubs making silk screens are given the same import or value as the Cubs engaged in boxing. They are rendered with the same care and visualized with the same respect. Vocat reminds us that these intensities by nature are not easily coded, and cannot be organized in one overriding paradigm of the nature of man: their relationship to each other is necessarily open and ambivalent. As much as the male images occur as closed and complete, either through commercial culture or through the homosocial environment of the Scouts, Vocat reminds us the act of being a man is a polymorphous one that may be best understood as de-centred in practice.[60]

Throughout his work Vocat offers re-interpretations of information and images that create breaks in pervasive symbolic cultures. There is a challenge to dominant codes of maleness implied in this approach to art. When one is a boy or man in a world saturated with imagery, it may not be as useful to claim identities in the abstract, but rather to begin to understand and situate oneself within the context of the images and their social demands. Vocat suggests we can experience and express desire within those dominant symbolic cultures and addresses the concerns of the alienated boy by reinterpreting the instruction about maleness he is getting in groups like the Scouts. Through reinterpretation, he suggests one can construct a new form of desire and difference and, therefore, a new form of art and learning that allows us to conceive of genders not yet imagined. There is no handbook for such an understanding of maleness and desire.

# 4 Troubling Role Models: Seeing Racialization in the Discourse Relating to 'Corrective Agents' for Black Males

CARL E. JAMES

## Introduction

In an effort to address the educational, social, and cultural challenges of Black youth,[1] particularly males, educational and social service institutions have in recent years initiated mentorship programs through which so-called 'successful' adult Black males are paired with younger counterparts to help with their educational assignments, family issues, and social concerns. The assumption behind such programs is that boys require male role models and mentors – 'corrective agents,' to borrow Patrick Shannon's term[2] – if they are to do well in school and become socially responsible, productive citizens. Role models and mentors are people who are seen to have taken full advantage of the opportunities and possibilities in life. In the case of Black male youth, mentors and role models are meant to provide evidence that despite any limitations and barriers Black youth may face, it is still possible for them to achieve what they want to achieve – these days, even in Canada, American President Barack Obama is put forward as an example. The message seems to be that racial and socio-economic barriers are personal constructs which can effectively be navigated, negotiated, and even overcome if young people heed the teachings, values, and examples of their mentors and role models. Furthermore, any challenges or 'setbacks' these young people might face are seen as opportunities for building character and strength.

Some time ago I received an invitation from a high school teacher to visit his media class, about one-third of which was composed of Black students. The teacher was concerned both by the students' apparent lack of ambition and by the negative images of Blacks to which they were being exposed. He wanted them to meet, as he put it, 'someone who holds a position in a university.' To this teacher, I represented a successful Black male who, like his students, must have experienced racism first hand, and so would be able to show them that 'they too can be successful by focusing on their academic work.'[3]

More recently in a graduate class, we watched the movie *Invisible City*,[4] which documented what life had been like for two young Black men, Mikey and Kendall, and their mentor teacher Mr Morgan, all of whom had grown up in one of Canada's oldest low-income, racially diverse neighbourhoods in downtown Toronto. The teacher, a Black male in his late thirties now living in a middle-class suburban Toronto neighbourhood, nurtured and supported Mikey and Kendall from the time they were in his Grade 7 class until they were eighteen years old. (The film covered a four-year period of their lives.) Mr Morgan was shown in conversation with the young men – sometimes individually, sometimes in a group – about their legal troubles and how to navigate the justice system, their education and the importance of paying attention to their school work, and about their respect for their mothers – both were only children who lived with their mothers. The movie also showed Morgan's return to the apartment (in a building now slated for demolition) in which he had lived with his younger brother and his mother, who had immigrated from Jamaica five years before she sent for her two sons. Morgan reminisced about sharing the room with his brother and noted how small both the bedroom and even the apartment now seemed. The scene was made more meaningful after we saw Morgan with his three young children (including two boys under the age of ten) and Mikey and Kendall at Morgan's big house in the suburbs – a long way physically and socially from his old neighbourhood. The mentorship and role-modelling Morgan provided was clear: Morgan was able to show Mikey and Kendall evidence of the success they might have if they applied themselves to their school work, kept out of trouble, and listened to their mothers. He also showed sensitivity and an understanding concerning the young men's plight, growing up in a neighbourhood where, as he put it, 'manhood comes early . . . [and] being weak is not an option.' In the film Morgan saw himself as a positive force in the lives of Mikey and Kendall. As he put it: 'Every child needs to have someone in their world that he or she does not want to disappoint.'

In the class discussion that followed the movie, one young Black female student commended Morgan (who was our class guest), saying:

'We need more men like you. We need more role models and mentors like you.' Her comment was prompted in part by the noticeable absence of the boys' fathers in their lives, and a direct comment from one of the boys that his father had had little time for him. By contrast, Mr Morgan was seen as a 'good man' and father serving as an appropriate male role model for Mikey and Kendall to emulate. After all, he played with his sons and daughter, and he had no problem telling Mikey and Kendall, as they were parting, 'I love you.' The need for male figures, and more precisely father figures, for 'fatherless' Black boys looms large in the discourse of mentorship and role modelling. In fact, it is widely just assumed that men like Mr Morgan can be instrumental in 'fixing' the lives of young men growing up without fathers.

Over the years Toronto media, in an effort to explain the violence and the poor educational performance of Black youth in parts of the city, have gone as far as to blame their problems explicitly on the fact they are 'from fatherless homes.'[5] A 2005 *Globe and Mail* article entitled 'The Many Fatherless Boys in Black Families' asks:

> Who is doing the killing and who is being killed in the wave of reckless public violence that has struck Toronto? Black boys and young men with no fathers in their homes. Yet as politicians at all three levels and black community leaders scramble for answers to the anarchy, no one has dared talk about the crisis of fatherlessness in the black community. The silence is inexcusable. Growing up without a father present is now the norm for many black children in Canada, particularly those of Jamaican ancestry. Nearly half of all black children under fourteen in Canada have just one parent in the home, compared to slightly under one in five Canadian children as a whole, census figures from 2001 show. Two in three Jamaican-Canadian children in Toronto are being raised by a single parent. The U.S. trend of 'radical fatherlessness' – in which the majority of children in an apartment building, on a street, or in a neighbourhood lack fathers – is hitting Toronto like a tsunami.[6]

In a similar 2007 *Toronto Star* article, 'Where Are the Men?,' based on visits to and interviews with single mothers – mostly Black – in public housing, community groups, and churches, Linda Diebel reported that for the most part the women were 'raising children on little money, often in public housing where kids are exposed to greater risks, because it's all they can afford.'[7] Diebel went on to underscore that a great number of the women interviewed were themselves raised in fatherless homes, had themselves become teenage mothers, and struggled financially to support their children while also protecting them from the constant threat of violence, drugs, and gang activity. Diebel cited the experience of one mother who worked two jobs to support her three children – one of whom, her oldest, had been to jail on a gun-related charge, something for which this mother took responsibility. As Diebel put it, the woman 'beat herself up for not spending more time with her son.' This mother was also quoted as saying:

> We are single mothers working two and three jobs to keep bread on the table, and they don't care . . . The fathers aren't helping and the kids are turning to crime . . . But fathers make a big difference . . . I hear the kids and they're always talking about their fathers, and how they're not there. That's what these fathers have to realize. They must step up to the plate. They must. Because when they're not here, they're replaced by other factors like gangs. Kids need role models, not deadbeat dads.[8]

The notion that Black boys need fathers (and Black male teachers) as role models was also expressed by Charles Johnson in his work about the 'Black American Condition Today.' There he writes that 'without strong, self-sacrificing, frugal and industrious fathers as role models, our boys go astray, never learn how to be parents (or men), and perpetuate the dismal situation of single-parent homes run by tired and overworked Black women.'[9] Chris Spence, director of the Toronto District School Board, would agree. A proponent of a *Boys to Men* program that is structured around role-modelling and mentorship for 'at risk' Black boys,[10] Spence has recently advocated for an all-boys elementary school as a response to lower test scores and higher rates of school suspensions and expulsion for male students. Based on his teaching experiences, Spence suggests strong mentors for boys can likely offset the 'fatherless worlds' from which they come.[11]

This call for mentors and role models is built on a notion that the problems Black boys face are largely a product of their individual attitudes, values, actions, and sense of purpose. By extension, it also reflects on parents – mothers who are unable to provide the appropriate and necessary support and guidance; and fathers whose neglectful and irresponsible behaviour evident in their absence has allowed the boys to go 'astray,' having failed to learn positive models of maleness from the person believed to be best suited to teach them. The fact that the media, politicians, educators, social service workers, parents, and community members – white and Black – are touting the merits of mentors and role models strongly suggests a prevailing opinion that the problems of our Black young men are best addressed through individual efforts, and not through systemic changes.

In this chapter, I argue that this focus on mentorship and role modelling in addressing the problems of young Black males is premised on the liberalist notion of individualism that holds these young males, their parents, and their communities responsible for their situation. Meanwhile the disproportionately poor educational performance and worrisome social circumstances which contradict the assumed equity, democracy, and accessibility in our society are explained away by the 'common-sense' notion of fatherlessness (understood as male father figure absent from the home). If one common characteristic among these young men is that they are raised by single mothers, it only seems logical that providing them with 'substitute fathers' – mentors and role models – would help ameliorate their situation. But I would argue this simplistic approach is more a case of 'blaming the victim,' an attempt at holding individuals responsible for what are, in fact, larger social problems. This common-sense approach is part of a new racism which operates to obscure the obvious systemic or structural impediments facing these young men and their parents, thereby leaving the status quo intact.[12] Gender itself is also understood to be central as a factor in racism. As Abby Ferber puts it, 'gender is constructed through race, and race is constructed through gender; they are intersectional and mutually constitutive.'[13] In what follows, I define this notion of new racism, go on to explore how it operates in the construction of Black males as 'deficient,' and discuss the role of the media and minority group members in this process.

**New Racism**

New racism can be defined as an inconspicuous, even covert approach to issues of inequity that unambiguously accepts racial preconceptions pertaining to issues of minority group members. In today's societies, 'old-fashioned' racism – that is, overt segregation, educational streaming, antagonism, name-calling – is widely thought to have been all but eliminated, and it is believed that race and racism no longer play pivotal roles when it comes to accessibility to societal resources.[14] According to Etienne Balibar new racism is 'a racism whose dominant theme is not biological heredity but the insurmountability of cultural differences, a racism which, at first sight, does not postulate the superiority of certain groups or peoples in relation to others but "only" the harmfulness of abolishing frontiers, the incompatibility of lifestyles and traditions.'[15] Historical forms of racism were explicit in suggesting biological or hereditary bases for individuals' superiority or inferiority. The racism of the twenty-first century proffers simultaneously a colour-blind ideology and a cultural difference epistemology, what Balibar terms the 'idea of racism without race.'[16] Vala Jorge would go further, suggesting that the covert attitudes, beliefs, and behaviours of new racism position the *other* as deeply different and inferior.[17]

Many scholars hold that the post – civil rights era in North America ushered in a shift in racism, through the outlawing of overt legal practices of white supremacy and the recognition of legal claim of minorities and Blacks in particular, to the principles of liberalism – democracy, equal opportunity, meritocracy, justice, and fairness.[18] Nevertheless, the new racism that evolved remains firmly wedded to the ideology of white supremacy: it merely operates with 'practices that are subtle, institutional, and apparently non-racial.'[19] In the new paradigm, racism is widely considered a thing of the past, yet the social and racial order of things remain. Frances Henry and Carol Tator use the term 'democratic racism' in reflecting on how and why white primacy remains intact despite claims of a post-racialist society. Democratic racism, they write, 'results from the retention of racist beliefs and behaviours in a "democratic" society.'[20] Its distinguishing feature remains its 'justification of the inherent conflict between the egalitarian values of liberalism . . . and the racist ideologies reflected in the collective mass belief system as well as the racist attitudes, perceptions, and assumptions of individuals.'[21]

Colour-blindness is a major tenet of new racism. In this new democratic racial system, white privilege remains untouched while even the suggestion that racism still exists is immediately rejected. Indeed, as Eduardo Bonilla-Silva writes with reference to the United States (of course, this can be applied to the Canadian experience as well),

> Compared to Jim Crow racism, the ideology of color-blindness seems like 'racism lite.' Instead of relying on name-calling, color-blind racism otherizes softly; instead of proclaiming that God placed minorities in the world in a servile position, it suggests they are behind because they do not work hard enough . . . And the beauty of this new ideology is that it

aids in the maintenance of white privilege without fanfare, without naming those who it subjects and those who it rewards.[22]

What is particularly troublesome about the misleading colour-blindness of new racist discourse is its practice of seeking out and referencing 'successful' Blacks (in dominant culture terms) like President Barack Obama, American media star and talk-show host Oprah Winfrey, American basketball player Michael Jordan, and former Canadian Governor-General (representative of the Queen of England) Michaëlle Jean as examples of the efficacy of the system of meritocracy and in turn, a justification for the elimination of equity and affirmative action (employment and educational) programs.[23] In the new paradigm, the failure of individuals to live successful lives no longer is attributed to racism but to 'the moral shortcomings of minority group members.'[24] The message becomes that it is hard work and not privilege that determines success. But this belief ignores the systemic barriers which render many opportunities inaccessible to people of colour while conveniently absolving whites, and others who operate on their behalf, of any responsibility in the maintenance of white privilege.

The presentation of Blacks who have 'made it' further reinforces the common-sense notion that individuals can create their own destinies and opportunities, irrespective of whatever structural impediments they face in the society. As Patricia Hill Collins notes, writing of the United States context, 'the joblessness, poor schools, racially segregated neighborhoods, and unequal public services that characterize American society vanish, and social class hierarchies . . . as well as patterns of social mobility within them, become explained solely by issues of individual values, motivation, and morals.'[25]

Lack of acceptance and respect for the cultures of minority racial groups based, in part, on presumptions of immorality due to individual failures, violence, and/or underperformance replaces the arguments of biological differences used in racist models in the past.[26] These new explanations comfort those who benefit from their race privilege, as they can take solace in believing that 'they are not involved in the terrible ordeal or in creating and maintaining inequality.'[27] At the same time, as Eduardo Bonilla-Silva argues, those who benefit from race privilege are 'charmed by the almost magic qualities' of the hegemonic discourse and the representation of 'people like them who have made it.' They point to the successes of minority group members, the so-called 'model minorities,' to argue that it is group and cultural deficiencies[28] that are responsible for the low performance, the feelings of inferiority, and the low self-confidence of racial minority group members as they confront the evidence that their lack of success as majority group members is their responsibility.

Several scholars have discussed the role of the mass media in manufacturing and recycling such common-sense ideas until they become part of the dominant popular imagination.[29] Everyday images and representations of minorities serve to remind people of the 'truth' of the common-sense notions about their poor education and antisocial behaviour. Indeed, the media's role in the constructed images of minority members is, in part, supported by schools, courts, law enforcement agencies, arts organizations and cultural institutions, human services, governments, politicians, and businesses.[30] Such institutions operate in a context where racist ideology and related racist discourse produces (in some people) a constant tension created by the contradiction between their own experiences with stereotyping and racism, and the notion (often internalized) that they are the cause of their own misfortune. This tension stems from an expectation that all members of society conduct themselves according to the morality and values of 'individual self-reliance, obedience, discipline and hard work' seen to be white European male middle-class norms.[31]

New racism, in the words of Paul Gordon and Francesca Klug, is 'a cluster of beliefs which holds that it is natural for people who share a way of life, a culture, to bond together in a group and to be antagonistic towards outsiders who are different and who are seen to threaten their identity as a group.'[32] As such, people whose language and actions are racist will claim that they are not, 'nor are they making any value judgements about minority group members, but simply recognizing that they are different.'[33] In this context the disadvantages minority group members experience as a result of their race are seen not as discrimination, but as a consequence of their inability to conform to the prevailing values and norms of society.[34] In this sense, to say that Black youth require mentors and role models in order to lead successful lives and to develop a healthy sense of what it means to be a man (masculinity as defined by prevailing norms, values, and morality) is to use the language of difference to conceal a systemic racism by which Black males are essentialized on the basis of cultural difference.

## Young Black Men, Corrective Agents, and the New
## Racism Discourse

In her article 'The Construction of Black Masculinity,' Abby Ferber raises a question with reference to the condition of Blacks in the United States: 'How can a White supremacist nation, which subjects Black men to ongoing racism and demonization, at the same time admire and worship Black men as athletes?'[35] Insofar as Canada is a culturally similar White supremacist nation, a similar question could be asked.[36] But here I would ask another question: How can we explain the fact that coaches, teachers, principals, students, and the media all appreciate and support Black student athletes whose profiles compared to those of their white athletic peers regularly include low grades, temper tantrums, and sometimes fierce, violent behaviour both during games and in the community? Often we read only of these athletes when they are potential scholarship winners at American universities.[37] Is it that coaches, educators, and sport reporters accept the athletic abilities of Black males as 'natural' as compared to their white peers, who have gained theirs through practice?[38] From a new racism perspective, the answer would be that 'natural' in this case does not imply genetics, as would have been the case previously, but an assumption that sport is an inherent part of Black culture – something into which Blacks are socialized. But why would sports be linked to Blacks over others, when we do see other ethnic and racial groups similarly involved in sports? Why is it that sport tends to be more often identified with keeping Black students in school than it is with other students? Are the *cultures* of Black people not just as diverse, dynamic, unpredictable, and adaptable over time as other cultures? How is it that Black youth seem to maintain cultural values and aspirations uninformed by the prevailing European, middle-class, male, heterosexual norms and mores?

Ferber argues there is a 'naturalization of racial difference in sports discourse' that argues for the natural athleticism of Black men, at the same time as their masculinity is seen as inferior, overly physical, driven by instinct, aggressive, threatening, prone to violence, and hypersexual.[39] The enduring historical 'naturalized' images of Black males not only perpetuate fear of the Black male body but are used to give credence to the idea that they must be controlled or tamed. The message is that Black males are 'essentially bad boys,' but that some can be transformed into 'good guys' if tamed.[40] In this sense, sport serves as a mechanism through which coaches[41] and sports figures, operating as mentors and role models, send Black male youth the message that it is possible for them to succeed in this society in spite of their colour. Successful athletes are used as models. Young Black males are told that if they live by the discipline and moral codes of sport the opportunities are there for them to succeed. It has become common to see athletes taking this colour-blind 'bootstrap message'[42] to students in schools in North America. And young people, mesmerized by the perceived success – the scholarships, money, clothing, women, and travels of these 'role models and mentors' – fall for the message. They try to emulate their heroes, wearing sports attire that bears their names and numbers. The irony is that many of these same role models and mentors who today encourage young people to 'stay in school' did not in fact apply themselves to their own education – secondary and postsecondary – as they would have their young protégés believe. Missing in the message of these successful athletes are their own struggles to find meaning in their own alienating, inequitable schooling experiences. Absent also are the stories of many of their athletic peers who did not make it in sport. And little is said about the limits that focusing exclusively on sport put on their time to pursue other possibilities, or on developing knowledge and skills that would prepare them for life after their sporting careers end.

Mentors of all kinds are often presented as stand-in fathers for the many 'fatherless' Black male youth about whom there are growing concerns, particularly when it comes to gang membership and the related violence. Reporting on the question of 'Why Kids Join Gangs' in 2006, *Toronto Star* article reporter Moira Welsh writes:

> These high-risk boys are poor, often from dysfunctional homes or ones where one parent has left, usually a father. Many fail in school, where teachers cannot cope with unruly, unfocused students. At home, there are no rules. Some of their mothers work fourteen-hour days, and when their sons say they are at a Boys and Girls Club playing basketball, they believe them. The neighbourhoods they come from are populated by blacks and other minorities, as are the schools, in pockets of the inner city.[43]

Such concerns about young Black males have been much discussed in various media reports and editorials. For instance 2005 has been referred to as 'the Year of the Gun' because of the shootings involving young Black men both as victims and perpetrators. The *Toronto Star* ran a series of articles focusing on what they called 'gang violence' within the Black community. In many of the news stories, editorials, and letters to the editor, fatherlessness was put forward as a primary cause of the delinquency among Black males. The situation was described as a 'moral panic' the Black community needed to address. In this same period, CBC Radio held a number of interviews, town hall meetings, and online moderated discussions with members of Black and non-Black communities on the topic 'Growing up without men.' In addition to the prominent Canadian community members and scholars invited to speak on the issue, as always happens with the Canadian media, notable African Americans were also brought into the discussion. For the most part, the guests on various programs agreed that fatherlessness or not having a father figure in the home was responsible for the behaviours of the young members of the Black communities.

For example, Dr Orlando Patterson, a prominent African American scholar, proffered that many of the traits and behaviours taken on by young Black men were related to the culture of 'hyper-masculinity and sexual prowess' which included 'being a father – [or] at least having children.'[44] He agreed that the absence of their fathers from their homes was a reflection of the culture within the community. Another American, Rev. Eugene Rivers of Boston, commented on 'a high correlation between father absence, single parent households and criminal behaviour particularly on the part of young males.' He also contended that 'Canada's black community faces a crisis. A generation of poor, predominantly black youth is in violent rebellion against their fatherlessness and, by logical extension, against law and order and an established middle-class black leadership that purports to speak for them.' Rivers, like the other people who participated in the series, blamed the problems Toronto was experiencing with its Black youth on both their families and the Black community, suggesting that these groups needed to take responsibility for the violence. 'Internally,' Rivers said, 'the black community has to make a decision that it will move beyond excuses, asking for funding to do programs which can be initiated without funding.'[45]

Some four years after that record number of gun-related homicides among young Black men in Toronto, the media continued to give voice to those who identify Black youth problems with a lack of positive role models, particularly among youth living in 'inner city' neighbourhoods. For example, in 2009 the *National Post* carried an article by Wendell Adjetey, who wrote,

> Young, Black males are falling by the wayside primarily because they lack positive male role models. Census data reveals nearly 60% of all Black Canadian children live with a single parent mother. For this particular reason, it is imperative that social service providers focus more specifically on establishing mentorship networks that would provide inner-city males with positive role models who are also family oriented.[46]

This call for institutionalized mentorship and role model programs by members of the community is consistent with a longstanding media message. It also suggests that the media do not feel the need to call into question the skills and abilities of the single mothers who seem incapable of raising their children. And the media, other institutions, and non-Black members of the society are not the only ones raising concerns over fatherlessness, and by extension, the moral implications of the way Black men supposedly practise masculinity. Insofar as members of the Black community are raising similar concerns, and seeing the problems as largely 'internal' to the community, as Rev. Rivers suggested, then it seems that the problems are more a product of particular cultural values and mores in the Black community rather than systemic racism and inequity. And since there are Black men who have demonstrated that it is possible to live honest, productive, and respectable lives – Barack Obama, Bill Cosby (comedian, television star), Chris Bosh (basketball star), Michael 'Pinball' Clemens (football star, coach, and president within Canadian Football League), not to mention doctors, professors, and police officers, many of whom are willing and able to become mentors and 'positive role models' – then the implicit message is that individuals are responsible for their own destinies. The point here seems to be that there is no excuse for fathers not to be taking responsibility for their children.

Following the premise that Black youth are equally capable of living successful lives within the current structure, and that 'corrective agents' are in place to support parents and young people who are willing to take advantage of such opportunities, we are seeing a proliferation of mentorship programs in schools and social service agencies. One such program is *Boys to Men*, in which male teachers and other volunteer mentors work with 'at risk' Black middle-school and high-school students in the Toronto area, providing them with 'positive images' of

Black males designed to change their 'negative attitudes towards life and academic achievement' and revive a self-esteem that, as Spence writes, has been 'battered by the pervasive negative images of people like themselves.'[47] While Spence did not explicitly say it, his call in the fall of 2009 for a boys-only school seems designed to build on the *Boys to Men* model.[48] But it would appear that while institutionalizing a gendered approach to addressing the needs of boys – all boys, Black or not – is acceptable, such a school exclusively for Black boys would likely be summarily rejected if we consider the recent negative reactions to the establishment of just such an Afrocentric school. The different reactions to a male-focused school versus a Black-focused school have to do with the fact that the latter is still seen as a form of 'segregation' while the former is in keeping with the discourse of multiculturalism – that is, not having a program of study in which race (specifically Blackness and related issues of racism and colonialism) is identified as having a defining role in individual's experiences.[49]

Ontario Premier Dalton McGuinty was vehemently opposed to the Afrocentric school, calling it a form of segregation, but quickly endorsed the idea of a boys-only school, saying 'our boys are not doing well as our girls when it comes to reading and behavioural challenges . . . You can put in place a curriculum that speaks to their special needs and opportunities and that focuses on some of their challenges, including reading and behavioural.'[50] When asked about having a school that would to do the same for Black students as for boys, the premier responded in this way: 'This is an all-boys school – not a some-boys school. All colours, all faiths, all cultures, all heritages, and traditions. All boys.' Putting aside the fact that there is no way of knowing which boys would attend a 'boys-only' school, it seems the idea of having a school that would focus on the experiences of Black students and engage young Black males in an education program and curriculum that would speak to their experience is unacceptable to many white people; even seen as a form of racism, perhaps. But the implicit message continues that there is nothing wrong with the schools – Black youth can succeed in the present system, but only if they are disciplined and apply themselves to their school work – and there is ample evidence of that belief. But that same evidence is not applied in the same way to meeting the needs of Black male students; instead, mentors and role models programs are expected to suffice.

Indeed, many male teachers enter the profession hoping to become just that – mentors and role models. For instance, in her recent study of male teachers working in elementary schools, Kimberley Tavares-Carter observed that one of the key ways these teachers felt that they could positively affect the interests of young Black males was through mentoring. Martin, she writes, 'feels that mentorship is about working with and for students to provide the "aggressive, proactive intervention" he and others felt is needed to support Black males as they navigate the school system. This is why they became teachers.'[51] It was noted that five of the eight teacher respondents looked at working in elementary school as a 'proactive measure' as opposed to 'reactive' – as Martin remarked, 'trying to get them [young students] on track when they're in grades 8, 9, 10, it's a bit more difficult.'[52] Speaking to this desire among teachers to be mentors and role models to young Black males at a stage in their lives when they are still 'save-able,' Tavares-Carter writes:

> Martin felt that he had to "cultivate a sense of self and cultivate this very confident progressive person in students." Omar sought to enrich the lives of the next generation by helping kids who are marginalized . . . For Kevin, being a teacher gave him the opportunity to "create a different experience for people who experience the world from the same place as me." Roy wanted to ensure that students "know that you are not coming just to talk about sports, but trying to help them with life itself."[53]

What is particularly interesting in Tavares-Carter's work is her starting point. She had set out to assert the need to have Black male teachers working with Black male high school students. As a Black female teacher she felt she was only able to partially connect with her Black male students and attributes this to gender differences. The students, she assumed, could more fully relate to male teachers. That assumption is consistent with the general common-sense belief in the need for father figures in the lives of young Black males. But the experiences of the people Tavares-Carter interviewed should themselves signal that the lack of males, and more precisely, the absence of fathers, does not mean Black boys could not live respectful and ambitious lives and have important, successful careers through the strong support of their single mothers. In fact, Tavares-Carter noted that six of her eight respondents, all teachers, 'grew up solely with their mothers who nurtured, guided and gave them a solid foundation' that helped to guide them through difficulties in the education and social systems.[54] One talked of having 'a strong mother and grandmother who pushed him,' and several spoke of doing things to make their mothers 'proud' of them.[55] Ainsworth Morgan from the movie

*Invisible City,* now a successful parent, teacher, and role model, also talked of growing up with his single mother, from whom he was separated for about five years, and of the significant role she played making him the person he is today – an experience he uses to prompt the youth he mentored to appreciate the efforts of their own mothers. Similarly, Conrad (a pseudonym), who participated in a study I conducted with about twenty university students from a low-income, high-density, largely racial minority community in Toronto, spoke of his mother as someone who 'understood you go to school, do your homework, you do well.' This was an idea he internalized, and which has contributed both to his success as a Master of Business Administration graduate and now in his early stages of practising corporate law.[56] Indeed, as Lawson-Bush writes concerning the participation of Black mothers in their sons' lives, 'no aspect or component of Black male life eluded these mothers in their ability to teach lessons that were necessary for manhood or the development of masculinity.'[57]

While male mentors and role models clearly do have a role to play in the lives of Black boys, the evidence suggests that simple exposure to 'corrective agents' will not in themselves result in young Black males pulling 'themselves up to social respectability by their bootstrap.'[58] It is also simplistic to suggest, as one of Tavares-Carter's respondent did, that 'no other than a Black man can teach a Black kid how to be responsible Black adult.'[59] Such thinking ignores the structural inequity that restricts opportunity and possibilities for individuals on the basis of race – a reality that persists despite the colour-blind message of institutionalized Canadian multicultural discourse. Further, the idea that Black male mentors and role models are best positioned to provide Black youth with a specific moral education is built on an assumption that their racial or cultural identity alone would make those corrective agents effective translators of the prevailing moral ethos; that they would be able to solve all the problems confronting disempowered Black youth and their communities; and that without changing the social order, they alone could 'eradicate racism or have special knowledge about how to effectively challenge it.'[60] This idea of Black corrective agents having 'special knowledge' is premised on a racializing discourse that treats minorities, in this case Black youth and adult mentors and role models, as homogeneous. In the end, white teachers, social service workers, and others are neither expected nor asked to do anything but point Black male students in the direction of Black male role models and mentors (that is, teachers), let alone address or evaluate how white teachers, social service workers, and most importantly, the system, contribute to the marginalization and racialization of Black youth.

## Conclusion

Let me be clear. While there is certainly some value to having or presenting Black males as mentors and role models for Black youth, having Black mentors and role models is by no means all that is needed in a society where inequity, marginalization, and racialization still exist, and where new racism, now couched in cultural terms, suggests that it is simply individual disposition or community cultural standards that are responsible for the reduced circumstances of Black and other minority youth. Liberal notions of colour-blindness and individualism voiced by media, educators, social services, and government institutions would have us believe everyone has access to the same quality of life and opportunity in society. The evidence suggests otherwise. Hence, corrective agents cannot simply work within the existing social and educational system and produce uncritical young people who conform to the status quo in terms of prevailing values, role expectations, and beliefs about the society. Mentors and role models will need to give attention to the complexity and contradictions of those young people's lives in a society where they do not feel the same sense of belonging as white youth.

Furthermore, as I have written elsewhere, unless mentorship and role model programs interrogate the 'hegemonic structure of the normalized white male masculinity into which Black males are being socialized and expected or forced to fit'[61] then they are unlikely to be effective. The starting point in the re-education or re-socialization of young Black males need not be about their 'single mothers' or about their 'fatherlessness,' but an education that gives them the critical skills and tools to understand and assess how the cultural forces in school and other socializing environments might help to shape their race and gender identities, school performance, and marginalization, and how they construct and perform their Black heterosexual masculinities in relation to that hegemonic social structure. The real responsibility of role models and mentors is to help young Black males with whom they work to recognize both their agency and their social and cultural capital, and to gain a critical understanding of their relationship to the power structures of society and the ways in which these structures inform their responses, and construct their identities and experiences.

# 5 Queering Asian Masculinities and Transnationalism: Implications for Anti-Oppression and Consciousness-Raising

GORDON PON

## Introduction

I write this chapter from my position as a Chinese Canadian, heterosexual, able-bodied, Christian,[1] middle-class man, who is a professor in the School of Social Work at Ryerson University in downtown Toronto. Our school is committed to anti-oppression, a critical approach to social work that is concerned with the pursuit of social justice and eradicating oppression.[2] In Asian American studies, one of the most contentious topics has been Asian masculinities. I find linking debate around Asian masculinity with anti-oppression discourse very useful, strengthening the engagement of anti-oppression perspectives with consciousness raising, queerness, globalization, and transnationalism. Moreover, this merger helps anti-oppression activists to grasp how local spaces of Toronto, such as bubble tea houses and locally performed cappellas, can be inseparable from the global circulation of culture, capital, and knowledge. This chapter therefore aims to combine scholarship around Asian masculinities with anti-oppression perspectives in social work.

Anti-oppression discourse emerged in the 1980s and 1990s as a response to social work theories that had been called into question for ignoring phenomena such as racism and sexism.[3] Viewed as a more inclusive approach compared to its predecessor, anti-racism,[4] anti-oppression is eclectic in its borrowing from earlier influences of Marxist, socialist, and radical ideologies,[5] and in its current engagement with and enrichment of fields of study such as anti-racism, feminism, postmodernism, and poststructuralism. Anti-oppression emphasizes self-reflexivity[6] which critiques personal privilege, biases, power, and oppression as they relate to social differences such as race, class, gender, sexual orientation, and dis/ability.[7]

One method endorsed by anti-oppression as a way to affect social justice is critical consciousness-raising,[8] which combats oppression by helping people understand how oppression operates in their lives and in the world. Consciousness-raising or critical pedagogy, with its roots in the ideas of Brazilian educator Paulo Friere,[9] is critiqued for possessing an underlying ideological motive to change people's awareness.[10] The method assumes that if the 'right narrative is privileged' people will change,[11] an assumption premised upon innocent and rational notions of the self,[12] which minimize the irrational elements of social violence such as racism, homophobia, and sexism.[13] Thus consciousness-raising often seems to stumble when knowledge is refused and resisted by learners.[14] The realization that some might rather not know or talk about racism presents a challenge for both consciousness-raising and anti-oppression.

Here, I look at the debates surrounding Asian masculinities and highlight how David Eng's[15] queer approach offers anti-oppression an escape from its presumed rationalistic pitfalls. His approach also helps anti-oppression discourse engage with concepts of diaspora, globalization, and transnationalism. By drawing on interviews with two Chinese Canadian youths in Toronto, I grapple with how they understand and experience globalization and transnationalism, a phenomenon full of contradictions, limitations, and pain, as well as possibilities and pleasures.

## Methodology

This chapter is based on doctoral research I did between 2002 and 2004 in Toronto. I interviewed eleven Chinese Canadians (six women and five men). Participants were recruited through word-of-mouth referrals and the 'snowball technique.' The focus of the research was the attitude of wealthy young Chinese Canadians toward anti-racism and globalization. Semi-structured interviews followed a guide which covered areas such as attitude toward anti-racism education, personal history of schooling and discrimination, employment equity, global capitalism, and neo-liberalism. After the interviews, I provided the participants with my written analyses for review. Celia Haig-Brown argues that researchers should bring their theorization of the data back to the research participants in this way; not necessarily to find consensus but to acknowledge and engage in dialogue about its contestable nature.[16]

This chapter focuses on two of these eleven interviews, the first with Matthew (a pseudonym), a gay Chinese Canadian man, and the second with a heterosexual Chinese Canadian man named Taye Shih (a pseudonym).

## Orientalism

Race and sexuality remain highly contentious topics among some Asian North Americans, especially as it relates to Asians dating white people.[17] Toronto writer Terry Woo deals with this topic in his novel *Banana Boys*.[18] Daniel Yon points out that the concept of interracial dating is dependent on discourse that sees races as fixed, essentialist, and separate entities.[19] The concept of sexuality is socially constructed and historically contingent, discursive, and fluid and inextricably linked to discourse related to race, gender, and 'heteronormativity.' Heteronormativity refers to the belief systems and practices that regard heterosexuality as the norm, and constructs sexuality that deviates from this norm as pathological, immoral, and in need of regulation.[20] Within heteronormative society, gay, lesbian, transgendered, bisexual, and sexually fluid individuals are deemed to be deviant, and/or pathological. As discourse on sexuality is situated historically, it has been argued that white and Asian sexual partnerships are potentially influenced by dominant western racialized discourses such as orientalism and colonialism.[21]

Wah-Shan Chou argues that white males who date gay Asian men exclusively (the pejorative term Rice Queen is often applied to the white partner) have a tendency to fetishize or orientalize Asian gays as submissive, feminine, and deferential. The fact that many Asians not only internalize racist discourse such as orientalism, but also are loathing of other gay Asian men,[22] speaks to the colonial and unequal relations of power implied by white males' relations with gay Asians. Likewise, power imbalances can be exacerbated, since the white male may be more financially established than his Asian lover.[23]

My use of popular cultural terms such as Rice Queen is not intended to reify or essentialize categories; instead, I call attention to Queer theorists who point out how identities are socially constituted, fluid, contingent, and performed. In Judith Butler's seminal text *Gender Trouble*, she argues that reiterative performative acts operate to regulate and consolidate identities. It is through continually repeated performances, she contends, that heteronormative and gendered identities come to be seen as essential or natural.[24] Thus, while I make reference to popular slang such as Rice Queen and Rice King, I fully see these as essentialist, modernist, and pejorative categories in need of deconstruction. But my hope is to call attention to the prevalence of inter-racial dating discourse in the popular imagination.

Much debate continues to frame tensions within Asian North America as being related to Asian women dating white men. Rice King is sometimes used to refer to a white male who exclusively dates Asian women, and implies that the relationship is based on the orientalist fetishization of the female partner. The imagined orient as 'other' to the west conflates with an imagined idea of 'oriental sex,' in which eastern women are stereotyped as exotic, sensuous, mysterious, and forever eager to service men.[25] Tania Das Gupta argues that these women are 'seen as soft, romantic objects for white men, ultra-feminine, delicate, and welcome alternatives to white, liberated women (a stereotype in itself).'[26] Rana Kabbani argues that the fetishization of Asian women is inextricably linked to how ideas associated with orientalism contributed to western domination and control of the orient.[27] Thus, orientalism, colonialism, and the geopolitical separation of Asia from Toronto become inextricably linked with the discourse of sexuality.

Orientalism operates to otherize Asian bodies and historically position those bodies as belonging outside nation-states such as Canada. The right to vote was denied to the Chinese in Canada until 1947. The infamous Chinese Head Taxes and Chinese Exclusion Act of 1923 were racialized government policies.[28] After the construction of the Canadian Pacific Railway, during which many Chinese men died, the Canadian government effectively barred further immigration from China by passing the Exclusion Act of 1923,[29] which was not repealed until 1943. Toronto historian Mona Pon contends that exclusionary practices like the 1923 Act were based on discourse that constructed Chinese men as a 'Yellow Peril' – fiendish, effeminate, cunning opium smokers who secretly fantasized about raping white women.[30] More recently, the Yellow Peril discourse has been superseded by the social construction of Asian men as laudable 'model minorities' – successful and non-complaining individuals who have overcome historical barriers by working hard, investing in education, and building strong nuclear families.[31] Thus, discourse about Asian men's bodies is connected to the vicissitudes of exclusion and inclusion from the nation-state. This discourse is implicated in the process of racial formation of Asians in Canada.

Eng argues that Asian North American men are both materially and psychically emasculated by discourse such as orientalism.[32] This feminization of Asian men is predicated on differentiating them from the normative western male, who is white, masculine, and heterosexual. Normative gender roles, or the socially constructed hegemonic roles and expectations accorded to males and females, are central to this process of emasculation. Asian males are conflated with the stereotyped female, who is seen as weak, timid, and demure. This renders the Asian man as 'other' to the hegemonic notion of the normative heterosexual, masculine, white male. The psychic castration of Asian men in the popular imagination is further complicated by Richard Fung's query: 'If Asian men have no sexuality, how can we have homosexuality?'[33] Hence the sexualization of bodies demonstrates how racism and sexism are unintelligible without the notion of the other.[34]

## The Limits of Cultural Nationalism as Response to Oppression

The positioning of Asian bodies as being outside of the nation-state has fuelled much debate in Asian North America in the past four decades. Scholars contend that these responses from activists, artists, and writers have been driven by an intense desire to claim home within America.[35] Accordingly, they have often been framed within a paradigm of cultural nationalism,[36] which can be understood as the belief that nation-states can be associated with separate imagined communities comprised of individuals who share a homogeneous culture, collective identity, and political beliefs.[37] Cultural nationalism is often used as an organizing strategy to unite individuals for collective political action. Gayatri Spivak calls this strategy 'strategic essentialism'[38] or the practice of uniting individuals for political action according to socially constructed identity categories such as racial or ethnic markers. This strategy tends to involve the erasure or minimization of differences within groups.

*Aiiieeee! An Anthology of Asian American Writers*, an American literary anthology edited by Frank Chin, Jeffrey Chan, Lawson Fusao Inada, and Shawn Wong, is a well-known example of cultural nationalism at work.[39] The authors rejuvenate the 'real' Asian classics of the heroic (male) tradition and attempt to restore the 'lost' manhood of

Asian men. In the sequel, entitled *The Big Aiiieeeee!*, the authors celebrate Chinese and Japanese heroic traditional classics that championed the martial arts expertise of Chinese male warriors and outlaws.[40] The title "Aiiieeee!," I believe, is supposed to suggest a Chinese verbal outburst of anger, pain, and frustration.

*Aiiieeee!* and *The Big Aiiieeee!* have spurred tremendous debate over the editors' questionable strategies for recuperating Asian American manhood. Scholars have critiqued such strategies as sexist, homophobic, culturally nationalist, and Eurocentric.[41] The tactics employed by the *Aiiieeee!* group recall the limitations of consciousness-raising strategies articulated by Deborah Britzman and Jen Gilbert.[42] Chin et al. believe that privileging the 'right' narratives of Asian manhood will change people's attitudes and beliefs about Asian men.[43]

In the next section, I discuss Eng's queer approach as a way out of the cultural nationalist trappings of essentialized and heteronormative views of race and sexuality.[44] His approach draws on queer analyses of racial formation processes within the nation-state, on the one hand, and with diaspora, on the other. Eng's approach does need to be connected to consciousness-raising, but it does invite a capacious understanding of globalization and transnationalism.

## Eng's Queer Approach: The Public/Private Binary and Claims to Nation

Eng argues that in their struggles to claim America as home, the *Aiiieeee!* group 'reinscribes a dominant system of compulsory heterosexuality and attendant misogyny and homophobia.'[45] This is evident in Chin and Chan's bemoaning that Asian American men have been portrayed by popular discourse as 'efficient housewives.'[46] This complaint, argues Eng, reveals Chin and Chan's willingness to reproduce dominant discourse that recreates a binary notion of public and private, whereby the public is commonly valorized, associated with men, power, status, paid labour, and the nation-state; while the private is devalued, associated with the domesticity, femininity, unpaid labour, and homosexuality. He contends that critics of cultural nationalism have failed to remark on the connection between the *Aiiieeee!* group's focus on the domestic and on heterosexuality: 'a public Asian American identity is purchased through the emphatic possession of a popularly devalued private realm of the feminine and the homosexual.'[47] In other words, the *Aiiieeee!* authors, in claiming America as their rightful home, effectively declare 'we're not homosexuals and we're not women.' Eng argues that a queer approach exposes the political practices embedded in compulsory heterosexuality, misogyny, and homophobia.

Eng buttresses his queer approach by noting Michael Omi and Dana Takagi's failure to recognize Asian American contributions to queer activism and the AIDS movement.[48] Omi and Takagi are associate professors of Asian American and Ethnic Studies at the University of California, Berkeley. They reviewed Asian American practices in the 1980s, concluding that radical politics had waned during this time period. Eng contends that such an observation implies a disavowal of, and a failure to recognize, the tremendous contributions by Asian Americans in the 1980s to queer activism. He concludes that such a denial is only possible when Asian American scholars continue to have difficulty integrating 'systematically issues of not only queerness but of sexuality into our critical vocabulary and theoretical discussions.'[49] His queer approach, on the other hand, situates queerness and sexuality in the Asian North American scholar's critical lexicon.

In Toronto in the past few decades, Asian Canadian queer activists have made similarly significant contributions to matters of social justice. For example, Toronto video artist and activist Richard Fung, who teaches at the Ontario College of Art and Design and whose films have been widely screened across North America, has made important cultural contributions in the area of race and queer sexuality.[50] Toronto professor Maurice Poon, who teaches in the School of Social Work at York University, is also the chair of the Research Advisory Committee at Asian Community AIDS Services (ACAS). Poon and his colleagues work to promote equitable and accessible services for queer and non-queer Asian youth in Toronto.[51] ACAS also has a youth-led Youth Advisory Committee which conducts research.

### Diaspora, Transnationalism, and Globalization: Eng's Queer Approach

Eng's queer approach is not only helpful for critiquing cultural nationalism but for understanding, in a global context, claims to the nation-state as home. His approach takes into consideration globalization, diaspora, and transnationalism. Since the *Aiiieeeee!* group began their writings in the 1970s, there have been profound changes associated with the rise of global capital, the collapse of communism in the Soviet

Union, and the decline of the Keynesian welfare state. These changes prompted Asian American academic circles to shift away from class-based analyses of racial formation, and toward a focus on concepts such as diaspora, globalization, and transnationalism. This new emphasis attempts to grapple with the implications of transnational movements of flexible labour; the increasing permeability of national borders through new technologies such as the internet, electronic communications, and international travel; and the global dispersal of Asians.[52]

In light of such global changes, Eng believes studies of the nation-state must now critically analyse how the domestic is linked to the global. For example, with respect to the Rice Queen phenomenon, Eng argues that globalization has created new articulations of race, class, and sexuality, whereby wealthy gay Asian men in America can be complicit with transnational management of capital, resources, and labour. This, he argues, destabilizes essentialist notions like the Rice Queen. Furthermore, Poon contends that in our new global times, gay Asian American men may not always be the subordinate members of the Rice Queen dyad. He cautions that there is 'no monolithic gay Asian Community, no normative gay Asian identity' any longer in which all members are necessarily oppressed.[53]

The global restructuring of capital since the 1980s has resulted in transnational migrations that have reconfigured the class standing of many gay Asians, in North America in general and in Toronto specifically. The class standing has mediated gay Asian men's relations with Asian women. For example, drawing on Ang Lee's film *The Wedding Banquet*,[54] Eng discusses how the protagonist, a gay Asian man named Wai-Tung, is wealthy and dating a white man (Simon). Wai-Tung is also a slumlord who exploits his tenant (Wei-Wei), a poor, undocumented Chinese woman. Chiang suggests that Wai-Tung articulates a 'transnational patriarchy of capital [that] is fundamentally dependent on the subordination of women and labour, and these are conflated in the film so that woman becomes the very sign of labour.'[55] Eng's queer approach provides a better understanding of the enabling and disabling violence that attends to globalization and the ongoing struggles of contemporary Asians in America to claim the nation-state as home.[56]

In the next section, I introduce Matthew, whose understanding of globalization and neo-liberalism in relation to sexuality resonates with Eng's queer approach, while also calling consciousness-raising assumptions into question. Matthew articulates how transnationalism intersects with queerness to turn Toronto youth spaces such as bubble tea houses queer.

## Matthew: 'Culture Isn't a Monolithic American Imperialism'

Matthew is a Canadian-born twenty-two-year-old who is university educated and lives in Toronto. He is an activist and film maker who identifies himself as a gay Chinese Canadian man. He espouses leftist values and commitments to social justice. He reports his class background as middle class and has travelled to China, Shanghai, Hong Kong, and Thailand.

In the following statement, Matthew calls attention to issues of power that are implicated in race and desire:

> Desire is very political. Not only queer desire in the face of heteronormativity, but race and desire is very political . . . A lot of gay Asian guys seek the older white male. Have you read Chou, Wah-Shan? He is a writer/theorist in Hong Kong or China . . . The title of his book is *Tongzhi, the Politics of Same-Sex Eroticism in Chinese Societies.* He uses postcolonial theory and looks at race and desire and how it has been informed by, in Hong Kong in particular, British colonialism. He argues that a lot of things are based on power. A lot of the older white males have more money, so they have a lot more power in different ways over the young Asian person. So it's a phenomenon [the Rice Queen] that is everywhere, all over the world. But there is now also a strain of resistance. It's called 'Sticky Rice.' Asians in general are actively seeking Asians in resistance to the Rice Queen phenomenon. In Toronto there is a larger movement of Sticky Rice than elsewhere.

Matthew contends that there is a vibrant and large Sticky Rice movement in Toronto. He sees Sticky Rice as a political practice that resists colonialism and racism on one hand, and challenges compulsory heterosexuality on the other. I define Sticky Rice as a discourse that relates to the ways of knowing and being of Asian Canadians, who choose to respond to histories of anti-Asian racism and colonialism by dating, more or less exclusively, only other Asians.

It is important to note that Sticky Rice as anti-racist practice is vulnerable to criticism that this approach perpetuates racism and colonialism simply because it is premised on racial exclusivity. To critics, proponents of Sticky Rice seem trapped in modernist racial categories and, to be sure, the contradiction is evident. Yet, the dynamic recalls

Barbara Heron's[57] contention that subjectivities are by definition always already caught up in contradictory discourse and desire. Moreover, individuals regularly take up identification with complete contradictory subject positions made available through discourse.[58] But while proponents of Sticky Rice make active identification with modernist categories such as 'Asian,' with its attendant racial limitations, they also attempt to transform racialized discourse into a liberatory one by signalling a counter-hegemonic move toward solidarity and Asian pride. Heron's poststructural analysis of subjectivity jibes with Matthew's understanding of Sticky Rice.

Matthew's analysis of the Sticky Rice and Rice Queen phenomena suggests a critical analysis of sexuality, colonialism, and racism that is attentive to global dynamics. His analysis also subverts the public/private binary implicit in the cultural nationalist claims to the nation-state as home. In other words, nowhere in Matthew's political practice is his Asian queerness predicated on devaluing women. He offers analyses of desire that are inseparable from considerations of power and the struggle over scarce resources like money in a global context.

Matthew also expresses positive feelings about some aspects of globalization, while being careful to differentiate the concept from neo-liberalism. It's globalization, he admits, that has permitted him to establish contacts through international conferences and travel to, for example, gay Asian clubs in San Francisco and New York. Matthew's transnational mobility and privilege recall Eng's queer approach, which aims to understand privileged gay Asian males' relations to transnationalism and the global restructuring of capital. Matthew says:

> I think globalization is really good. It's great as opposed to neo-liberalism. There is often confusion between those terms. Activists use globalization all the time to build global networks. The spread of culture isn't a monolithic American imperialism. I have a lot of really good contact with people of colour around the world, through travel, internet, and through organizing conferences. Neo-liberalism is the economic policy, the capitalism, and that has had more of a negative impact. Neo-liberalism is a concept that favours free trade and liberalized markets. It is based on bottom-line driven, capitalist economic policies, that have had negative impacts globally, but especially in the so-called Third World.
>
> For example, neo-liberalism has led to the migration of people and indirectly to the creation of the Pacific Mall [a large suburban Toronto Asian shopping centre]. These spaces are important for new immigrant

communities who can't get jobs in the mainstream because of language barriers and qualifications. They don't have Canadian experience, so these are very important spaces because they can find a living in those spaces. But at the same time there is a lot of exploitation within those spaces. People of colour are in the service positions. They work long hours and under the table deals are struck with immigrants and they don't have work benefits. There are good and bad things, so it's not monolithic in that way.

Matthew seems to understand how a transnational, privileged, gay, Asian man such as himself nonetheless always needs to think about the spectre of localized neo-liberal class exploitation. In other words, while he is able to engage in social relations across national borders, he sees that globalization trades on exploitation of transnational migrant labour. Here, Matthew articulates a subjectivity in which his transnational queerness will not be purchased at the price of disavowing the brutality of neo-liberalism and persistent racialized exploitation of people marked as Asian. Matthew's way of being and knowing also shows a willingness to live with complex contradictions in which the questions of sexuality and diaspora can escape the trap of cultural nationalism. His statement that the 'spread of culture is not a monolithic American imperialism' echoes Eng's call for an analytic shift from cultural nationalism to a transnational culturalism.[59]

Matthew speaks directly to local effects of transnational spread of culture in his critical understanding of bubble tea houses, a global youth cultural phenomenon originating in Taiwan. A flavoured tea-based beverage containing tapioca 'bubbles,' bubble tea is consumed through large plastic straws. Bubble tea houses have proliferated in Toronto, especially in suburbs such as Richmond Hill, Markham, and Scarborough. Matthew explains how suburban bubble tea houses become spaces of resistance and comfort for many Asian Canadian youths. These spaces resist racist exclusion from white mainstream culture, he suggests, but are not anti-capitalist:

> Just in terms of the reality, a lot of people are not against capitalism. Because Asian youth are not really included in a lot of mainstream places, they find their own spaces within suburban Toronto . . . Because they are so heavily populated with Asian people, these spaces, like bubble tea spaces, become very important social spaces. Here you barely

ever see white people. It's a space of resistance or a space of comfort, a comfort zone. It's not overtly political or politicized but it's a good space nonetheless. [These ideas] disrupt several notions that the suburbs are a white place full of gigantic houses, full of rich people. But that is not true, if you look at Scarborough, for example. There are also a lot of class differences [within the suburbs].

On a related point, Matthew says that contrary to heteronormative discourse, Asian Canadian queers also carve out spaces of resistance in suburban bubble tea houses. Commenting on a short film which Matthew directed on bubble tea houses and queer Asian Canadians, he states: 'It's a queer story within the suburbs . . . queer spaces [bubble tea houses] and how they are carved out in the suburbs.'

In summary, Matthew alerts us to not only the important distinctions between globalization and neo-liberalism, but how transnational movement of culture and bodies results in Toronto suburban phenomena like the queering of bubble tea houses. In one scene of Matthew's film, the young gay Asian male protagonist is shown sitting across a table from another young Asian man, both sipping bubble teas. They are shown laughing and ostensibly enjoying each other's company. The film ends with the exchange of an affectionate caress between the two youths. The seeming pleasure and enjoyment the two are sharing recalls Matthew's contention that the bubble tea house is 'a space of resistance or a space of comfort, a comfort zone . . . it's a good space' for young Asian Canadian queers. Indeed, the film depicts the suburban bubble tea house as a triumphant site of resistance for both queer Asian men and women. For instance, in another group scene in the film, there are queer women sitting at the table in the bubble tea house. Juxtaposing this group scene with the one featuring the two men, Matthew explains that, in many ways, 'the group scene is, in some ways just as (if not more) powerful as the scene between the two men, since a large group of queer Asians more triumphantly queers the suburban heteronormative space.'[60] For Matthew then, the queering of the suburban space of the bubble tea house evidences hospitality toward non-heteronormative sexualities, and in so doing, offers him relief from the racism of mainstream queer spaces. He also signals that any projects of consciousness-raising aimed at, for example, trying to change his critique of globalization and capitalism would be misguided, ideological, and would fail to recognize his awareness of the contradictory nature of subjectivities in global times.

In the next section, I introduce Taye Shih (a pseudonym). Taye's art work articulates an alternative masculinity that is ambivalent toward racist portrayals of Asian men, but hospitable within a range of Chinese masculinities. I grapple with how his ambivalence unsettles assumptions of consciousness-raising.

## Taye Shih: 'Everybody Look at Me, I'm the Model Minority'

Taye Shih, twenty-four years old, was born in Taipei, Taiwan, came to Canada in the early 1980s, and resides in Toronto. He identifies as a heterosexual, middle-class, Chinese Canadian man. Taye speaks English and Mandarin, is university educated, and is an artist who illustrates comics, writes poetry, and performs cappellas.

Taye understands his identity through postmodern concepts and the limits of essentialist categories. His thoughts about identity are consistent with the writings by Gilroy, Gosine, Hall, and Carl James.[61] The term 'postmodern identities' refers to an understanding of identity as fluid, contingent, socially constructed, multiple, and hybrid. This notion is typically seen as being at odds with modernist notions that regard identity as constituted by essential, rigid, unchanging, and absolute characteristics. When Taye was asked, 'How do you identify?' he cautioned me immediately about the limits of identity categories, instead emphasizing the fluidity, instability, and dynamic nature of any given identity: 'when you come up to issues of self-identity . . . you describe yourself a certain way . . . it is a self-constructed story which changes day to day, month to month, hour to hour.'

In the following cappella titled 'Model Minority,' written by Taye, he illustrates this double consciousness and an ability to manipulate and engage with contradictions between his postmodern identity categories and cultural absolutism. W.E.B. Du Bois's legendary concept of double consciousness can be understood as an acute ambivalence felt by racialized individuals, who have a double knowing – an awareness of both how they see themselves and how they are perceived by others.[62] The following is an excerpt from Taye's cappella:

> Spreading like butter invidious distinctions
> Between minority classes, exalting the Asians
> Ooh, look at him think, he's so intellectual
> We better cast him as completely asexual
> At least for the men, it's not the same for our women

They fall under a different distorted perception
North Americans love a woman who's Asian
. . . I don't wanna be Black, I don't wanna be Chinese
I wanna be white, rule with luxurious ease
I want maximum social fuckin' mobility . . .
I'm an artist, a slave, an angry authority
Everybody look at me, I'm the model minority.

Taye recognizes that his subjectivity is full of ambivalence, rage, and pain. The rage he feels is linked to his awareness of orientalism and racist and sexist portrayals of Asian men and women. He builds on this meta-awareness or double consciousness in the following comment:

This illustrates, sort of, the complexity of the situation and the fact that many of us are aware of this complexity, those who are more inclined to be introspective and analytical. It also makes a statement on, I think, 'intellectual slippage' . . . but sometimes you just wanna say, 'Fuck it all,' right? Like, 'Fuck him. He's doing this all to me.' Even though at heart that's not really what's happening. From that standpoint, you shouldn't be saying this at all, but sometimes you do.

Here, Taye expresses the anger he feels as someone subject to oppressions such as racism. What is particularly interesting, however, is his contention that he may not really be an entirely innocent and passive victim of racism:

Sometimes we act like victims because it's fun to act like victims . . . There's more to it . . . we all know CBC [Canadian-born Chinese] guys who do quite well with any kind of girl, or most of us know them . . . There are inadequacies to acknowledge. The fact that even though we know what the problem is, we find it very difficult to overcome this shyness, this lack of confidence, this meekness. And ultimately most of the anger and the pain that we have, in my observation of people around me and myself, is really aimed at ourselves. We know at some level that if we were to just change, which is difficult, but if we were to just be able to come up and talk to the girl, to do this and that, these problems would disappear.

Taye is giving voice to an internal struggle of confidence, of risking the self in order to connect, or 'talk to the girl.' This candid admission by Taye recalls what Cheung calls the decoupling of 'masculinity from paramountcy and invincibility that is the traditional burden of manhood.'[63] When Taye admits to his shyness and meekness, he reveals a vulnerability Cheung cautions should not be regarded as weakness. Rather, Cheung notes that hegemonic masculinity glorifies invincibility. Thus Taye has subverted hegemonic masculinity through his candidness, articulating the possibility of an alternative masculinity. Cheung would probably see Taye's disclosure as heroic because he has had the courage to reveal his vulnerability. Alternative masculinities in Cheung's view should not be viewed as effeminate and certainly not emasculating. To be sure, the queer approach cautioning against the devaluation of the feminine and the queer would be effective in guarding against such slippage.

What might the ambivalence and contradictory nature of Taye's cappella mean for anti-oppression and its reliance on consciousness-raising? It shows how ways of understanding Asian masculinities can be articulated in the poiesis of art. However, this art is not invested in privileging the 'right' or innocent narrative and changing people's views. Instead, his cappella reveals a hospitality, a kindness of sorts, that is caring even toward 'the model minority.' Yet, to grasp this welcoming of vulnerable and non-invincible masculinities requires, as Taye makes clear, a refusal to cling to victimhood or innocence. These are possibilities of alternative masculinities that might dwell in the arts of diverse individuals in a city such as Toronto.

To fully appreciate these artful expressions of alternative masculinities, anti-oppression requires a healthy scepticism toward consciousness-raising techniques that rely erroneously on privileging the 'right' narratives. The extent to which this scepticism could be buttressing of anti-oppressive perspectives might be measured by anti-oppression's ability to embrace the arts with their double consciousness, contradictions, ambivalence, and beautiful rage. Moreover, such an embrace of art would steer clear of underlying tendencies to promote the 'right' as opposed to the 'wrong' art.

## Conclusion

Asian masculinities continue to be widely debated issues. Historically, cultural nationalist responses to racist portrayals of Asian men have been predicated on the devaluation of the feminine and the queer. Eng's queer approach escapes the pitfalls of cultural nationalism and consciousness-raising, in that it does not aim to privilege certain narratives as a path to social change. Instead, Eng makes room for contradiction and fluid identities, as in his explanation of how Asians in America can find themselves complicit with capitalist exploitation of vulnerable populations such as migrant woman. Extricating oneself from the limitations of cultural nationalism and consciousness-raising opens space for alternative masculinities that can, as with Taye, express outrage at racist portrayals of Asian men on one hand, and recognize the beauty, complexity, and sensitivities of Asian men's subjectivities on the other. Moreover, the queer approach might aid anti-oppression in exploring how youth in Toronto such as Matthew and Taye understand and experience globalization and transnationalism as being full of contradictions, limitations, and pain, but also possibilities and pleasures.

Critical consciousness-raising continues to be promoted by many proponents of anti-oppression.[64] The efficacy of this approach likely rests on the willingness of practitioners to continue to call into question our own passions and visions of a transformed world. A cosmopolis such as Toronto offers insight into how local spaces like bubble tea houses and Asian-themed malls are never fully outside of the global circulation of racialized, gendered, and sexualized discourse. Moreover, it is vital that anti-oppression proponents grapple with how our visions might fail to recognize how cosmopolitan youth today, with their youthful ways of knowing and their eagerness to accept difference, may not fervently identify with anti-capitalism. The local youthful co-existence with global culture and capitalism, like the ongoing debates on Asian masculinities, might serve, then, as a barometer of anti-oppression's capacity to confront its own ambivalences and epistemological limits.

# 6 'Keeping It Real': The Art of the Masculine

PHILIP LORTIE

> There are advantages to remaining less than intelligible.
>
> *Judith Butler*

Since 2000, I have visited many Toronto-area high schools in different capacities: as a theatre artist working in drama classrooms; a university instructor coming to observe student teachers; a researcher; and, most recently, a teacher. When students see me for the first time they often think I'm a *cop*. They will whisper loud enough for me to hear, 'Popo,' slang for police officer (also, coincidentally, a family nickname of mine from childhood, derived from my oldest sister's adaptation of 'Phileepo,' my mother's pet name for me). At 6'4", 240 pounds, I'm a big, white guy, and I usually ride my bike to school, so I'm wearing a helmet and, if it's raining, a yellow slicker and weatherproof pants. But this mistaken identity still takes me by surprise, not because I don't look like a cop, but because I don't feel like a cop. It is a predicament familiar to every student walking the school's halls: saddled with an unwanted label, I must build an identity from an unanticipated starting point. How I move from this false impression to some place more authentic in my dealings with the students will define who I am to them, and they to me.

Daniel Yon describes schools as discursive spaces in which the practice of naming oneself as a member of a category (White, Black, male, female) can be both productive and constraining in that 'identity categories and labels are often unable to satisfy the desire to be recognized as complex subjects. Identity is therefore always partial, capable of telling us something but unable to tell us all.'[1] In his study of a

Toronto high school, Yon argues against 'culture as an attribute,' instead urging us to see it as an 'ongoing process attuned to the ambivalent and contradictory processes of everyday life.'[2] As will be seen below, this latter approach is consistent with a view of gender as something 'performed' and highlights the myriad ways students experiment and play with the supposedly stable identity markers of race, gender, and class. If, as Yon says, identity is 'always relational'[3] then it may be a worthwhile exercise to look at those relations in a creative and critical way. By presenting them theatrically, we might better understand the power that discourse has in shaping one's performance of self.

Social scientists have made good theoretical use of theatre, ritual, drama, and performance as a way to explain everyday life in a culture, most notably the sociologists Erving Goffman,[4] who coined the term 'social drama' in describing personal and cultural phenomena, and Victor Turner,[5] who introduced the notion of 'liminality,' a territory between reality and fantasy, in his exploration of how societies change. According to Richard Schechner, a leading practitioner of performance theory, 'for both Turner and Goffman the basic human plot is the same: someone or some group begins to move to a new place in the social order; this move is acceded to or blocked; in either case a crisis occurs because any change in status involves a readjustment of the entire scheme; this readjustment is effected performatively – that is, by means of theatre and ritual.'[6] The notion that art and life mirror each other can yield surprising insights, though, as Clifford Geertz notes, often 'at the expense of making vividly disparate matters look drably homogeneous.'[7] Contemporary scholarship in the social sciences has largely shied away from the modernist view of human behaviour as a performance conforming to narrative archetypes. Here the concept of performance helps to challenge the orthodoxy of a stable division between our social self and inner, or 'true,' self, and posits instead an open-ended, constantly revised constellation of selves – never settled, never fully knowable.

The study of gender, in large part due to Judith Butler's reading of Foucault, has been a leading force in fleshing out this new vision of performance. Theorists and researchers have used the concept of performativity to explore the ways in which repetition, incompleteness, and parody are implicit in our understandings of gender. In this view, our gender precedes and exceeds us:[8] there is no such thing as a pre-gendered, neutral subject choosing or learning a given role, rather, we are born into a pre-existing web of meanings in which we are at once and forever enmeshed and given coherence. Carrying this point further, Butler argues that 'there need not be a "doer behind the deed," but that the "doer" is invariably constructed in and through the deed,'[9] the 'deed' here being the enacting of one's gender. As to who is in control of the process, she invokes the notion of signification as a repetitive act, since this implies that the subject (whose construction starts at the moment someone asks 'boy or girl?') might do it differently next time: 'the task is not whether to repeat, but how to repeat.'[10] Gender is therefore not a play put on by biologically typecast actors acting out memorized scripts, but 'an improvisation within a scene of constraint.'[11] Gender ideologies, in their repressiveness, produce the possibility for parody, for example, drag, which Butler sees as a subversive act whose thoroughly convincing enactment by implication calls into question the naturalness of its 'straight' counterpart.

My dramatic work with high school students has proven fertile ground on which to examine some of this still-evolving view of gender, and to delve directly into the notion of gender-as-performance by asking students to represent themselves in a new way to an audience of their peers. Perhaps predictably, that inquiry has yielded moments of true insight along with great frustration about how difficult it is to change or transcend prescribed gender roles. My goal is to examine the experience of gender hierarchy in schools and take a deeper look at what propagates these performances by framing three moments from my life as dramatic scenes. They draw upon my experience as a student, an educator, and a researcher, respectively. My objective here is 'authenticity,' an attempt to capture textually the 'essence and resonance of the actors' experience and perspective through details of action and thought revealed in context.'[12] But, beyond this, the theatricality of my writing is intended to simulate the types of openings, contradictions, misunderstandings, confrontations, ambiguities, and silences I live as a man, knew as a boy, and must negotiate as a teacher and researcher of boys in school. In so doing, my hope is to apply Butler's thinking about gender to real world instances of masculine performance in schools and to provoke new ideas about how to constructively engage with boys in settings where the idea of straight-male privilege goes unchallenged.

An important point made by those studying gender today is that it is a phenomenon that does not occur in isolation from other aspects of one's identity. The category 'Man' or 'Woman,' Butler explains, is not

sufficiently descriptive 'because gender is not always constituted co-
herently or consistently in different historical contexts, and because
gender intersects with racial, class, ethnic, sexual, and regional modalities of discursively constituted identities. As a result, it becomes
impossible to separate out "gender" from the political and cultural intersections in which it is invariably produced and maintained.'[13]

The recognition that this is so has led to the widespread use, in
men's studies, of Robert Connell's term 'masculinities.' He, however,
takes issue with the idea that these cultural and political factors are intersections, arguing instead for the term 'interactions' to emphasize
the shifting, contradictory effects their combination has on one's subject position.[14] As an example, in his detailed study of masculinity
and school culture, Máirtín Mac an Ghaill found that Black students
were aware of the historical and current contradictions of Black masculinity, seeing as the patriarchal privileges of power, control, and
authority that are ascribed to the white male role are denied to the
Black male.[15]

While this negative experience should certainly be understood as
contributing to the disaffection of those considered 'ethnic' by whites
whose own ethnicity is erased, so-called 'additive' models used in
class- or race-based analyses of masculinity cannot explain why homi-
cidal 'school-shooters'[16] are most often affluent white boys, the very
picture of privilege. To come up with an effective explanation of gender, therefore, one must discuss the interrelated roles of gender, class,
and race/ethnicity within social practice.

The stakes are high for adolescent boys in proving themselves as
masculine subjects. Despite dogged efforts by a generation of educators, homophobic harassment and violence are as stubborn a fact of
school life as they were fifty years ago. In patriarchal societies, a boy's
display of his maleness is performed almost exclusively for other
boys. Because homosocial relations among boys are of paramount
importance in establishing one's position relative to one's peers, the
stigma of homosexuality is all the more pronounced in the policing of
gender boundaries.[17] Any sign of nonconformity to these rules is auto-
matically read as feminine, therefore *not* masculine, and punished
accordingly.[18] These are the circumstances under which boys, striving
to appear fully masculine, work at 'keeping it real,' a common phrase
among young males, which denotes toughness, dispassion, as well as
membership in a mythic brotherhood. Effectively, 'keeping it real'
means keeping it quiet, keeping it to yourself, keeping it down.

The following scenes, in their deconstruction of real-life experiences, seek to 'keep it real' by doing the opposite: by showcasing the pretence of normative masculinity, and shaking up the traditional gender hierarchies found all too commonly in high schools. The three scenes presented in this chapter are based on my personal experience but have also been stylized in different ways. The first scene recalls an experience of mine as a freshman (Grade 9) when an older boy who was on the football team bullied me. The scene consists only of the words spoken by him. The second scene uses a more pronounced theatricality to deconstruct an episode I experienced as a visiting theatre artist at a downtown Toronto high school. The third scene, inspired by an incident I witnessed as a researcher – at the same high school as the second scene – is comprised of invented monologues, thought or spoken, from a sampling of the parties involved.

## Scene 1

*1978. The capacious atrium of a large, predominantly white high school in the suburbs of Chicago. It is lunchtime, and following the custom, two hundred or so students have filtered out into the atrium to hang out with their friends, idly chatting and watching the goings-on. At the bottom of a very wide staircase we find George, sitting squarely with elbows on knees, amid a buzzing, shiftless group of Senior (Grade 12) athletes. The text of this scene is comprised solely of the words George speaks to others.*

Look at that stupid little Frosh sitting over there in his overalls. Doesn't have his big sister with him today. He makes me sick. Don't tell me to relax, Kevin, YOU relax. Dickweed.

What? What are you looking at? Look at him, he looks like he just ate a lemon. Asshole.

Hey, hey, holleee shit, look at this. HEY SWEETHEART – YES YOU. WHAT'S WRONG? YOU LOOK SO SERIOUS, COME HERE AND TELL DOCTOR GEORGE ALL ABOUT IT. Damn, have you seen her before? Nice. I might have to get on that. What? What'd you say? Shut up, faggot.

Tony, come here. You got any change on you man? Let me have it.

HEY SHEILA, DON'T SAY HELLO OR ANYTHING. NICE SHIRT. Slut.

Andrew, hey man, let me see your homework. What?! You *told* me you were going to hand it in today.

That's all you got, Tony? No quarters? I want to bean that little fuck. Over there, the farmer in his overalls. Andrew, gimme a quarter, man.

HUSKIES! ALRIGHT DOMER, SEE YOU OUT THERE.

'Member that kid you nailed with a ketchup balloon last week? Yeah man, let's do that again. Q, you are such a pussy. "We're going to get in trouble," wanh wanh wanhhhhh. It's Parker, dude, he won't do shit. Look at him, he's hitting on Olson again. He's such a faggot. That's hilarious.

Wait, wait, wait, who's that with Tina? What the fuck? Who is that? Who? Never heard of him. I'll be right back.

TINA. TINA. YEAH, HELLO, IT'S GEORGE. What the fuck, baby, who's this? Shut up, man, I'm not talking to you. Don't touch me, just tell me what the fuck you are doing talking to this asshole. Yeah that's right you little fairy, get on outta here. Fairy. FAGGOT. DON'T LET ME CATCH YOU TALKING TO MY GIRLFRIEND AGAIN, ASSHOLE.

Come here, Tina. Sit over here with us. Cuz I want you to, that's why. Because I love you so much, Snookie-Ookie Pie. Is that what you wanna hear?

I know, I know, did you see him run? Swee-eet.

Oh shit, where'd Ferguson come from? Alright, I gotta do this quick. No, I'm gonna use a penny; I need the quarters for a Coke. Check this out, this is gonna be sweet.

La la la la, how's it going buddy? Nice hat.

La la la la la. And . . . bullseye! Yessss.

Yeah? Where'd I get him, in the eye? What? Even better. He is? Where? Oh hey, the Farmer wants some more. Stupid little turd.

What? I don't know what you're talking about. Yeah, that looks bad, your lip's bleeding and everything. I told you, you have the wrong guy. Maybe you didn't hear me. Let me show you something, okay? Look. Got it? Good boy.

Almost time to go. Drew, you going to class? Yeah, me neither. Let's book.

What? Where?

Oh man . . . he's dead. I'm gonna kill that little fucker. It's Ferguson too. *Damnit*. C'mon, let's cruise. Tony, let's *go* man. Aw shit, too late. He's coming. Thanks a *lot*, guys. Drew, take my knife, man. Here, here . . . hide it!

What? Me? Sure. How are you doing today, Mr Ferguson? Good. Sure, what is it? Who? That's absolutely untrue, sir. I don't why he's lying like that. Honestly. You can ask anyone here. Well, I think some-one, one of these people, of all the people here, don't you think some-body would have seen it if I did? I dunno, maybe he's jealous. I've seen him looking over here before like he was getting ready to say something. Yes, sir. I know, I know. You can search me if you want, I don't even own one. Well, if I hear anything I will let you know, but it wasn't me, I promise. I won't. We were just sitting here waiting for the bell to ring and then you came over. I will, sir, thank you, sir.

That little fucker has had it. I swear to God, I'm gonna fucking kill him. He could have gotten me expelled. I don't care . . . I'll do it off school property.

DREW, wait up.

## Afterword

This scene removes the voices of the bully's peers to keep the focus squarely on the various strategies he employs, but this device (it is hoped) also calls attention to how much of this is done for the benefit of the audience, his friends. The framing of this incident in dramatic terms also highlights the familiar in the bully's masculine perfor-mance: while acutely self-conscious, it seems to work wholly without conscience. The instigator in this scene might as well be Shakespeare's Richard, Duke of Gloucester (Richard III), gleefully explaining how he will wed the widow of a man he has just slain: 'What though I kill'd her husband and her father? / The readiest way to make the wench amends / Is to become her husband and her father / The which will I; not all so much for love.'[19] All the bully's energy is directed outward; the last question to be asked is 'why?' Totally devoid of empathy, the aggressor operates within a moral vacuum in which anything that can be done should be done to establish superiority. In their watchful but silent acquiescence to the bully, his friends are indispensable as wit-nesses who create a context in which violence is mediated and under-stood. Masculinity is ever a performance, one that subjugates both actors and viewers in a proscribed set of responses.

Also implied in the action is the school's use of disciplining techni-ques to sort and divide the student population into small, manageable groups, or streams,[20] which only contributes to the pack mentality. Without even attempting to, students can find themselves identified and categorized on the basis of their affiliations, or the lack thereof –

Stoner, Jock, Loner being a just a few of the more common labels. Among those groups of boys where physical prowess and/or an inclination toward violence is a prerequisite to membership, picking on isolated peers is a way to simultaneously establish dominance and rebel against what is, in their view, an anti-masculine ethos of obedience to school authority.[21]

## Scene 2

Though the setting for this scene is borrowed from an actual event, the action is transformed via an overtly theatrical turn.

*Present day, a drama classroom in a downtown, working-class Toronto high school comprised of students from almost every continent on Earth. Two male teachers, one sitting behind the desk reading a newspaper, while the other, Phil, a visiting theatre artist, is trying to capture the attention of about twenty-two Grade 9 students, all boys.*

MATT: This is boring.

PHIL: Matt, I told you only to say that if you think you are speaking for the whole class.

MATT: I am. This is boring.

PHIL: Does everybody agree? Or should we give it a little more time?

MATT: Everybody thinks it's boring, sir, trust me. Even Peanuts thinks it's boring, don't you, Peanuts?

[*Loud, sustained laughter from classroom.*]

TEACHER: Be quiet, everyone. Give Mr Lortie your undivided attention, please.

PHIL: Okay, Matt has spoken. Then what I would like everyone to do now is find a partner.

MATT: Stupid.

PHIL: Matt . . . I haven't even finished telling you what I want you to do.

MATT: Doesn't matter. Finding partners is stupid.

[*Assorted guffaws from students to* Matt's *immediate left and right.*]

PHIL: Maybe not though, maybe not. Give it a chance. Here's what I'd like: once everyone gets a partner, find a space anywhere in the room and stand facing each other.

MATT: That's gay. This is stupid!

PHIL: You can't know until you try it. Come on everybody, get up, and find somebody to work with. Let's see, do we have an even number? Yes, we're fine.

[*None of the students move.*]

MATT: Sir, Phil, sir, this is boring. I'm the spokesman. You said you would stop no matter what. So, move on – next!

PHIL: Not yet, not yet. We're going to give this a try. (*Most students are sitting, and the ones that are not, begin to.*) Ah, ah, ah – no sitting! You're going to have to move for this one. Come on, guys, it's just like gym only you don't have to wear a cup. Look at you sitting there like a bunch of old men, get on up!

MATT: What are we going to do? Dance?

[*Laughter.*]

PHIL: I'll show you once everyone has a partner.

MATT: Peanuts, dance with me!

[Teacher, *feigning ignorance, does not look up from his paper. Students laugh.*]

PHIL: It's too bad, I had some things planned that I know you guys would really enjoy, but, oh well, I get paid no matter what you do, so . . .

MATT: Speaking of getting paid . . . Peanuts! Where's my money, eh? What's this guy get paid to just sit there and read the paper and he can't pay up on a bet? (*Sucks his teeth loudly, a show of disrespect.*)

TEACHER: I told you, Matt, it wasn't a bet. I'm not going to tell you again. Mr Lortie has asked you all to stand up and find a partner. Do it. Now. I want to start seeing some cooperation. Now.

MATT: I don't feel like dancing. It's only guys here, I don't dance with no guys.

PHIL: All right, can we just get over this? Nobody is going to have to dance. If you get into pairs we can do a few activities that are no big deal, and might even be a bit fun.

[*Nobody moves. After an uncomfortable silence,* Matt *brazenly begins a conversation, completely off-topic, with a group of boys next to him.*]

*The fluorescent lights, which have been flickering throughout, begin to flicker more noticeably, faster and faster, until they achieve a near-strobe effect. Simultaneously, the voices of the students, talking to each other in scattered groups, transform into low grunts, high-pitched squeals, and finally, into a kind of demonic rallying cry, over which can be heard:*]

PHIL: That's it, that's it. Here it comes. Yes. Do you feel that? Matt? Peanuts? Everyone? Do you see? YES! Your power. It's awesome; it's awful. They will tell you what to do and you will say, no. They will expect you to beg, they will want to see you grovel, and you will say, I refuse. You have that option. The freedom option. You are locked in now, and blood will have to be shed to move you from your stance. Come on, boys! Men! YES! The power is yours and it is terrific. Yours is the eternal truth of the beauty of destruction. Burn it down, boys! Burn it down! You will return to your homes as heroes. The packs you carry will be laden with mementos of your conquest. You will make history! You thought I came here to teach you fear, to punish you, to discipline you. Hah, yes, I could see it in your eyes. You blinkered oafs. *Educare* – I have come to *lead you out*! You must only throw off this girlish indolence if you wish to grow to be men of action in this embattled age. Action, my boys! The alarm is raised! Action! YES! Now – I command you: GRAB A PARTNER. PAIR UP. FIND A SPACE ANYWHERE IN THE ROOM. FACE EACH OTHER. WE HAVEN'T A MOMENT TO LOSE.

[*The boys have arranged themselves perfectly. Lights return to their original rate of flickering. The teacher remains seated, reading paper. Smoke from fog machine (if available) has engulfed the classroom. A low mechanical hum hovers, then fades.*]
BLACKOUT.


## Afterword

The authoritarian turn the scene takes at its climax – with the teacher addressing the students as a sergeant would a platoon – brings to mind the increasingly militaristic mindset among urban school principals and superintendents, who view anti-school sentiment as insubordination that demands increased regimentation as a response.[22] Underachieving, at-risk students in this racially diverse, working-class high school in downtown Toronto are commonly subjected to heightened surveillance,[23] police interrogation, and 'tough love' strategies by administrators who are convinced the best way to reach them is by scaring them into compliance.[24] Perhaps partly in reaction to – or parody of? – this regimentation and the wholesale application of the term 'at risk,' a sameness takes hold in the performance of the antagonistic student. Although the classroom upon which the above depiction is based contained students from a wide variety of racial, ethnic, and cultural backgrounds, I observed comparatively little difference in how these students presented themselves by means of clothing, posture, gait, and preferred forms of verbal expression.

Matt, the ringleader, leads the other students in foiling the teacher's attempts to engage the class. His leadership depends on being a jokester, a role he plays with accustomed ease. Though he no doubt works hard at making fun of everyone around him, the content of Matt's jokes is less important than what is achieved by their use. His jibes at the visiting teacher and the teacher are time-killers: as long as he can keep up the barrage, his classmates fully realize, the lesson cannot proceed, and they will be free to lounge in their chairs. Nullifying Matt requires an appeal to something greater than the promise of a free ride. The teacher, Phil, has to convince the students that the drama exercises will be worth the energy they put into them if he is to get the boys out of their supine state. Matt's actions are perhaps best understood as an instance of what Foucault called a 'technology of the self' – a 'regime of normalizing practices through which specific gendered discourses become mobilized.'[25] His performance serves to push conformity to a masculine ideal: he chastises the teacher for backing out on a bet, for being less than manly by not keeping his word (a shortcoming he physicalizes with reference to his genitalia), and uses homophobic humour to disrupt or pre-empt the lesson.

In this scene, Matt is given direct control over what can be said or done. Not surprisingly, he decides almost everything the teacher is asking them to do is an affront to their collective masculine identity. His jokes are an iron fist wrapped in velvet; he incites the group's derisive laughter as a way to enforce a code of heteronormativity. The typically silent resistance adolescent boys demonstrate when asked to defy the definition of what is acceptably male is given voice here. The manner in which Matt disrupts the teachers' efforts, however, reveals something more about the norms of the group: 'By resorting to jokes and sometimes insults . . . young men allow "for the intimate closeness of male peer cultures to be sanctioned, without compromising on an overtly heterosexual group identity."'[26]

Of course, very few people who've participated in this kind of revelry would recognize, or agree with, the above as a description of what they were doing. To an unreformed class clown and someone who worked as an improvisational actor and comedian, this is the kind of statement that only seems true of *other people*. Were I and my friends told that our joking allowed us to be intimate without being thought of as gay, we quite likely would have made a joke about that, too. Humour is important – and not just for adolescent boys – because it involves ambiguity. When people are laughing it may be a form of aggression, or escapism, or even cruelty, but it can also suggest a shared consciousness that exceeds the present moment. As the epigraph for this chapter suggests, there are good reasons for wanting to be less (or more?) than intelligible. Matt's joking was troublesome and it shut down the lesson, yes, but part of why it worked is because humour can be such an effective tool for resistance.

## Scene 3

This is a collection of monologues I created based upon an actual incident I witnessed while working as a research assistant for a study of social relations in drama classrooms. My representation of the students' voices should not be understood as equating these attitudes with any given racial, ethnic, or cultural group of students. The scene depicts a phenomenon sadly familiar to students and teachers everywhere.

*Each of the following monologues is enacted by a different actor; a change in typeface represents a change in actor. The setting is a downtown Toronto high school, with the monologues taking place in various areas of the school, that is, bathroom, classroom, hallway, outside school grounds, etc.*

It ain't shit, Angie, you hear? It was Jason and them, you can't listen to what they say. We did great, our scene was the *bomb*. Ms C. really liked it, I could tell. Forget them. Seriously, don't mean shit what they say. They just clowns. We know it, and they know we know it, so it ain't nothing. Did you hear Martin, though? I love him. 'Shut up y'all, stop being ignorant.' He stood up to all them – Jason, Ritchie, Park, all them. I love him.

*Stupid fucking zits. Why am I so ugly? Goddamnit, Goddamnit. Shut up, Angie, shut up. You beautiful, fuck them. What they know? Stupid assholes think they on Springer or something. I ain't never goin' up on stage again. I can't. I hate them, I hate them so much. Why they hate me? What'd I do? Get yourself together, girl, they just trash. You did good. Stop feeling sorry for yourself, you better than all them. I can't help it I got zits. What they think, I put these ugly-ass scars all over me? They were so mean, though. Why? Why they hate me so much?*

Yo man, yo, it was deep man, you shoulda been there, I'm telling you. No, check it, check it. Angie and Nadine was up there, they was doing they scenes, they monologues? Yo, Angie up there crying, dude, I'm straight, she crying about how she can't get no date on Friday night. Yo, dude, we was buggin. Jason, dude, that boy's crazy, he go 'you can't get no date cuz you ugly.' I ain't lying. Naw man, it was sick, I'm sayin'. Yeah. Yeah, she fat and got all them zits. Dude, it was deep, yo. Ritchie be like 'crater face, shut yo cryin' ass up.' Fah real, dude. She run out the room. She be cryin' fah real now. Straight. Drama be deep, yo.

*I hate this so much, my heart just aches for Angie. Poor thing. Hanging on by a thread as it is, and now this. Dammit, dammit, dammit. I honestly have no idea what to do about this. It makes me sick. And the research team there to witness it all, of course. Those boys are impossible. They know what they're doing too, they pick on her because she's the weakest one. I'm not sure she's coming back; I honestly can't blame her. No grade is worth exposing yourself to that. They egg each other on. I just want to scream when they act out like that. But I don't, I try to intervene, to be 'fair,' which does no good at all. I swear, sometimes it feels like Drama only makes things worse. Thank God for Martin, at least. The way he spoke out against them, that was wonderful.*

Angie'll be alright. She got her feelings hurt by a bunch of dumbasses. Trust me, those guys? They in Drama for one reason and one reason only: easy marks. Ms C. know that. I'm just keepin' it real. I ain't afraid of them; I ain't afraid of nobody. For me, it's about the work, you know what I'm sayin'? I want to act, so I'm here to learn, straight. All them guys, strollin' in here twenty minutes late or whatever, talkin' shit – they ain't serious, they don't pay attention. I hate school as much as they do, trust me, but Drama, this here is my lifeline. I want to work and that means it is time for those fools to quit it. Leave it at the door, that's what Ms C. always says, leave it at the door.

*Why that girl always be cryin' every time she get on stage? She think she J. Lo or some shit. Damn. She get up there, be readin' her monologue about how she can't get no date. And there she go, cryin'. She need to be told, she think she Hollywood, but she ain't even Dogwood. Ugly and crazy. So, I told her.*

*'You can't get no date cuz you ugly.' Now sit yo ass down. She did. Sat right down. Plunk. And she ain't done neither, I don't care what nobody say. She comin' back. Trust me. Next class, she gonna be up on that stage cryin'. And I gonna be there telling her to sit her ass back down. I ain't playin' – Angie need to be told.*

## Afterword

'Verbal abuse [is] a central part of teenage sexual morality. Homophobic and misogynistic discourses were key resources used by boys for the collective construction and policing of heterosexual masculine subject orientations. Central to this form of regulation was the subordination of girls and any boy who failed to conform to hegemonic heterosexual masculinity to ensure the reproduction of male power.'[27]

Most every drama teacher who has tried to make a 'teachable moment' out of how a class reacts when an 'ugly' girl or a gay boy volunteers to play a leading role will be all too familiar with how hard it is to break down the social dynamic described in the above quote. The only humane position to take in regard to these kinds of events is a commitment to talk through them, to build up enough trust and understanding among the students that hurtful, hateful comments are no longer tolerated by the group; however, experience has shown that it takes a prohibitive amount of time and energy to keep to this commitment. The scale of the problem overwhelms many teachers, who, besides, may themselves view such harassment as the inevitable consequence of stepping outside a gender paradigm they too have accepted as normal or natural. According to the code of hegemonic masculinity,[28] a boy is compelled to defend himself and his peers from any threats to manhood posed by its opposite, femininity, or its lacking, homosexuality.[29]

Fiona Leach's analysis, based on a reading of the relevant research, adds to the picture of schools as sites typified by hierarchical organization and gender-specific roles, where 'pupils come to see differentiation by gender, race (or ethnicity) and class as normal features of social relationships.'[30] Emerging trends in school disciplinary strategies add another unfortunate dimension to this stratification as students are increasingly slotted into one of two categories, 'harmless' or 'dangerous,'[31] with poor, dark-skinned males placed disproportionately among the latter. Set at odds with the complex and contradictory aspects of identity, such surveillance techniques result in reductive, prejudicial readings of their subjects, and, in so doing, represent an abandonment of the founding principles of liberal education. Stuck in the binary trap of such reductive thinking, 'bad boys' enact an anti-institutional masculinity that simultaneously gives credence to and struggles against the stereotype of incorrigible criminality.

## Boys in School

Those concerned with boys in school have made efforts to turn around the historically poor academic outcomes for boys who display anti-schooling behaviours, but, as Louise Archer and Hiromi Yamashita suggest, this is hardly an easy task:

> popular public, educational and political discourses have put forward the notion of male "laddishness" (and its associated "bad" or "naughty" behaviour) as a possible explanation for boys' underachievement at school (and resistance to participation in education more generally). We would suggest, however, that "bad boy" identities are far more complex constructions, being specifically located, classed, and racialised masculinities.[32]

Archer and Yamashita conclude that boys' resistance to schooling might derive from their adherence to a 'globalised and diasporic'[33] discourse on masculinity that does not have its origins in the school yard, but in the wider community. Thus, educational initiatives to re-integrate these boys into the schooling system fail because they 'do not address the boys' strong emotional attachment to identities grounded outside of the educational context.'[34] Such analysis of the school culture's connections to the broader community dovetails with a wider call for research that does not place the blame on boys for their unease with the academic establishment, or treat them as toxic.[35]

Since mainstream masculinity is a performance that cannot tolerate being viewed as such,[36] the bad boy works to conceal his awareness of his audience. But, of course, his efforts are for their benefit. The bad boy performance, despite outward appearances, is an instance of anxious masculinity.[37] To maintain control, the bad boy must expunge any feminine characteristics from his persona, at the same time 'keeping it real' by naturalizing his performance to the greatest extent possible.

In most ethnographic accounts of school-based gender relations, researchers report that the mainstream student view is that masculinity *is* heterosexuality.[38] Boys are conditioned to define and defend their masculine position through discursive practice that valorizes hetero-sexuality and demonizes gayness. One must only walk down a school hallway to see masculine claims being validated through both the deg-radation of homosexuality and open heterosexual activity.[39] As one might imagine, these acts of domination involve a great deal of sexual and verbal harassment, behaviours likely more prevalent in schools than is commonly acknowledged. Studies have shown that school per-sonnel who have come to regard such bullying as an unchangeable aspect, however lamentable, of schoolboy culture have a tendency to dismiss complaints by students about this kind of teasing.[40] This jaded acceptance by educators of 'boys being boys' and the hurtful consequences of their behaviour support Butler's definition of gender as 'a construction that regularly conceals its genesis,' one that '"com-pels" belief in its necessity and naturalness'[41]

The problems of violence, bullying, underachievement, and disrup-tive behaviour associated with boys in school have moved researchers to look outside the classroom in trying to discover ways in which our society's heteronormative and patriarchal ideas of what it means to be a man can be interrupted and respectfully engaged in high schools. For all the work that has been done in the area of gender equity, the detailed study of how hegemonic definitions of masculin-ity are implicit in the maintenance of oppressive hierarchies of race, class, and disability has only just begun. As Wayne Martino and De-borah Berrill,[42] citing Apple, observe: 'the challenge that still remains relates to how the complexities and nuances of the social construction of masculinities in boys' lives can be translated and deployed strategi-cally in ways which speak, in practical terms, to the everyday realities of teachers' classroom experiences of teaching boys.'

The effort is to understand how the specific cultural politics of schooling affect or interact with local and global cultural politics of identity, to see how schools and masculinities are mutually consti-tuted,[43] and to suggest how we might construct policies and practices that critically engage, rather than catalyse, the performance of anti-school adolescent male identities.

If the schools are to act as sites of liberation rather than intimidation, we will need to seriously rethink the dynamics that are reinforced in the everyday life of schools. As it stands schools are, to a disturbing extent, places where students are exposed to, and participate in, some of the most extreme gender regimes in our society. As an educator interested in issues of gender, I see the quest for a non-threatening, effective way to interrupt or interrogate such scenes of gender privilege as an ongoing project. Too often I have had the experience of having my lesson for the day or week come to a crashing halt because I have dared skate on the surface of the usually unquestioned gender roles, played especially by the boys. In my work as a researcher, I naturally gravitate toward finding some way to work within the dramatic medium to deconstruct gender performances and expose them to productive examination.

I believe there is great potential in researchers undertaking creative collaboration with high-school boys to turn their life histories into performance texts. Such research could incorporate insights gleaned from focus group and individual interviews, field observation (the researcher's and the participants'), journal writing, and dramatic role-playing. There is significant liberatory potential for this type of hands-on research to provoke a rethinking among all participants of what they make of their masculine identity. A staged presentation of the material developed during the research collaboration could stimulate local, sub-cultural debate concerning the range of masculine positions; conversations which could further contribute to the development of the students' writing and performance.

The performative writing in this chapter has tried to suggest that there are ways dramatic engagement with youth might, one day, have such a function. By framing scenes of masculine performance *as* performance, for example, space is opened up to encounter these scenes either as different ways to depict and analyse issues relating to gender identity, or to use them (or their likeness) as the basis for working with selected youth, the terms of whose own masculine performance might benefit from a decidedly theatrical turn. Either way, the assumption here is that if masculinity is indeed a performance, then we should encourage young males to consider the vast range of parts they might be able to play.

So now the last Drama class of the day is almost over. The students are putting their shoes back on, hanging around the door waiting for the bell to ring. I can tell from their body language that they had fun. Some boys who do not normally participate got involved, to the point where a few of them had to be reminded to give others a chance. Watching them now, seeing how easily they are talking and joking, the fear that stood between us seems to have vanished. But it was real; I started out as a cop, turned into a supply teacher, and, finally, became a recognizable person to them. It took work to travel that distance. Sometimes, when things don't go so well, I have told myself I do not belong here, that these kids really need more teachers who share their background and can understand things about their experiences that I never could. And maybe I'm not the right one to be teaching them, but there are times, times like today, where that seems to be the whole point: I'm there as someone who wants to be there, to speak from difference, to the difference, to say, 'I am not a *cop*, and I am not exactly like you. I am a man who does not have to put others down to feel good about myself. What do you suppose we can do for each other today?'

# 7 Dancing without a Floor: The Artists' Politic of Queer Club Space

KEN MOFFATT

In Toronto club events have been an important element of queer culture through which gender can be explored. At times the club culture of dancing, music, and socializing has been treated as insignificant to the understanding of queer cultures and gender. At other times, queer club culture has been criticized as non-political and superficial in nature. In the following chapter I document a specific queer club space, Vazaleen, and argue that the space can contribute positively to queer transformative politics through the reconstitution of gender when the conception of space is based upon an ethics of change that refuses ontological foundations. The club space, properly envisioned, makes a significant contribution to a culture of diversity for queers. I describe the historical context of Vazaleen, conceptualized and organized by Will Munro, an artist, impresario, activist, and community organizer. The elements of the space that exist alongside one another at Vazaleen contribute to concrete sensuous, specific relations that are both real and acted out as fictions. The taken-for-granted is turned inside out due to Munro's interest in ephemeral, open-ended, communal space. His refusal to rush to judgment has been influential in participants' experiences of rebellion and revolt. The politics of the space are a challenge to the abstract, the transcendent, and to conceptual purity we are accustomed to when thinking about gender and sexuality. Social critique and experimentation are important to participants who value the subjective construction of local culture in the present through the historicity of the moment.

The analysis of Vazaleen was accomplished through participation over a three-and-a-half-year period, and extended interviews with the

founder Munro. I have also reviewed articles about Munro and Vazaleen in Toronto's alternative press for a two-year period.

### Blurring Boundaries through the Event *Vazaleen*

Vazaleen was first held in January 2000 at Toronto's rock and roll bar
the El Mocambo on Spadina Avenue. Due to the success of the initial
night, meant to commemorate the Millennium, Vazaleen became a regular monthly event, eventually moving to Lee's Palace on Bloor Street,
a club with a reputation for booking progressive and alternative rock
and roll bands. At the new location Vazaleen grew in popularity from its
initial small gathering and attracted as many as a thousand people taking over two levels of Lee's Palace on major dates, such as New Year's
Eve and Gay Pride Week. The last monthly event was held in 2006.

The importance of queer space within commercial venues is well
documented in the queer history of Toronto. Commercial for-profit
bars and bathhouses have been places where queer community members have met and created relationships for generations.[1] In these
commercial spaces people have been able to experiment with gender
while experiencing contact across differences according to gender
identification, class, and race.[2] The organizers of Vazaleen respected
this history by organizing the event in a commercial venue. At the
same time, however, Vazaleen was meant to be a community place
where emphasis was on contact rather than consumption.

Munro's intention was to embrace this history of queer spaces and
based Vazaleen's creation on the perception that a number of commercial queer spaces had resulted in a homogenized capitalist culture
for queers. At times, the homogenizing influence was experienced
through the imagery within the commercial space and at others because diversity, particularly by gender, was discouraged. Munro was
intent on constructing a not-for-profit event within a commercial
space. The imagery, explicit politics of the organizers, and the not-for-
profit character of the event was meant to allow for a unique mixing
of people that led to a different experience of engagement among community members. In particular organizers were careful to avoid organizing events so that they became the exclusive preserve of men.

Although Vazaleen was collaborative in nature, its conception and
implementation was the passion of Munro. In the same manner that it
is impossible to separate Andy Warhol from the Factory, it is impossible

to write about Vazaleen without considering Munro's vision of the event.

Munro, an artist and impresario, moved to Toronto from the suburbs to attend art school. Underwear was Will Munro's primary medium for artistic expression. He reconstructed undergarments from items discovered in thrift stores to challenge concepts of gender, intimacy, and sexuality. It is also a medium that makes the private public.[3]

The abject, all that is expelled due to its perception of perversity and 'being outside,'[4] is present in Munro's art. According to Julia Kristeva, social rites exist to 'separate this or that social, sexual, or age group from one another, by means of prohibiting a filthy, defiling element. It is as if dividing lines were built up between society and a certain nature, as well as within the social aggregate, on the simple basis of *excluding filth*.'[5]

Both Munro's art and his events such as Vazaleen defy this form of ritual. At times, he purposely stained the underwear with bodily fluids.[6] The limits of gender and the body are challenged through the reconstruction of the underwear so that gendered expectations of the items are overturned. The presence of bodily fluids on the underwear suggests a type of 'grotesque' defined at the limit of the body and the blurring of boundaries.[7] Ambivalent and feminized garments are vilified in western culture, since they challenge the closed non-porous body of the male. Munro's art is a challenge to all that is represented as 'pure and clean,' in particular the 'straight' male.[8]

Upon his graduation from art school, Munro hoped to create a new social scene in Toronto. He wished to create a 'downtown space with a mixed crowd' in a place that was known to be a straight space. Since Munro associated himself with the rock and roll subculture, he preferred to place the event in a rock and roll club.[9] Munro hoped to contribute to a 'more humane' environment for queer people by offering spaces outside of the established urban 'gay ghetto' at Church and Wellesley streets. By situating Vazaleen in rock and roll clubs throughout the city Munro intentionally expanded the urban boundaries within which queer people can feel safe. He challenged the exclusion that queers experience in neighbourhoods outside the 'assigned' central ghetto.[10]

While challenging the lack of spatial alternatives for queers in Toronto, Munro also challenged the nature of queer space itself. In planning for his events he appealed to 'all sorts of queer subcultures' because most gay male public spaces did not reflect the diversity he knew existed in Toronto. In reaction to the type of homogeneity that existed, particularly in bars catering to males, he endeavoured to create 'a space that was mixed up'[11] – a space where people could be 'as queer and freaky or crazy as they wanted to be.' Munro 'just wanted to have a party and celebrate with more of a queer mixed thing.'[12]

Nurturing this alternative space marked by diversity came out of an overtly queer community whose membership included punks and activists – a community that places a value on including outsiders.[13] According to Scott Treleavan, a Toronto queer zinester/artist/filmmaker/short story author, the Toronto punk scene has an ethos that had an 'inclusive, overarching leftist stance. It revelled in difference, defiance and personal expression.'[14] Members of the community continue to be involved in social causes that reflect their social, political commitment – Munro volunteered at the Lesbian, Gay, and Bisexual Youth Line. Another member of the community, the DJ Miss BarbraFisch, is a sex worker activist who works at a shelter for women.[15]

The cultural, musical element to the queer punk community is made up of an international network of homocore groups. In cities such as Vancouver, New York, San Francisco, and Chicago parties are held with performances by bands such as Gossip, Limp Wrist, The Butchies, and the Skinjobs.[16] Vazaleen is a result of Munro's concern as a queer punk with inclusivity, outsider status, and difference.[17] He arranged for bands from the queer punk community to perform at his events.

Munro took his 'experience as a punk kid' and as someone who went to house parties to conceptualize Vazaleen as an expression of punk ethos. Munro credited punk rock with teaching him how to be a critical thinker. His older brother's punk records were a seminal influence on his thought. The 'do-it-yourself' ethos of punk culture with its emphasis on self-sufficiency appealled to him. Popular local forms of communication such as punk zines were influential to his mode of communication.[18] The promotion of Vazaleen as an event was about the promotion of punk cultural values such as respect for diversity and local autonomy in art.[19]

The early posters and flyers for Vazaleen were hand-made. Later on the Vazaleen posters were designed and created by a variety of local artists and served a number of purposes beyond promoting the event. They championed local art through the do-it-yourself aesthetic as art works.[20] Michael Comeau, a Toronto artist and printmaker, created a number of posters for the event that challenged gender expectations. At times his expression of maleness in the posters was so extreme as to be ironic. The images of men such as in Figure 8 are so macho as to make one wonder whether they were masculine in a conventional sense.[21]

In addition posters, such as Figure 8, created queer visibility through imagery that questioned public expressions of maleness. Queer images were posted on walls, mailboxes, and telephone poles where least expected in the streets of neighbourhoods outside of the 'gay ghetto.' A queer, punk aesthetic was created on the street while playfully questioning public imagery of maleness.

Munro was also a member of Toronto's Queen Street West art scene that has flourished in Toronto since the 1970s. The scene is named for a street in Toronto where artists' events were held in a variety of spaces including galleries, parks, shop windows, and bars. The spirit of the Queen Street scene continued to exist in events such as Vazaleen. The Queen Street artists and community members are an amorphous group of people who have created and nurtured an art presence that defies mainstream interpretation of both art and social relations. The subversive nature of the scene is expressed through creative experimentation in all art forms, as well as a credo of tolerance for multiplicity and difference. Galleries such as the S.P.I.N. Gallery, Paul Petro Gallery, Katharine Mulherin, and Zsa Zsa Gallery represented the ethos of this community. Vazaleen was one of the spaces in which members of the Queen Street community were able to socialize.

Historically the club space has taken on an important role as an intermediary space between the street and the commercial gallery. Within such venues a form of artistic immediacy is apparent.[22] Smaller clubs or special events within larger night-clubs have become urban institutional phenomena within North America. Performance art and art installations in night-clubs have been elements of this cultural scene.[23] These institutions within commercial establishments created a place for self-defined bohemians, such as musicians, artists, and queers to socialize and mix. During the 1970s and 1980s the New York club scene was an integral part of the art scene. Clubs such as the Mudd Club, C.B.G.B.s, and Max's Kansas City were meeting places where partying mixed with networking. The social milieu encouraged the sharing of artistic ideas while participants experienced a social alternative; the contagious mix of art and social experimentation encouraged creativity.[24] In Toronto, events such as Dyke Night and KGB parties at the Boom Boom Room drew crowds made up of participants who might not attend a regular night at the club.

Munro's struggle to create and nurture queer space was part of militant contemporary Canadian queer organizing.[25] The right to queer

Figure 8: Michael Comeau, Poster for Vazaleen (November 18, 2004). Courtesy of the artist.

space, a space that is defined by the mores, norms, and standards of the queer community, has been central to the fight for Canadian queer liberation.[26] In 1981 demonstrations by gay, lesbian, bisexual, trans-gendered, and transexual Torontonians and their allies marked the beginning of an extended period of community organization for queer space. The demonstrations were protests against the police raids of bathhouses and the mistreatment of the men who had been arrested through the raids.[27] Similarly, lesbians were involved in community organizing in 2000 to challenge police raids on the Pussy Palace, a lesbian-organized bathhouse.[28]

Tom Warner argues that those queers who demand the right to self-defined space are members of a radical group of queer organizers.[29] The fight for queer space has challenged the assumptions about Canadian social institutions and community moral standards. The limits of tolerance and inclusivity within both mainstream and gay cultures have been challenged through this battle.[30] Public space for contact among queer people has been gained only through 'cumulative victories against repression.'[31] The spaces have been created based on the willingness of queers to fight for and to inhabit those spaces on their own terms.[32]

Munro's conceptual, artistic experimentation with gender, diversity, and boundaries is key to understanding the event Vazaleen. Munro imagined a space in which all that is normally perceived as grotesque and abject is openly explored. The bodies of participants at Vazaleen are imagined to be open-ended and irregular rather than symmetrical and balanced. Participants can relax into the communality of imperfect bodies and porous boundaries rather than the individualizing forces of fastidiously perfected beauty.[33] Through staged events such as *Vazaleen* geographic, gender, artistic, aesthetic, and commercial/non-profit boundaries have been blurred. The brilliance of the event was the blurring of boundaries through the focus on difference.

## The Borderline between the Everyday and Art: Sense-Based Specificity of a Local Cultural Space

*Vazaleen* drew participants of all genders including women, men, and transgendered persons. As well, the appearance of participants suggests a diversity of sexual types were in attendance at the event. The gendered diversity of the participants has contributed to the characterization of Vazaleen as an alternative space[34] and a 'queer fringe thing.'[35] Bruce La Bruce, artist, filmmaker, pornographer, and social commentator, remarked enthusiastically that due to the radical nature of his events 'Club impresario Will Munro has put homosexual Toronto on the international map.'[36] The Vazaleen crowd reflected a number of the subcultures within Toronto's queer culture. Munro explained that the mix of participants at an event was

> like your gay rock and rollers um as well as your dyke kind of like punks um also you get into like leather subcultures. So you have like dykes who are into leather . . . as well as fags who are into leather. As well, you get all those sort of trans subcultures – so your [*sic*] getting tranny boys and tranny girls. You are getting people who are into gender fuck, um you are getting like bear subcultures, you're getting swingers, you're getting cool straight hipsters, music kids. Um, it's pretty shook up . . . I've seen most sexual subcultures. I think there's also a pretty strong bi contingent

that shows up . . . You get a lot of people who come out who have wanted to ah explore queer things and they identify mostly as being straight and will come to this event specifically.[37]

The social contact within the space had fluidity both by purpose and type. Vazaleen was a social space where people of differing classes, professions, and work status mixed. Members of the Toronto arts community including authors, visual artists, gallery owners, curators, collectors, musicians, journalists, and critics attended. Attendance by the unemployed, hairdressers, labourers, civil servants, academics, lawyers, social workers, architects, clerks, computer programmers, sex trade workers, and salespeople was equally significant. Cultural workers networked, negotiated, and collaborated on new artistic ideas. Many participants were as likely to flirt, cruise, and pick up prospective sexual partners. Due to the diversity of the crowd and the queer punk ethos, Vazaleen was a space where 'life [is] at its most rewarding, productive and pleasant when large numbers of people understand, appreciate and seek out interclass contact and communication conducted in the mode of good will.'[38]

Vazaleen was best understood as a scattering of social fragments. Depending on your focus, Vazaleen could have appeared to be a leather bar, a transgendered space, a discotheque, or a rock and roll club. Vazaleen lay at the crossroads of a network of social possibilities, such as the Queen Street art scene, the punk subculture, and any number of gender subcultures. The presence of the diverse social influences within the space informed the nature of the event. The unpredictability of the consequences of the social mixing defined Vazaleen as an art event.[39]

Munro valued social experience between people such as those relations 'between the young and old sharing knowledge.'[40] He worried that experiential relations across difference were eroding: 'Instead it's all about fucking. That's great. That's fine. But if you don't have anything else then what's gonna happen to our culture? Is our culture gonna become *Queer as Folk*?'[41] The principle of encounter was key to the form of experimentation at Vazaleen. The social relations were constructed so that sense-based phenomena and the abstract were integrated. Forms of relations were created so that thought, art, and social life were informed by the sense-based experience of another person.[42]

The 'artistry of being' at Vazaleen was based in a practice of 'unworking' or de-transcendence of a gendered heterosexual culture. Participants were involved in the contradictory exercise of undoing the work of culture while demanding a culture based on specificity[43] and the sense-based experience of others. New York City's rock and roll musician and DJ Jayne County demanded a type of sensible recognition by explicitly explaining to the crowd, 'I am a transsexual with drag queen tendencies.'[44] Furthermore, she claimed a specific subjectivity by declaring at Vazaleen, 'I am not Alice Cooper, I am not Marilyn Manson . . . I am Jayne County.' The approval of the audience to her declaration of gender identity connoted the recognition of her specificity.[45] Jayne County coupled her specific claim of identity with stories of Lou Reed's and David Bowie's manipulation of identity through playing with gender and sexual ambiguity that was controlled by the business of market-driven rock.[46] By separating herself from pop stars, Jayne County situated herself and Vazaleen's participants outside the capitalist play of surface realities such as identities defined solely by market forces.[47] The sense-based phenomena and the specific of her gender were honoured in the space. The queer punk emphasis on local do-it-yourself culture was reconstituted in the space as is the possibility of multiple genders.[48]

Similarly, the club participants were invited to engage in the outsider status whose productivity was tied to their sense-based experience of each other.[49] Jayne County cried out to the crowd: 'I want to see the freaks. Where are the freaks? Are you a freak? Good for you.' Similarly the lead singer for the Skinjobs called out for a response 'from the queers' so that they could join the band on stage. The club participants were reminded their politics were not so much about abstraction or transcendent referents for social comprehension;[50] rather the politic of the club was

A metamorphosis or a passage, in any case a movement, from pathos to affectivity . . . from the interiorities of subjectivity and identity to an exteriority that is not merely the outside of the inside . . . from community to the being in common of whatever singularities, from history to historicity, from society to sociality, from authority to power, from communication to significance: from the cultural to the political.[51]

As one of the DJs for Vazaleen, Munro kept alive the politic through his choice of music. He relied heavily on 1970s rock and roll in his playlist because he associated the music with a decade of social change. His choice of music was a lesson that informed the historicity of the moment. Often he played music because it was unexpected and surprising in a queer club. The queer connotation in 'straight' rock and roll music was made explicit when played at Vazaleen. Queers in the club took back music that had racist, misogynist, and homophobic connotations in order to free the revolutionary potential of rock and roll.[52] This music was one of a number of elements of the event including queer-positive video projections and/or stage presentations. The interaction of the elements subverted the original intent and meaning of the music or, at least, brought it into question.

The DJ is key to the creation of contemporary performance space as she or he sculpts aural soundscapes to the tone of the event. Toronto artists such as Andrew Zealey, Luis Jacob, Don Pyle, and Will Munro spin records as an art form that is part history lesson, as it refers to other aural artists, and part soundscape. At the same time, a key role of the DJ is to facilitate the social mixing of people with diverse identities through the use of sound. In this manner, DJs such as Denise Benson at Toronto's Dyke Night have taken on a socially significant role as icons of difference and outsider status. In New York City, Wayne County was the DJ at a New Year's show starring the Ramones and the Heartbreakers.[53] In 2003 she was the DJ at Vazaleen as Jayne County.

Specific activities within the space of Vazaleen promote performance by both guest stars and the club participants. Munro offers a description of the event:

> You are going to see sheets projected on, that are hanging from the ceiling on two sides of the room. You are going to see all kinds of different projections: slides, super eights, sixteens, video. Sometimes, video mixing. And there is a stage where a lot of performances happen, ah people in the audience are encouraged to, you know, come on stage and participate in certain themes or events . . . as well as performers who are brought in as a main act. Then sometimes we will set up things that are more interactive in another corner of the space by the side of the stage. We've done various different photo shoots . . . we once did a biker shoot with a low rider bicycle . . . Other things happen in the space we've done roller derbies, we had drag races once, drag queens and drag kings racing on bicycles . . . all sorts of things that happen . . . the audience is participating so in a sense the performance is happening everywhere . . . For example, when we had the prom night massacre . . . forty per cent of the audience was wearing some kind of weird gore or prom outfit so that then makes the whole space a kind of performance.[54]

Some performances at Vazaleen demanded a reconsideration of social expectations within both the gay and the mainstream cultures. In this manner, the performances were a type of artistic agitational propaganda (agit prop). Historically in Toronto agit prop has consisted of activities such as short political sketches, drama, choral speeches, poetry readings, and street performances often with a socialist or anarchist message.[55] During Toronto's Gay Pride week, Munro challenged the corporate sponsorship and consumerism of the Gay Pride Event by holding an event entitled Shame. A confessional was located on the site of Vazaleen during the Roman Catholic Church's World Youth Symposium. During the SARS outbreak men showed up at the event dressed in protective gear. The week after a raid by Toronto police on the Pussy Palace, a lesbian bathhouse, a performance was held by drag queens 'that was totally about cops busting up queer spaces.'[56] In a performance by drag kings, male-identified women dressed as male police officers arrested male-identified women dressed as gay men in a public washroom. This performance was based on real-life events during which men were arrested in St Catharines, Ontario, and one of the defendants committed suicide. These performances make transparent public anxieties and challenge the taken-for-granted nature of the media coverage and public perception of social issues. At times the critique is implied, at other times the performance explicitly takes to task social forces such as gender expectations, capitalism, liberalism, and social conservatism.

Agit prop need not be severe and sombre. In fact, much of the performance at Vazaleen was remarkable for how it incited laughter as well as the celebratory tone. Playful performances are means of addressing social, political issues. According to Munro,[57] a Vazaleen event focused on so serious a theme as challenging the war in Iraq is done in a 'fun and very playful way.' The intent is to help the survivors of government policy to be 'political in a bit of a different form.' Social roles are experimental while politics are unveiled 'without oppressing people." Participants who have not been critical are encouraged to become critical for the first time.[58]

In this respect the performances contribute to the Bakhtinian carnival flavour of the event. Vazaleen was an oppositional culture based on alternative cultural production and expression of desire. All that has been marginalized becomes the centre of activity and awareness.[59] Vazaleen was a form of carnival as understood by Bakhtin: carnival 'is by no means a purely artistic form nor a spectacle . . . It belongs to the borderline between art and life. In reality, it is life itself, but shaped according to a certain pattern of play . . . Carnival is not a spectacle seen by the people; they live in it . . . During carnival time life is subject only to its laws, that is the laws of its own freedom.'[60]

Dogmatic or repressive relations and concepts become incomplete and open, so that all that was formerly fixed including gender becomes fluid.[61] Eccentricity is encouraged as a form of challenge to the external, hierarchical ordering of gendered social relations.[62] Munro was interested in relations that are non-conventional, sensuous, and experimental in spaces that are elusive and transitory. While political consciousness and social identities are based on good will, communality, and a critique of corporate capitalism, they also multiply in all their eccentric permutations.

## Art Space Defined by the Encounter in the Planar

The politic of *Vazaleen* is best understood by a logic that involves the encounter[63] in the context of planar relations.[64] The 'planar,' purposefully placing elements beside one another, serves an important queer politic. By placing elements such as sexual identities, gender identities, performative acts, and symbols in proximity to one another, one avoids a dualistic interpretation of social life. Dichotomous categories of subject versus object, antecedent versus precedent, cause versus effect are subverted. Furthermore, the 'spatial positionality of *beside* . . . seems to offer some useful resistance to the ease with which *beneath* and *beyond* turn from spatial descriptors into implicit narratives of, respectively, origin and telos.'[65] The shift from dichotomous thought opens the possibility of multiplicity in gender subjectivities and expressions of agency. Juxtaposing the various elements makes possible 'a wide range of desiring, identifying, representing, repelling, paralleling, differentiating, rivalling, learning, twisting, mimicking, withdrawing, attracting, aggressing, warping, and other relations.'[66] Space, in this case queer club space, has a rich dimension[67] from the philosophical, artistic, social, and moral points of view.

The ephemeral quality of the space further enriches the experience of the planar (beside) rather than the historical origins of the event (before) and/or the psychology of the participants (beneath). By its nature the rock and roll bar is a transitory space, since the crowd changes according to the event and the performer; people coming for a particular show constitute the culture of the space at that time. To place a queer event in a straight space is still more elusory.[68] The principle of encounter in the moment is heightened as other explanations for the social politic are diminished. In fact, Toronto critic and author R.M. Vaughan argues that too much has been made of seeking philosophical interpretations and historical antecedents for Vazaleen. He argues that the success of the event was the music. However, he is forgiving of those of us who seek a cultural interpretation of Vazaleen, because, according to Vaughan, queer culture is elusive, if not repressed, and when not documented it is too soon forgotten.[69]

Through events such as Vazaleen the aesthetics of the self, that is, making oneself present, taken-for-granted social codes are challenged.[70] The unfolding takes place in a form of *heterotopia,*, a place where signs, languages, interpersonal relations are incongruous, disordered, and multiple.[71] Unfolding a diversity of selves allows for the 'violation of the usual.'[72] Rather than ask why our selves exist or what they do, we are interested in the negotiations involved in the empirical existentiality.[73] We are not present to serve capitalist production through preoccupation with exclusion, safety, security, and predictability.[74] Rather, we are interested in productivity of the self and the expression of eros which 'undoes the work of culture altogether. It is the unrecognizable face of the stranger each us is at the brink of pleasure – or death.'[75]

Coexisting with this openness is comfort with 'a discovery of the new and as yet unseen things.'[76] Within the dramatic 'being in common'[77] at Vazaleen, an open-endedness of gender subjectivity is possible. Support for each other occurs even as personal subjective possibilities are uncertain.[78] According to Munro,[79] journalists, authors, and performers commented on how 'mixed up' the audience was. Some commented that they 'have not seen a slice of life like this since the early 80s.' Cultural codes are rewritten without yet understanding the outcome of the change. Underlying this risk, however, is a good will marked by openness – a refusal to rush to judgment of others.[80]

Freed of a preoccupation with origins and telos, an experimental space, an art space is created. Within this space all participants perform in the context of anarchic social relations based on situatedness, specificity, and historicity. The performative within such an experimental space challenges bourgeois values such as monogamy or consumerism. In fact, the concept of fundamental precepts or values is challenged. Brought to task is 'a model of humanity that had absorbed into itself the transcendent ideal (God) and which, from his immanence[,] was in hot pursuit of values and objects.'[81]

A solidarity is created based on 'awareness of one's discontent,'[82] rather than a stable code of values.[83] Change occurs in the revolt against the ongoing capitalist ethos of calculation and management.[84] Within the queer punk community members are 'always politicized . . . There are problems facing our community and . . . there are issues that are "pissing people off." '[85] As Kristeva states: 'I revolt: Therefore we are still to come.'[86]

 Munro was interested in the construction of the self in a play of productive, amorphous, and desirous relations.[87] Like Deleuze, he avoided the problems of 'the retreat into metaquestions of judgement – a symptom in fact of . . . a "weak period, a period of reaction." '[88] In his article 'Pride Terrorism,'[89] Munro questioned the tone of Gay Pride celebrations in Toronto. He challenged the reader to reconsider that Gay Pride events were born of revolution and riot. He stated: 'Probably over a million people will converge on Toronto for Pride this year. With attendance figures like this it's really hard to imagine that Pride used to be a radical and serious underground event that was part of a larger struggle.'[90] Even as he engaged in his polemic based on an acknowledgment of history (before), he still maintained the importance of the present (beside) by writing: 'I do not wish to judge or alienate those involved, my focus is to encourage change.'[91]

When encouraged to judge the mainstream audiences over their ignorance about the queer nature of stadium rock and roll, since queer bands such as Freddy Mercury's Queen are often used at sporting events, he responded with hesitancy. When pressed to make a judgment about how blinded straight populations are to many queer cultural influences, he responded: ' I think people know' and 'maybe they just don't mind so much. It is just about the unspoken . . . they don't want someone to beat it over their heads.'[92]

The success of his events eventually created a difficult contradiction for Munro and the participants. The events were so well attended that lines formed and at times people could not be guaranteed entry. The popularity created difficult questions about whether the space should be allowed to spill over to the street or to other venues or whether it should be contained to carefully ensure the original subversive character of the space. Some of the original participants became alienated. Shannon Mitchell,[93] interviewing members of the Skinjobs, characterized the event as increasingly mainstream. She asks:

how do you feel about playing such big events such as Vaseline [*sic*]? You've got the queer punks but over time it's become the cool thing to do with that you get the corporate yuppie queers coming to it . . . It used to be really awesome but now it's gotten so big, there are even VIP cards! The line-ups are insane with lots of people who aren't even there to see the bands, and half the time unless you get there early you can't get in. Queer punks finally got their space, to do our own thing but then it gets taken back. Community gets replaced by scenesters.[94]

Another question for revellers at Vazaleen was whether the mixing of people by race fully represented the racial diversity of Toronto. While the event was predominately attended by white people, part of the mixing within the event was across race. Performers were not exclusively white and narratives within performance invariably attempted to be inclusive. Regular attendees were of all races. Still, since Vazaleen was 'about the music,' the focus on rock and roll may have limited racially mixing.

Due to its utopian nature, the culture of laughter as a part of carnival may or may not lead to full rebellion and fully defined opposition. According to Bakhtin: 'The consciousness of freedom . . . could only be limited and utopian . . . It would therefore be a mistake to presume that popular distrust of seriousness and popular love of laughter, as of another truth, could always reach full awareness.'[95] At the same time I would argue that the polyphonous voices of Vazaleen allowed for an open interpretation of gender codes that allowed for multiple forms of rebellion.

In fact I rethought my own masculinity as participants at Vazaleeen treated me as if I was a rock musician, a beatnik, a revolutionary, a middle-aged man, and a scholar. At Vazaleen I had the honour of being mistaken for an artist, a critic, a curator, and a truck driver. Perhaps in the space that was Vazaleen I was an *artist of myself*. Either I encouraged these interpretations of myself or they were based in confusion born in the clash of difference. I think this re-experiencing of myself as a man in the face of difference was a form of social change. In this queer space that played with boundaries I was freed from imposed anxieties of capitalist corporate culture and from self-imposed anxieties over sexuality. At times the ego of the man is irrelevant in the expression of desire between difference on the planar.

The social at Vazaleen did not seek to be authorized outside the placement of elements beside each other at the event. The 'social seeks no authorization in any putatively ontological ground that, as a solicitude subject to no necessity whatever, anarchic sociality founds the ethico-political as such. The very fact that unauthorized protocols and etiquettes exist here at all is the foundation of ethicality altogether.'[96] So, Munro refused to rush to judgment, and he continued to speak to the importance of the planar. He stated: 'I go to spaces that I do not personally inhabit to encourage people to come.'[97] If someone who is not normally comfortable within the queer "underground" chooses to "come to this space and think it's cool and interesting" then the value lies in the fact that 'something is changing, you know.'[98]

## Conclusion

While the careful eye, the welcoming attitude, and loving presence of Will Munro is no longer present, Vazaleen continues on an occasional basis. Within the space that is Vazaleen, performance challenged the taken-for-granted. By focusing on the planar (*beside*) and the encounter, Vazaleen is a queer space that allows for the *unworking* of assumed cultural codes. The radical nature of the space is due to the refusal to seek ontological understandings outside the experience of the elements of the space. The politic of the space is created through staged performances that comment on social anxieties, social welfare, repression, and death, alongside the randomness of social encounter in the context of difference, including gender difference. The masculinities, at times self conscious of hegemonic masculinity, are articulated in that social space in fragments through brief encounter and unexpected social encounters. In addition, masculinity is articulated through intentional performance on the stage, through symbol recreation in the video projection, as well as through the playful presence of the participants. As with Munro's underwear art, gender, intimacy, and sexuality are reconsidered as abject yet beautiful. In the messiness between spaces and the refusal of rigid judgment new masculinities might come into play. The space in its entirety becomes an art space as people seek out sense-based phenomena including the experience of the specific other person. The performance is focused on the present due to its lack of concern with psychology (*beneath*) and its ephemeral treatment of time (*before*). Experientially, participants are artists of their own gender while intellectually they are 'dancing without a floor.' In this manner, participants begin to imagine productive life and an aesthetic of existence outside the calculation and management of the bourgeois, capitalist western culture.

# 8 Boy to the Power of Three: Toronto Drag Kings

BOBBY NOBLE

Let me make a confession at the outset: I love drag kings. I am what you might call an academic fan. I saw my first drag king show on 29 June 1995, when the Greater Toronto Drag King Society staged a 'Drag King Invasion I,' at a Toronto drag bar called El Convento Rico to an audience of about six hundred screaming fans. It was quite a ride that night and, as an out lesbian, it was beyond just about anything else I had seen before. The performers were equal parts campy, sexy, outrageous, raucous, and utterly tenacious. The crowd was whipped into a kind of queer frenzy, and together, in a bar designed for drag queen performances, lesbian public culture was permanently transformed.

This chapter will explore those transformations through three different waves of drag kinging in one major urban centre: Toronto. I borrow the wave metaphor from feminism and find it a useful way to characterize three different historical moments in what I will begin to document here as the evolution of drag king culture in Toronto. These are not easily characterized as generations; age ranges may not differ dramatically between groups and some kings travel comfortably between each wave, mentoring young generations of upcoming kings. But what is significant about these waves is the social, historical, and epistemological context each maps. The first wave – the Greater Toronto Drag King Society – is easily situated in but not of lesbian performance contexts, such as those mapped by lesbian performance theorists Jill Dolan,[1] Kate Davy,[2] and Sue-Ellen Case.[3] Even as these drag king performances challenge the work of the lesbian theorists, historically, this first wave overlaps with changes that each notes in the development of a body of literature on lesbian performances, such as those of the WOW Café and the performances of Lois Weaver and

Peggy Shaw of Split Britches. Drag kings do not fit easily into the work of Dolan, Davy, and Case but are significant in the sense that they began to mark the rupturing of lesbian discourse, theory, and identity by what I call the butch-femme renaissance. This first wave of kings, then, in Toronto, began to expand the circles around 'lesbian' to map an imbrication with the then emerging queer theory and nation.

The second wave – The Fabulous Toronto Drag Kings – emerged, as waves do, on the end of the first wave. With the emergence of this troupe, drag kings are dis-identified with lesbian cultures, even though they perform in lesbian contexts. What began to emerge instead was an entirely different set of relationships marked by affiliations with both gay masculinity and transmasculinities. Where the first wave engaged in mimicry of masculinity, the second wave began to complicate that mimicry through an increasing identification with masculinity and dis-identification with lesbian subject positions. I trace these identifications and dis-identifications but also trace the ways that a second wave began to foreground a consciousness of race, especially of whiteness, into performances. Finally, I explore the work of one king in particular – Deb Pearce – and her alter ego, Man Murray.

With the dissolution of the Fabulous Toronto Drag Kings, a moment that overlaps with the emergence of a third wave, which includes a variety of groups including Big Daddy Kings and United Kingdom, and then with a fast fourth wave – Bois Will Be Boys and King Size Kings – what I will develop as 'boys to the power of three,' discernible gender identifications and affiliations are all but rendered incoherent. What exists instead are both self-referential (performances that signal the representational practice of the first wave and earlier lesbian cultures) and a plethora of gender identities that are off known gender maps. These are productively incoherent genders in No Man's Land. Moreover, what makes each wave newish, in addition to the existence of a new group of performers, is also physical performance space as discursive as well as geographical location, particularly bars in a large urban centre like Toronto, where different neighbourhoods with varying demographics lend to each wave an entirely different character through its fan base.

One of the things that links these waves, even through some pretty significant differences, is their proximity to discourse of masculinity and a kind of dependence upon this larger problematic for its condition of possibility. While not every performer identifies with masculinity, even dis-identification marks a persistent relation to larger, cultural scripts of gender. 'The "I" who would oppose its construction,' Judith Butler told us back in 1990, 'is always in some sense drawing from that construction to articulate its opposition; further, the "I" draws what is called its agency in part through being implicated in the very relations of power that it seeks to oppose. To be implicated in the relations of power, indeed, enabled by the relations of power that "I" opposes is not, as a consequence, to be reducible to their existing forms.'[4] She reminds us that thinking in excess of social construction renders any subject, and masculinity in particular, incommensurate with self-knowledge or unable to know that which makes it its/self. Self-consciousness, in other words, is not in and of itself the remedy as consciousness is conditioned by language and is a product of language all at the same time. Curiously, then, it's often what the subject cannot know just yet that conditions what it can know. Two points here: these reconfigurations of ours are always already ambivalent but also thinking in excess of what we think we know is where we find out what we still cannot think. Drag kings draw out this ambivalence and stage it for both pleasure and parody. The work I want to do with drag kings is located at the meeting point of these ambivalent contradictions and paradoxes – a space I am hailing as yet another No Man's Land. If we cannot deny or disavow masculinity, as Homi Bhabha suggests we cannot, then what we can do, within the larger ideological and discursive economies of essentialism, racism, and heteronormativity, is disturb, or trouble its manifest destiny, deny, at the very least, its invisibility. By drawing attention to masculinity as a free-floating signifier we rearticulate it, again to quote Bhabha, as prosthesis – a 'prefixing' of the rules of gender and sexuality.[5]

## At the Butch-Femme Lesbian Bar: Drag King Invasions

I want to situate my reading of the 'Drag King Invasion I' as lesbian cultural production at the crossing of 'performativity and the loose cluster of theatrical practices, relations and traditions known as performance,' and more precisely for my purposes here, 'lesbian theatre.'[6] It is precisely the tension between performativity and performance that fuels the erotic intensity of the drag king show. In other words, it is precisely the tension or ambiguity between the so-called 'reality' of the performance – its parody of both the 'hyper-masculine star' at his most contradictory and illusory 'stardom' as a technology of desire – and performativity, or the identificatory processes themselves, that marked the show that night as such an important and pleasurable event.

Second, my reading of the show foregrounds the axiomatic, discursive, and historical slippage between the terms 'camp' and 'drag.' On the one axis of my rather oppositional taxonomy rests earlier lesbian feminist 'performance' theorists Davy, Dolan, and Case, focusing on the woman-run performance spaces Split Britches and the WOW ('Women's One World') Café. To conflate the arguments of these three theorists would be a mistake; however, they not only share similar questions, but they anticipate issues foregrounded in theories of performativity, and provide a lens, as it were, through which I want to read the drag king show. Those are the problematization of the field of representation itself, an interrogation of reading practices vis-à-vis performer-audience dynamics, and finally, the outing of butch-femme subjectivities as constitutive of a 'lesbian aesthetic.' As Kathleen Martindale suggested, much of this early work held high hopes for articulating both a radical and political aesthetic. 'While the utopian appeal of such anti-realist hopes for aesthetic activism is compelling . . . even the critics most responsible for producing these determinist readings concerning the new lesbian spectatorial communities came to acknowledge that they hadn't paid enough attention to the contradictions within discourses and within spectators.'[7] Nonetheless I agree with Martindale's assertion that the demands on lesbian avant-garde writing/performance art for political accountability can be traced back to early feminist theory and practice, and so I will set the stage, as it were, by revisiting that work.[8] I will return to those 'contradictions both within discourses and within spectators' a bit later.

Kate Davy attempts to discern an essential difference between what she identifies as gay camp, and a lesbian performance aesthetic. In her 'Fe/Male Impersonation,' Davy disparages what she identifies as the misogyny inherent in camp, arguing that it not only says 'something about women' to the men it is intended for, but it effaces women in the process. Moreover, Davy suggests gay camp doesn't translate on the 'lesbian' stage, as camp is driven by 'a fierce masculine-feminine heterogendering' that cannot work for a lesbian aesthetic. Finally, Davy begins the outing of butch-femme subjectivities as a solution to the problems posed by male impersonation. Defined in opposition to female-to-male cross-dressing, butch-femme doesn't 'hide the lesbian beneath' and as such 'dismantles the construction of woman . . . challenges male sexuality . . . [and] challenges the heterosexual contract.'[9]

In other words butch-femme as the motor of lesbian performance is 'lethal.'[10]

Dolan is also concerned with both the field of representation itself and the reading of lesbian theatre, that is, with the relations between the performer and the reader/spectator. In ' "Lesbian" Subjectivity in Realism: Dragging at the Margins of Structure and Ideology,' Dolan eschews realism as a strategy of representation, arguing that realism offers 'unhappy positionalities for lesbians . . . the ideological inflections of which are crucial to mark.'[11] One of the inflections that Dolan marks is not only the denial of butch-femme generally, but the feminization of the butch herself: 'By the mid-1970s, the sexual lesbian who engaged in butch behavior as a subcultural resistance to the dominant culture's gender and sexual ideology was silenced by feminism, her transgressive sexual desire "femininized" through the woman-identification that neatly elided active sexuality as a pre-condition for lesbianism.'[12]

In 'The Discourse of Feminisms: The Spectator and Representation,' Dolan goes on to theorize the position of both the individual spectator and spectorial communities in the making of a specifically 'lesbian' desire in representation. While Dolan posits a rather unitary and white spectator, undifferentiated by class, gender, and race, she does attempt to rethink the argument by film theorists Mulvey, de Lauretis, and Doane which suggests that the series of 'looks' built into the structure of film position the male spectator as subject, and woman as the passive object of the male subject's active desire. Dolan too deploys butch-femme in a rhetorical move which anticipates Butler's notion of 'citationality,' arguing that butch-femme 'quotes' gender, to appropriate the male gaze for the purpose of 'looking' and 'reading' queerly in the theatre and in the performance of the everyday as well: 'the drag role requires the performer to quote the accepted conventions of gender behavior. A woman playing a man . . . is quoting gender ideology, holding it up for critique . . . When the assumed gender role does not coincide with the performer's biological sex, the fictions of gender are highlighted.'[13]

Finally, Case herself fully outs the butch-femme couple as the definitive subject position in not just lesbian theatre, but in feminist theory as well. Paradoxically nodding in two directions at once, both through feminism and against feminism, Case's 'Toward a Butch-Femme Aesthetic' attempts to resolve a theoretical impasse in then current (circa 1988) thinking about the lesbian subject.[14] Case is in conversation with

Teresa de Lauretis, who argued in 'The Technology of Gender' that the female subject is always already trapped within the concept of 'sexual difference,' either a biologically overdetermined 'female subject' or an evacuated significatory effect. De Lauretis interrogates the limitations of both positions and offers another perspective – again, from the 'space-off,' a concept borrowed from film theory which identifies the space not visible in the representational frame but inferable from what that frame makes visible. This space then is where we find the terms of a new perspective which will allow the 'subject of feminism' to move between 'the (represented) discursive space of the positions made available by hegemonic discourses and the . . . elsewhere of those discourses,' at once both inside and outside of ideology.[15]

In a very clever rhetorical move, it is within the 'elsewhere' of de Lauretis's own 'subject of feminism' that Case finds her dynamic duo – the butch-femme couple: 'The butch-femme subject could inhabit that discursive position [where] the female body, the male gaze, and the structures of realism function as only sex toys . . . In recuperating the space of seduction, the butch-femme couple can, through their own agency, move through a field of symbols, like tiptoeing through the two lips (as Irigaray would have us believe), playfully inhabiting the camp space of irony and wit, free from biological determinism, elitist essentialism, and the heterosexist cleavage of sexual difference. Surely, here is a couple the feminist subject might perceive as useful to join.'[16]

As Bob Wallace notes, the other axis – 'performativity' – as signified in the last decade by queer theory generally, and Butler in particular, answers that of performance and its attendant identity politics, by suggesting that all identity categories are performatives, or acts of signifying systems that gain efficacy through stylized repetition.[17] Gender then is no longer an immutable and natural 'fact' waiting for articulation in discourse, but rather is a fictional and discursive effect of signifying systems. Moreover, Butler's work problematizes the distinction between 'sex' and 'gender' as it was read in feminist theory. If the two are no longer suggestive of a biology vs. culture split as feminism argued, then logically, to quote Butler, 'man and masculine might just as easily signify a female body as a male one, and feminine a male body as easily as a female one.'[18] Thus, while *Gender Trouble* suggests that gendered performances such as butch-femme are not pathological imitations of heterosexuality, but rather are a kind of fictional imitation for which there is no original, her next work, *Bodies That Matter*, through its interrogation of 'sex' suggests that it too is fantasy, the effect of the reiterative regulatory sexual regimes:[19] 'If gender is the social construction of sex, and if there is no access to this "sex" except by means of its construction, then it appears not only that sex is absorbed by gender, but that "sex" becomes something like a fiction, perhaps a fantasy, retroactively installed at a prelinguistic site to which there is no direct access.'[20]

While much of the work by the former lesbian performance theorists is very much grounded in its own historical moment – lesbian-feminism with its attendant essentialisms – what I find interesting here is that this body of work does attempt to map a kind of 'performative' which Butler polished in her later and highly influential works. What I am suggesting then is the interrogation of 'performance,' as very tentatively mapped by Davy, Dolan, and Case, can be re-constituted as the three lenses through which to read the work of this early wave of drag kings: first, butch-femme in its 1990s manifestation as parody of both a recognizable lesbian signifying system, and heterosexual gender roles; second, the function of an audience or authorizing witness for such performances/performatives; and third, lesbian drag in its proximity to larger technologies of heterosexuality.

An impossibility structures this citation of the performative event at the bar that night, indeed in any live performance. Peggy Phelan notes that nostalgia, or 'the wound of wishing to return,' structures any attempt to report, record, repeat that performative:

> even at the seemingly simple level of the linguistic sign it is impossible for writers to convey the complete context in which a[n] . . . act occurs. To report it back, to record and repeat it, is at once to transform it *and* to fuel the desire for its mimetic return . . . Much of the writing [about performatives] is a record of a living relation between the writer and the artists she sees. This seeing is, necessarily, a distortion, a dream, a hallucination; writing rights it back toward reason by creating enabling fictions . . . The effort to 'cite' the performance that interests us even as it disappears is much like the effort to find the word to say what we mean. It cannot be done.[21]

What my memory impossibly recorded that night was a range of mostly white masculinities staged in performance: Andy Gibb; John Denver and Placido Domingo; The Village People; Billy the Kid or other Nashville or Hollywood cowboys; Freddie Mercury; Guns 'n Roses' Axel Rose and guitar player Slash; and Anne Murray herself.

What underwrites these performances of masculine 'stardom' as well as the conventional live music show is how each 'star' signifies beyond just a 'genre' of music. Each constructs gendered subject positions, types of physicality, identities, fashions, in other words, *star texts*, intertextual constructs produced across a range of often contradictory media and cultural practices.[22] In other words, each of these signifiers listed above signals entirely different identity-based as well as musical discourse: disco (Gibb and The Village People); country ('Trouble'); folk (Denver); rock (Freddie and Axel); and whatever descriptor we might use to characterize the *star text* loosely organized around 'Anne Murray.'

What intrigued me about these performances was the obviously contradictory and at times hysterical visualization of the tensions of masculinity as heteronormative discourse. Contra Davy's assertion that male impersonation does not 'say anything about men' other than their erasure of women, I suggest that male impersonation speaks volumes about masculinity. But I do think Davy is right that we need to learn to read lesbian drag differently, and I offer the following very tentative speculations about that reading paradigm. The drag kings' performance suggested to me that lesbian drag, as opposed to camp, might depend not so much upon excess or an excessive send-off of heterosexual masculinity, but upon equivalency instead. To put this into other terms, if we define mimicry as 'the parodic hyperbolization of a gender identity,' and masquerade as 'the nonironic or unconscious assumption of that identity,' then it seems this dyke drag show did not spin around mimicry's distance from masquerade but rather upon its approximation to it instead. The drag kings' mimetic act takes masquerade, or the unconscious assumption of identity, as its object.[23] In other words, in targeting masculinity as a supposedly 'natural' identity, the show signalled both process and product at once, unveiling performance technologies, with 'technology' both as a discourse naturalizing identity categories as well as the illusion-producing apparatus of the theatre/stage itself, and the performative, or the fictive identities produced. While gay camp foregrounds the performativity and excess of traditional femininity through its 'over-the-top' parody, masculinity remains unmarked and underspoken. The drag kings foreground that cloaked status, and parody masculinity's own unspoken artifice, even though, as Butler rather paradoxically suggests, '[a woman performing masculinity] is perform[ing] a little less, given that femininity is often cast as the spectacular gender.'[24] Moreover, it seems that Davy was both right and wrong. Right, in that male impersonation puts a different spin on its object from gay camp, but wrong in that lesbian performance, at least in this particular manifestation in this moment, is as implicated in a 'masculine-feminine heterogendering' as gay camp.

Moreover, part of what this male impersonation speaks about masculinity is its contradiction and inevitable, and thus repetitive, failures. As Butler suggests, 'to the extent that gender is an assignment, it is an assignment which is never quite carried out according to expectation,' where the addressee never quite inhabits the ideal s/he is compelled to approximate.[25] In their parody of heteronormative masculinity as 'failure,' the drag kings flesh out Butler's assertion. For instance, the drag kings seem quite fond of hijacking musical acts that rely on either duets – Donny and Marie Osmond, John Denver and Placido Domingo – or groups – The Village People. The duet as a music convention is a form just asking for 'trouble.' And troubled it was. One of the most raucous points of the show that night occurred during the Domingo/Denver duet, when at the big climactic end of the song, John and Placido could no long hold back, and commenced necking onstage. Similarly, as Axel Rose and his guitar player Slash finished flailing around on stage, Slash fell to his knees and gave Axel a rather enthusiastic blow job. While seeming to be great fun for most folks in the audience, including the gay male waiters and bar staff working that night, these particular performances foregrounded and parodied masculinity's hysterical fear of 'feminization' vis-à-vis sexual desire between men. Finally, the penultimate group act poached by the drag kings was, of course, The Village People. Not to be outdone by the 'original' Village People and their parody of gay masculinity, the drag kings' Village People self-referentially parodied a mimicry in a performance that simultaneously signified masculinity, hyper-masculinity, and white notions of queer 'diversity.'

Furthermore, the drag kings' impersonation of masculinity and parody of sexual desire between men relies on but also shifts away from what Case identified as the butch-femme couple and toward what I have identified elsewhere as a continuum of female masculinity. Evoking those axiomatic epistemological tensions outlined by Eve Kosofsky Sedgwick in *Epistemology of the Closet*, that same-sex desire is 'understood' either as an expression of the essence of one gender (gender separatism), or as cross-gendering (gender transitivity), I suggest that what overdetermines the male impersonation at the heart of the drag kings' show is a shift from the separatist to the transitive trope, complete with its shifts in alliances and cross-identification.[26] To quote Sedgwick, 'under a gender-separatist [trope], lesbians have looked for identifications and alliances among women in general [while under] . . . a [trope] of gender [transitivity] . . . lesbians have analogously looked to identify with gay men, or, though this latter identification has not been strong since second-wave feminism, with straight men.'[27] Clearly, the drag kings' performance could be grouped under the latter, that of gender transitivity, and the proliferation of butch-femme subjectivities as anticipated by Case. (We will see later in the second and third waves that it is precisely this dynamic that these latter waves tease out; that is, there is a decided move away from lesbian affiliations toward ones with masculinity instead.) But fuelled by its referent 'butch-femme of the 1950s,' or Case's butch-femme couple, butch-femme of the 1990s, as I will argue a bit later, in many ways far surpasses its own history, demonstrated by the proliferation of female masculinity in all its complexities: ftm transsexuality, butch-bottoms, soft butches, butchy-femmes, stone-butch, fag-butch, etc. Subsequently, the masculinities performed on the stage signify in very contradictory but remarkably rich ways, simultaneously as 'butch,' and in excess of 'butch,' an approximation of heterosexual masculinity, and an outing, queering, and poaching of that masculinity as well.

Elspeth Probyn reminds us, in her essay 'Lesbians in Space,' to think about the question of human geography, or more precisely, the fact that bodies exist in relation to other bodies within socio-spatial sites as well.[28] And the space of the performance that night was a queer bar, not a theatre. If I were to limit my definition of 'stage' to what it was that we all supposedly looked at, then it would be difficult to go much further than discussing the kings on stage. But I want to suggest that we read the 'stage' as the front door of the bar instead. The drag kings' performances do not take place in isolation; the audience, especially but not exclusively its femme audience, is as much a part of the performance as those in the spotlight. In fact, I would suggest that audience, or femme desire, is the central condition of the performance.[29] The audience, or at least the many panties that land on the stage, are props in the performance as much as the performers are in the show staged by the audience. But this contingent authorizing and contingent community is not made up of Dolan's undifferentiated, unitary subject. Nor is it Mulvey's passive female subject, object of a masculine gaze. Rather, this was an audience made up of as many desiring and identifying boys and girls, actively reading against the grain of hegemonic gender and desire, desiring and authorizing not just the complex performances 'on stage,' but reading and read by the many other performances 'off-stage' as well. Thus, what is staged and negotiated then is not 'lesbian identity' as ontology, but the beginnings of a very queer and, eventually, post-queer desire as it's constructed through the multiple identificatory and dis-identificatory positions opened up through and across the performances in that bar as a queer space. Identifications within and across the show as performative event constitute its seductiveness, not ontologies.[30]

If Butler is correct, as Lynda Hart suggests, that the power of lesbian subjectivity may be not in appearance but in disappearance, in 'letting that which cannot fully appear ... persist in its disruptive promise,' then the drag king show that night was doubly potent.[31] The remarkable irony of the event was that, unlike the performances of Split Britches and WOW Café, this show did not have one single 'Lesbian' on stage, short of Anne Murray of course. Needless to say, there were lesbians performing both in, to, and around the bar. Indeed, 'lesbian' was the defining condition of the show. But I suggest that this was a very different performance of 'lesbians in space' from the realist, 'positive-images' school of lesbian representational politics. That apparitional creature, the Lesbian, lurked continually in de Lauretis's 'space-off' just outside of view, and no matter how hard one worked to catch a glimpse of her, she remained productively absent. The drag kings engage gender as 'an inevitable fabrication,' working gender against both identity and heteronormativity, staging, not 'representing,' lesbian desire.

I have been suggesting here that a reading of the Toronto drag king show through the enhanced lens offered by performance theorists Davy, Dolan, and Case as well as the complex and rigorous theories of performativity by Butler can serve to layer the drag kings' queer performances of masculinity. What seems to be at stake in both bodies of work is, as Butler notes, an 'increasing politicization of theatricality.'[32] What Davy, Dolan, and Case remind us is that such an increasing politicization has an important set of both performance and epistemological histories..

## Long Live the Queer Kings: The Fabulous Toronto Drag Kings

Where the 'Drag King Invasion I' suggested that heterosexual masculinity doesn't quite hold together, the Fabulous Toronto Drag Kings demonstrate that white masculinity doesn't always cohere either. The Fabulous kings, later known as The Toronto Drag Kings, held court in Toronto for the last half of the 1990s. Produced by Clare Smyth ('Flare'), also a drag king performer, both the Fabulous and Toronto Drag Kings became a standard feature in the Toronto queer, lesbian, and performance scenes for over seven years. This wave, made up of a fairly consistent group of performers – Flare, Zach, Stu, Deb Pearce ('Dirk Diggler' and 'Man Murray'), Jesse James Bondage, Christopher Noelle, Chris, Moner, and Mitch[33] – introduced Toronto to some of the most innovative and long-lasting king performances around. This was also the first group to represent Toronto in the International Drag King Extravaganza, in Columbus, Ohio, October 1999, and many of these same kings – Dirk, Christopher Noelle, and Flare – have developed a kind of notoriety which has bumped them to a national level. For instance, Flare and Christopher Noelle appeared on *Queer as Folk*; Jesse James Bondage, Flare, and Dirk all appeared on the *Maury Povich Show*; and Christopher Noel appeared in the Toronto Unity 2000 show with rock star Cyndi Lauper.

What this next wave of drag kings articulates in their performances is as vast and unique as the kings themselves. Themes include ironic spins on famous duets or groups; interesting or hyper-masculine characters from popular culture; famous musicians or artists; some, like the performances of Jesse James Bondage, perform songs which have had meaning at various points in time; especially popular are songs from a king's high school years. Other kings, like Mitch, imitate famous artists known for their genre-specific style or dance moves. As I discuss below in more detail, some kings emulated their favourite bands while others again, like Man Murray, impersonate famous Canadian icons rumoured to have queer histories (Anne Murray). While this group presented literally hundreds of performance scenarios, there are a few consistent tropes that I want to draw out here.

First, a stock favourite of a number of these kings is the places where masculinity, especially white masculinity, speaks volumes about itself in very ironic ways. That is, of course, through race and the operations of white supremacy. My understanding of whiteness is as a racialized identity that mis-recognizes itself as *the* human race, as universal mankind; then a consciousness of race and the processes of racialization start becoming standard features of the second wave of kings. Two of the white kings in this troupe target precisely that paradoxical hypervisibility and yet simultaneous invisibility: Zach does an impressive angry young white boy in his salute to Rage against the Machine. What makes this particularly effective is that Zach is wearing an 'Anti-racism Action' [ara] t-shirt that shows a young white boy jumping up and down on top of a swastika.

The effect is to mark whiteness from inside and articulate it against the invisibility of white supremacy. Moner too stages whiteness and stages it as a subjectivity simultaneously hypervisible and invisible. Moner performs a song called 'Pretty Fly (for a White Guy).' The lyrics of this song document the ways that white masculinity imagines itself in relation to men of colour who are read as 'hip' and 'cool.' 'Our subject,' so the lyrics tell us, 'is not cool but fakes it.' He dresses up, overcompensates as it were to fit the part, and to disguise the emptiness of whiteness: he 'listens to the right music,' Vanilla Ice, cruises in a cool car, a Pinto, and is 'trying too hard' to imitate masculinity. The song inverts a white racist gaze back at itself, and shows whiteness to be both vacuous and hyperbolic. Moner's version of this song forces attention onto the artificiality of the white subject in the song and both denaturalizes and makes ironic that artifice even further. As Moner said to me in conversation, 'it's important to work the white boy persona, that's what I am.' Whiteness is marked and articulated, that is, made to work by revealing itself. If you think about the verb 'to articulate,' it means to divide into words, to pronounce, or utter. But it also means to connect or mark with joints, that is, to be connected with sections. Thus, to articulate is both to express fluently and to manipulate a site where component parts join (as in a knee or hip), to bring segmented parts together to enable functionality. These kings disassemble white masculinity, break it down into its parts, and then reassemble those parts to make them work differently, to render them dysfunctional if you will. If white supremacy works best when it's hyper-visible and invisible, it cannot work in quite the same way when it is denaturalized, rearticulated, and most importantly decloaked.

In the same way that whiteness manifests itself and speaks through normative masculinity, gender is also spoken loudly through a queering of heteronormative male sexuality. A number of the kings stage the sexual failures at the heart of straight masculinity. For instance, during a skit where Kelly, Flare, and Zach dress, well, down to look like stereotypical ill-kempt, working-class men with huge beer bellies and perform 'I Am Too Sexy,' the men at one point drop their pants to show their butts to the audience. Two of the three are wearing men's underwear, which is what you might expect. But Flare's character is wearing

girl's panties and subsequently gets chased off the stage for it. Chris
and Stu do a similar routine, only their characters are hyper-masculine
soccer players, where one player (Stu) has a crush on the other (Chris),
who at first refuses him but then returns his advances and finally carries him off the stage. The song is 'The Cup of Life' by Mr Contradiction
himself, Ricky Martin. Ricky represents an entirely curious figure of
masculinity. He's racially marked but sings in English; he's hypersex-
ualized as a man of colour, but that over-sexualization is always
already overdetermined as simultaneously in excess of heteronormative masculinity. What's parodied in these numbers is the sometimes
very thin line between gay and heterosexual masculinity, where queer
and ironic reading practices articulate the contradictions that masculinity often disavows and yet is unable to contain. The first wave of
drag kings in Toronto similarly played with these tensions. Not to be
outdone by the 'original' Village People and their own parody of gay
masculinity, the Fabulous Toronto Drag Kings' Village People, as we
see in Figure 9, parodies a parody in a performance that simultaneously signifies masculinity, hyper-masculinity, failed heteronormative masculinity, and white notions of queer diversity all at the same
time. This wave of drag kings staged queer community when Flare,
dressed in a sailor suit, performed Kermit the Frog's 'Rainbow Song'
while the rest of the kings joined him on stage with rainbow flags in a
group finale.

Moreover, the drag kings' mimicry of masculinity and parody of
sexual desire between men relies on but also shifts away from what
we might identify as butch-femme sexual identities toward a continuum of female masculinity, and then off the map completely to what I
will call 'something a wee bit different.' What better ground to map
that difference onto but the female masculinity as open secret coded
onto Canadian songstress Anne Murray? Pearce's Man Murray has
been a stock and a clearly beloved feature of almost every drag king
wave to date. What makes Man so pleasurable is the way in which
Pearce's performance codes not just irony but layers of irony onto
each other. Layering refers to the way that drag kings will map a king
persona onto their own gender identities, allowing that identity to
show through cracks in the mapping.[34] What Pearce draws our attention to is Anne Murray's own layering of identity. Murray has long
been rumoured to have a lesbian past; this rumour is virtually unveri-
fiable. But what is far more interesting about this rumour is the degree
to which it is fed by a disavowed spectre of masculinity around

Figure 9: The Fabulous Drag Kings parodying the Village People. Courtesy of Bobby Noble.

Murray's gender identity, including her deep baritone voice. Despite the signifiers of femininity that accrue around Murray – make-up including requisite blue eye-shadow, earrings, long gowns, feminine pant suits, women's low-heeled shoes, and so forth – Murray's performance of white femininity always already seems to fail given it is layered onto a body which reads more masculine than feminine. That is, one could argue that Murray herself, as text, reads as a very toned-down male-to-female drag queen. It is precisely these already existing ironic layerings around Murray that Man Murray brings to the foreground.

As we see in Figure 11, a rainbow flag replaces an evening gown, but many of the other markers seem consistent with the codes around Anne Murray: the short masculine hairstyle, square jaw, broad face and smile, strong hand tightly gripping the microphone in a fist, pant suit with slip-on shoes, step-dancing where she moves awkwardly from side to side, etc. What make this performance so effective – that is, what make the irony so resonant – are the similar facial features that Anne Murray and Deb Pearce share.

Figure 10: Flare dressed in a sailor suit. Courtesy of Bobby Noble.

This is the face of white butch masculinity, accompanied by what for me, as a young teenage butch, was unequivocally the voice of female masculinity as well. How else might we characterize that deep baritone voice? Only for Anne Murray, femininity is layered – albeit unsuccessfully – onto female masculinity. But Man, of course, is not just layered, he's also queerly camped up. Man is packing a phallus not unlike the microphone Murray grips so tightly; Man draws out the awkwardness of body movements, dancing centred at the knees as they step from side to side, equally awkward facial expressions (the wink, complete with blue eye-shadow, and head nod, for instance), and continues to inhabit Murray's body through crowd favourite songs, such as 'Snow Bird.'

Clearly, such ironic and simultaneous reiterations of failed heteronormative femininity, disavowed female masculinity, and queered gay masculinity return us to Sedgwick's axiomatic epistemological contradictions and to a post-queer No Man's Land. I suggest that what

Figure 11: Man Murray. Courtesy of Bobby Noble.

overdetermines the male impersonation at the heart of the drag kings' show, such as Man Murray, is a shift from the separatist to transitive trope, complete with its shifts in alliances and cross-identifications.[35] In many ways, I think this latter turn, toward masculinity, has finally been taken.

Christopher Noelle, for instance, plays on the different expectations between looking like a girl and identifying as a boy in his number 'Sharp Dressed Man.' Noelle comes out in a tight black slinky dress with hair down and proceeds to transform himself into a John Travolta–looking man (from *Grease*) to the song in front of a mirror on stage. The transformation from femininity into masculinity in some ways defies the premise I began with, that is, that femininity is about hyperbole, masculinity about understatement. Noelle puts on the man using as many accessories and props as he takes off. And Chris too, formerly Ricky Martin in 'The Cup of Life,' returns to do 'La Vida Loca' as Ricky Martin, and referenced this turn when he told me,

'I am the straight man of the lesbians . . . it's hard for me to do the gay stuff on stage.' Moner and Jesse also do a song, 'Mr Roboto' by Styx, which re-articulates these identifications with straight men. The narrator of the song is a self-made man, who allegorizes the natural and ultimately defamiliarizes the liberal humanist 'man': 'I have a secret I have been hiding under my skin . . . I am not what you think / Forget what you know / I am the modern man who hides behind a man so no one else can see my true identity.' Clearly, the drag kings' performance could be grouped under the category of gender transitivity, and the proliferation of butch-femme subjectivities. But fuelled by its referent 'butch-femme of the 1950s,' female masculinity of the 1990s in many ways far surpasses its own history, demonstrated by the proliferation of female and male masculinity in all their complexities: transman, straight man, butch-boy, butch-bottoms, soft butches, stone-masculinity, gay masculinity, fag-butch, etc. The masculinities performed on the stage signify in very contradictory but remarkably rich ways, simultaneously as 'butch,' and in excess of 'butch,' an approximation of heterosexual masculinity, and queering of that masculinity, racialized masculinity, and the longer overdue racialization of whiteness.

Curiously, these re-articulations and performative deconstructions of masculinity are very telling of these affiliations with masculinity and dis-identifications with lesbian practices and identities. For instance, I asked nine of the kings one day if they identified or found themselves at all in the word 'lesbian.' All nine of them said no, including the one 'girl' who identifies as femme; they offered me a bevy of other words but not one of them said lesbian, suggesting that the history of lesbian politics has been both incredibly successful and a failure all at the same time. Barbara Johnson anticipated this kind of paradox when she wrote on the failure of success: 'If the political impulse of [lesbianism and/or queer theory and/or performativity] is to retain its vital, subversive edge, we must become ignorant of it again and again. It is only by forgetting what we know how to do, by setting aside the thoughts that have most changed us, that those thoughts and that knowledge can go on doing what a surprise encounter with otherness should do, that is, lay bare some hint of an ignorance one never knew one had.'[36] In other words, if we suggest that what's ironic about irony is not about controlled self-consciousness but the failure of self-consciousness instead, then these scenes of irony need to be read for what they reveal about ourselves and our identifications. To phrase this differently, what drag kings do is stage the things that whiteness and masculinity do not want to know and cannot know about themselves, to use irony to make these subjects strange and make their ambivalences work against what they think they do know. As a mode of critical politics, the scene of irony has to be inherently noisy and dialogic in the Bakhtinian sense, that is, engaged in many conversations all at the same time. As a discursive mode of the unsaid and the unseen, irony is the ideal form in which to stage ambivalences, ambiguities, and contradictions. Meaning is made and confused, reduced, and complex all at the same time. Drag king performances are inherently dialogic, in conversation with both conservative and oppositional politics of gender, with lesbian feminism, queer theory, homophobia, feminism, with race and racism, with transgendered politics etc., but also with the contradictions that fracture each. Irony troubles correspondence, it removes certainty that we mean what we say, or conversely, that reality is somehow reducible to some appearances. It also betrays the continuous and inevitable failure of the visual as an epistemological mode.

In addition to my arguments that drag kinging allows for the ironic re-articulations of whiteness and masculinity, especially of those things they cannot know about themselves, and that the culture of drag kings produces, indeed necessitates, new affiliations across gender and sexual identifications, my own interest as of late has been in those performances of more abject masculinities: the guys who perform, for lack of a better term, and I use this term affectionately, 'pond scum.'

I remember listening to a friend talk once about a king character she was creating and developing. In her non–drag king life, she's one of the best-looking, most charming gentleman butches around: 'He,' she said, referring to her drag persona, 'is nothing but pure pond scum . . . He's gross to women. He's entirely flirtatious in a way that is completely disgusting. He's constantly grabbing himself and making those offensive noises to women. He's a pig!' How might we begin to make sense out of these somewhat paradoxical articulations of a kind of masculinity that fifteen years ago we might have tried to intimidate into disappearing? What are the pleasures of watching, say, 'Jay,' who did a stunning non-musical performance where he impersonated an incredibly homophobic man who picks up what he thinks is a woman in a fag bar, has sex with her, then, upon discovering she is a drag queen, beats her up. Jay held his audience spellbound while he performed this scene. The larger question at stake in a performance like

Jay's is similar to one articulated by Stuart Hall, who rereads Bakhtin to ask the question: 'Why is it that the thing we deem socially peripheral has be[come] symbolically central?'[37] Why did Jay's character – a homophobic man – hold us spellbound that night in a dyke bar? Part of my answer lies in reformulating the question to ask what kind of cultural work the category of 'drag king' might do? My tentative answer is that when drag kinging emerged it worked toward articulating an unspoken tension inherent in identity politics that continually asks what we are.

Our political task must not be finding out what we are but instead understanding the relations between what we say we are and what we deny we are. I am not implying that female or trans masculinities are actually Mr Pond Scum at their core. But I do want to suggest that the power of the drag kings lies in their exposure of the impurity of categorization itself, especially those categories which have historically understood themselves to be bound, distinct, somehow discrete, and separate (for instance, our history of lesbian separatism, and for some of us, the history of white supremacy). These lines that are crossed are there to differentiate, say, lesbian from straight man, black from white, but that line already allows 'in' that which it is suppose to 'ward off.' It binds identities in the very same gesture through which it supposedly differentiates itself. By way of a conclusion then I suggest that the drag kings remind us, with Bakhtin, that 'when one finds a word, one finds it already inhabited . . . there is no access to one's own personal ultimate word . . . every thought, feeling, experience must be refracted through the medium of someone else's discourse, someone else's style, someone else's manner . . . almost no word is without its intense sideward glance at someone else's.'[38] If this is true of words, then, of course, it must be true of our identity categories at the same time.

## Kings to the Power of Three: Bois Will Be Boys

It is with this third, and likely, by now, even fourth or fifth, wave of kings that the proliferation of gendered subject positions moves beyond 'something a wee bit different' into something unrecognizable on our gender maps. Curiously, though, one of the stock features of continuing waves of kings is the presence of the boy. This boy – as either a lesbian boy, gay boy, or ftm boy – is an exceedingly popular trope performing either solo or with other boys (and hence the title of one of these new troupes, Bois Will Be Boys). Why is it that the boy bands – or, if not actual boy bands, then acts or performers that foreground *boyishness* – are such popular fodder for drag kings? Here in Toronto, as recently as 2003, several new boy acts appeared on the drag king scene including the utterly compelling trans-trio/ménage-à-trois New Cocks on the Block. But the boy has featured as a stock choice in drag king numbers – at least here in Toronto – for as long as drag kings have been performing. New Cocks on the Block is a case in point: its 2003 appearance at the bar Pope Joan signalled a new turn in the Toronto drag king scene where several incarnations of the boy converged. The event at a lesbian bar was a convergence of those who, across a spectrum of subjects, might identify with the term *boy*: butch boys, lesbian boys, trans-bois, the tranny-fag-boy, gay boys, and, judging by the demographics of the huge audience, the bio-boy (admittedly, in some instances, dragged out by their girlfriends for a night on the town, or so several of my straight female students later confessed).

If we agree that this boy is theatricalized, and by implication, denaturalized, soft, always already stylized, anti-heteronormative in his orientation to the imperatives of masculinity, then could we also agree, perhaps, that whether he appears on stage in a lesbian bar, or appears in a fag bathhouse, or in a (bio-)boy band, this subject is always already trans-gendered? That Brando and Dean types resisted such hyperboles of heteronormative masculinity is evident in the 'new' new boys of culture: Leonardo DiCaprio or the more numerous boy bands. These teen idols and objects of teenage girl fandom and consumption are sexualized through a feminizing gaze that is seductively threatened by the very thing boys supposedly lack: phallic power.

But one of the crucial triangulations that I am also seeing in this new wave is the way in which the figure of the boy/boi functions as a hybrid, anti-essentialist hinge point among three different kinds of resisting masculinities: lesbian boy; transsexual boy; drag king boys. This figure remakes manhood and gives us new vocabularies which are not just anti-essentializing but simultaneously a-essentialist; that is, they draw our attention to the ways that we remake gender every day as fiction through our reading practice and our desires. But even as we attempt to remake gender as a fiction, these fictions are still heavily and sometimes violently regulated with heteronormative cultures.

One of the results of that regulation is, of course, a particular relationship to cultural and political, and hence public, trauma. Ann Cvetkovich's book *An Archive of Feeling: Trauma, Sexuality and Lesbian*

*Public Cultures* argues a curious relation between trauma, sexuality, and public cultural production by suggesting that both power and trauma are productive rather than repressive. Unhappy with increasingly commodified self-help approaches to trauma, as well as with theories of trauma which overly individualize and decontextualize trauma from its socio-political frameworks, Cvetkovich provides a theoretical framework within which to theorize the role of trauma in the production of what she calls queer counter cultural publics. [39]

I do not want to get lost in theories of trauma at this juncture, nor am I suggesting at all that drag kings are working out private traumas on the stage. This has always been an accusation levelled against queers, trans-folks, gays, lesbians, bisexuals, etc., that is, that somehow these queer and resisting subjects exist as a traumatic response to and interruption of heterosexual identity. That is not at all what I am arguing here. Nor is it what Cvetkovich is suggesting either. But I do think it is necessary to draw our attention to a couple of axioms of queer theory and activism about trauma as they inform the performance cultures of female masculinity. First, of course, has to be that it still remains traumatizing, both individually and culturally, to live under any of these signs of difference. Whether it be 'queer' or 'lesbian' (two signs that I will not posit here as mutually exclusive) or 'gay,' and despite the many social and economic gains made, it is still a traumatizing everyday experience to be queer. Of course, the everyday experience that I detail here is always already mitigated by power vis-à-vis race, class, ability, ethnicity, nationality, and so forth. Moreover, both trauma and Lesbian, Gay, Bisexual, Transgender, Transsexual, Queer cultures have been marked by an unspeakability or unrepresentability in public cultures; both have had to aggressively insert themselves into the public domain, but each has also had to struggle to preserve histories and spaces.[40] Each has been marked by a permanent tension between 'official' and 'unofficial' narratives or knowledge; each has found/created language in a kind of ironic or unconscious re-articulation of public/heteronormative language. Finally, as Cvetkovich herself notes, the memories of each have been embedded not just in narratives but also in material artefacts, which can range from photographs to objects whose meanings might seem arbitrary but for the fact that they are invested with a particular kind of value.[41]

Quite apart from specificities of individual traumas (bashings, sexual abuse, loss, and so on), Cvetkovich posits what a number of other queer theorists including Sedgwick (shame) and Butler (melancholia and unmournable trauma) have stated, and that is that social and political traumas give rise to counter-cultural public spaces. But Cvetkovich takes this one step further, and it is this argument which interests me here in terms of drag king cultures: she particularizes these relationships to argue that if trauma presents an epistemological challenge, standing at the crossroads of the complex relation between knowing and not knowing, then it can be a particularly potent discourse with which to 'sort through the every day relation between categories rather than resolve them.'[42] Cvetkovich puts it this way: 'I am interested instead in the way trauma digs itself in at the level of the everyday, and in the incommensurability of large-scale events and the ongoing material details of experience . . . I hope to seize authority over trauma discourses from medical and scientific discourse in order to place it back in the hands of those who make culture, as well as to forge new models for how affective life can serve as the foundation for public but counter-cultural archive as well.'[43]

Among the things that continue to be brilliantly reiterated in the performance of the New Cocks on the Block/King Size Kings are the traumas of living in these incoherent bodies through which I centre a post-queer politic. I want to end this chapter on drag kings with their work because in the few performances I have seen, they struck a chord with me in the ways that they staged a kind of resistance to their trauma on the site of gendered bodies. As I noted much earlier in this essay, the return to previously viewed performance art is structured by what Peggy Phelan identifies as a kind of nostalgia, or 'the wound of wishing to return.'[44] These performances are ones I return to because, in many ways, they overlap many of my own experiences with an identity in transit. For me, as a trans-person, two sets of surgeries occurred during my time in Toronto: breast reduction and chest reconstruction. The butch body, and the ftm body, are each marked by different relationships to trauma: the first, at least in my experience, carried a profound ambivalence to breasts while the second alleviated the first, but was not itself without trauma. The first performance I saw by New Cocks on the Blocks staged these bodies in trauma and in, sometimes ambivalent, transit. Two of the then-original three performers of New Cocks came on stage with their chests wrapped in what was supposed to be the surgical tape used after breast reconstruction. Under that see-through material, drawn in red on their breasts, were bright red lines, again mirroring the incisions made to reduce breast size. At this point, not that long after my own surgery, I am not even sure I noted the song they performed, but I certainly made note of the trajectory of the performance. Where in the beginning of the performance they treated their chests as sites of wounding, by the time the number came to a close they had, in essence, dramatically removed the see-through bandage and the red incisions, and celebrated their breasts. The message of the number was a clear refusal of the traumatizing interventions of breast reduction and removal. These are three very queer, young, non-operative, transgendered youth with very unconventional bodies who, as part of a new trans-wave, clearly seize authority over traumatized incoherent bodies from medical and scientific discourse in order to place those bodies back in the hands of those who make culture with them instead. They are not only bodies of incoherence but they are also, quite literally, bodies on the line, embodying new possibilities for resistance.

# 9 Eyes of Excess: The Darkness and the Fire at the Centre of Growing Up Male in Toronto in the 1950s and 1960s

ALLAN IRVING

I'll take whatever breaks down beneath its own sad weight

*Charles Wright*

Scattered ruins same grey as the sand ash grey true refuge

*Samuel Beckett*

For the raw truth of an episode never ends

*Michael Ondaatje*

The first girl for whom I remember feeling a strong sexual desire was in my Grade 8 class at Whitney Public School; she had also been in my classes in earlier grades but now I couldn't keep my eyes off her. I thought about her constantly and a few years ago wrote a poem about how she affected me those many years ago:

**MAY 1958**
May 1958, grade 8, Whitney public school.
In the interests of intellectual enrichment
Our class taken for a day train trip
To see the St. Lawrence seaway project
I noticed little of the great project however
Sitting across from me wearing the cutest poodle skirt
Was Ann G.
She knew I could see and was excited by her
pink panties; my erection lasted for days.
Next month at the graduation celebrations

She asked me to dance and I wafted home
On that warm and fragrant June night and never saw her
Again.

Mesmerized by this cute, sweet girl sitting across from me on the train I was every inch the coming-of-age heterosexual male obsessed with an attractive girl.

Soon, fresher desires were tripping through, haunting me. Almost from the time I began cross-dressing at age ten what distressed me was that my eyelids were blotched and red, what eye doctors call blepharitis, which for me seemed to be an outward and visible sign for all to see that I secretly desired to wear women's clothes. Is it significant, I wonder, that the first female clothing I wore while masturbating was an abandoned red skirt of my mother's? I found it in a box of clothes in our basement at 250 Glenrose Avenue in Toronto and its allure took hold of me and pulled me into a shadowy underworld space of darkness and sexual excitement. Since those early attempts to be female, Nietzsche's phrase, 'the secret work of the instinct of decadence,' has often fluttered at the abyssal edges.[1] For me, crossdressing and my blemished and unsightly eyelids (I wear dark glasses now to hide them) have always represented the world's dark grace. Even now my eyelids fill me with shame and disgust. So often I want to suppose, as does one of Beckett's characters, 'as if to grow less could help, ever less and less and never quite be gone.'[2] Just disappear. For years I have lived with a horror that each day builds incrementally on others, heading toward ruin and a moment that will arrive lamenting the impossibility of 'ceasing before having been.'[3] Like most romantics (I have been listening to Sibelius's Symphony no. 6 in D minor the last few days) I will admit to finding some kind of unruly contentment in sorrow and darkness, in perpetual rain, in ashes and dust, in months like November.

Threading its way through my life is this question of vision, of looking and being looked at, symptoms of the tortured and weeping eye. In Georges Bataille's so-called pornographic novel *Story of the Eye* (1927) eyes are overvalued and denigrated. Eyes are afflicted and sexualized, the organ of excess and transgression; eyes weep over bitter memories, and are damaged by what they see. My eyes have always felt to me to be scarred and gutted with wounds. Bataille's novel brings us sharply to the realization that since the eighteenth-century enlightenment, eyes of excess resist modernist attempts to have a single, universal vision of the truth. To connect the damaged and repulsive eye to blood, tears, sex, and death, as Bataille does, is to say that vision is never totalizing, pure, singular, or comprehensive, that the eye is not capable of, as Nietzsche mockingly put it, 'immaculate perception.' As Nietzsche has Zarathustra ask, 'Is not seeing itself – seeing abysses?'[4] Bataille's cobra strikes in *Story of the Eye* annihilate all systems of meaning to fragment our subjectivity until we are broken into flecks of light that disfigure and blind the I who sees.

Today it's Schubert's String Quartet no. 14 in D minor, *Death and the Maiden*.

In the two years (1968–70) following my first marriage I went on a reading binge, perhaps as a way of avoiding the intimacy I still seem so incapable of. We lived in a one-bedroom apartment at 111 Oriole Parkway in Toronto and at the time I was working for the Ontario Ministry of Correctional Services as a parole and rehabilitation officer in downtown Toronto. On Sunday mornings my wife played the organ at a Baptist church in Thornhill, north of the city, and I used my time alone to indulge my cross-dressing fantasies and desires, trying on her skirts and dresses.

But read I did, and the way time always seemed suspended in Kafka's writing greatly appealed to me. Being pulled into Kafka's dark vision was exhilarating and, like most readers I suspect, for me *The Castle* became a theatre of longing, a place of profound sorrow and grief. In Kafka's novel Amalia discovers the horror of the 'truth' submerged deep in the castle. As her sister Olga remarks, 'she stood face to face with the truth and went on living and endured her life then and now.' This sentence had a profound effect on me, and from 1969 to the present I have striven, not always successfully, to accept the fact that so often in life one can do little but simply endure. Another affecting exchange in the novel occurs when Hans says to K: 'The day after tomorrow then.'[5] That day, as Heinz Politzer observes, is the seventh day K will have spent in the village, and the day the novel breaks off. 'Another name for this day is "never."'[6]

It is perhaps worth pausing to comment on what my intention is in writing this account of my early life. But first what it is not: it is not in any way an attempt to provide an explanation for my cross-dressing by relating it in a cause-and-effect way to depressions I have suffered; nor in reverse does it try to say my depression episodes are caused by my cross-dressing. It is simply to put together, and not in any linear way, the various moods, desires, life experiences, authors, who have arced through my mind and more particularly my body and created a life, a person. I view neither cross-dressing nor depression in any sense as pathological! There are some words that appear which carry an enormous freight for me: absence, desire, oblivion, pain, endure, darkness, eyes, fire, blood. It is minimally a story about the beating of my heart toward the end, toward darkness.

One of my earliest memories of life in Toronto is of my mother taking me to Moore Park at the corner of Moore and Welland Avenues, a few blocks from our house. The park had a wading pool, tennis courts, lawn-bowling pitches, a baseball diamond, and in the winter, a natural ice-skating rink, where I learned to skate and play hockey. I still vividly remember, age three, a November afternoon in the park with my mother, quiet and still, almost magical, the lovely oak trees now bare and acorns scattered on the ground. When I was older, I would go to Moore Park not just for sports activities, but to surreptitiously watch the teenage girls and women in their cute pleated tennis skirts and frilly panties. At the time I would have given anything to dress in their sexy outfits, and girly thoughts would frolic in my mind for days. How could I possibly be expected to concentrate on my high school homework?

By the time I entered Oakwood Collegiate in the fall of 1958 something else had my cross-dressing adrenalin working overtime. Walking by the school auditorium at lunchtime in early September, my eyes, getting ever redder, fixed on the stage where the school's cheerleaders, in the Oakwood colours of blue and gold, were practising their routines, handstands, and cartwheels in their very short, sexy pleated miniskirts and yellow panties. Getting through the afternoon classes became torture and I would rush home to put on a little flouncy skirt of my sister's and pretend with intense pleasure that I was a cute, appealing Oakwood cheerleader. I wanted so much to be attractive and wildly desired. I still do. A recent survey I came across on the internet about why men cross-dress applies completely to me: a liking for the feel of female clothing, it's sexually thrilling and exciting, it helps me to relax and deal with stress, a desire to be like a flirty sexy girl.[7] For Bataille it is only that which is shaped by the immediacy of erotic desire and experience that is meaningful. I have come to see my cross-dressing in this way. He viewed the work of de Sade, for example, as a 'heroics of perversion,' repudiating homogeneity and the binary antagonisms of good and evil as his own thought embraced a radical heterogeneity.[8]

Gender, as Judith Butler so brilliantly addresses in *Gender Trouble*, is not something that is fixed, essential like a 'fact,' but rather a social construction, a performance, or a repeated performance. We can recreate our 'gender' for moments, or for longer periods, or even permanently. In order to indulge and understand my cross-dressing I have had to reject myself as a stable subject, and acknowledge that I have never existed completely within a heterosexual 'male' matrix.

Michel Foucault writes that 'the freeing of differences requires thought without contradiction, without dialectics, without negation; thought that accepts divergence; affirmative thought whose instrument is disjunction; thought of the multiple – of the nomadic and dispersed multiplicity.'[9] Following Bataille, Foucault maintains that the eye of western philosophy which leads us to the truth 'out there' and locates us as sovereign subjects can internally be seen now as eyes of excess: 'sight, crossing the globular limit of the eye, constitutes the eye in its instantaneous being; sight carries it away in this luminous stream (an outpouring fountain, streaming tears and, shortly, blood), hurls the eye outside of itself, conducts it to the limit where it bursts out in the immediately extinguished flash of its being. Only a small white ball, veined with blood, is left behind, only an exorbitated eye to which all sight is now denied.'[10]

The gender confusion of my high school years was that exactly. While wanting much of the time to be a pretty and sexy teen-age girl, I also wanted very much to be brought back into a virile, dominant male social order. There was, therefore, a persistent anguish and an obsession with undoing both impulses that consumed vast amounts of emotional, sexual, and intellectual energy. At any given moment I could be male, female, neither, or both. Endless, excruciating parody? Perhaps. But there was no original or prior moment of plenitude for me to deform. This identity nexus marked the beginning of my realization that there is no simple ontology, only indescribable, shifting heterogeneity, a withdrawal from all predetermined identities. My high school years evaded identity, becoming a series of dark movements and flows of intensity perhaps similar to what Gilles Deleuze in *Francis Bacon: The Logic of Sensation* writes about the ways Bacon paints.[11]

One of the ways I tried to demonstrate my maleness in high school (1958–63) was to play on the football team, which I did against my parents' wishes for two years. During these years I regularly watched televised sports and my two heroes were the oak-ribbed running back for the Green Bay Packers, Jim Taylor, and the 'Golden Jet,' Bobby

Hull of hockey's Chicago Black Hawks. I'll never forget seeing Hull at Maple Leaf Gardens in the late 1950s unleash one of his blistering slap shots just after he crossed centre ice, a shot so powerful that it seemed to be in the net almost at the same instant he took it. It was a thrilling moment. Unlike the more elegant football player Jim Brown of the Cleveland Browns, Taylor revelled in running right at defending players rather than going around them. I remember once in an interview he said he wanted 'to sting' opposing players. This I found very appealing. Once when I was playing road hockey on Glenrose Avenue, a passing neighbour commented as I unleashed a slap shot, 'You look just like Bobby Hull.' For a second I thought I was, and I often wished I could be as manly and as hard-hitting as both Jim Taylor and Bobby Hull.

My mother was a social worker and my father a professor of philosophy. They met in 1938 when she was a student in one of his classes at the University of British Columbia. I was born the night of 13 March 1945 in Vancouver, an excruciatingly painful labour described in searing detail in my mother's journal. The day had been, by my father's account, 'dreary, drizzly, rainy and without sunshine,' and when the hospital phoned at 11 p.m. to tell him of my birth he went upstairs in our house at 1650 Wesbrook Crescent and looked out over the Gulf of Georgia. He wrote in his journal, 'the wind was blowing a terrific gale: there was a snowstorm and one could hear the wild waves roaring in the blue Gulf, beating at the cliffs of the Point Grey Promontory. Such was the night that Allan was born – wild and stormy like the world at war – and like the ordeal of human birth.' And like my life was to become. A number of studies have documented that from a seasonal perspective, March is the peak month for the onset of episodes of depression,[12] and given how much depression I have struggled with throughout my life perhaps it was an unfortunate month for me to be born. That same month, my father resigned from the University of British Columbia and accepted a position as professor of ethics at Victoria College at the University of Toronto.

'We live with those retrievals from childhood that coalesce and echo throughout our lives,' Anna says in Michael Ondaatje's 2008 novel *Divisadero*, 'the way shattered pieces of glass in a kaleidoscope reappear in new forms and are songlike in their refrains and rhymes, making up a single monologue.'[13] Our memories can become invention as we create self-consoling stories to be with us in our ochre dusks. But is it possible to find a form for sadness? I would say, yes.

Robert Lowell's confessional poem of negative transcendence, 'Skunk
Hour,' with its 'moonstruck eyes' red fire' full of longing, desire,
everything sick and stained with the 'red fox stain' of breakdown and
disintegration, is the darkest poem I know. The very spirit weeps:

> I hear
> My ill-spirit sob in each blood cell,
> As if my hand were at its throat . . .
> I myself am hell;
> Nobody's here[14]

Every time I read 'Skunk Hour' the poem drives to the heart of the
loneliness, loss, and abandonment that I have hidden in my body,
racking it with deep slicing pain like a knife cutting through me. I
have come to realize that the reason Lowell's poem rips into me the
way it does goes as far back as to when I was seven and a half months
old. At the end of October 1945, my mother and I left 1650 Wesbrook
Crescent, a house she loved on the campus of the University of British
Columbia, to begin the five-day train trip to Toronto. It was a trip and
a new life in the east she was dreading. I can only imagine through
the sadness and my tears, sixty-two years later now falling on the key-
board, my mother's own 'ill-spirit sobbed' that day. In her journal she
describes how she carried me from room to room saying goodbye to
the house. 'I was deeply sad to leave,' she writes, 'and all the beauties
and meaning of the places were sharp and called to me. The day we
left Vancouver a deluge came down and I left without seeing the
mountains.' In 1994 a brief poem I wrote about that day long ago was
published in *Queen's Quarterly*:

### 1650 Wesbrook Crescent
Awakened from the long repressed watery November light
By the thumping of an early morning foghorn
Bleating out its mournful two-toned warning
Brings back a primeval memory of that long ago
last wringing departure
Now raked into a bracketed postmodern sky.[15]

When she stepped off the train at Union Station in November 1945 my
mother's apprehensions about Toronto flooded over her, and years
later, she told me all she wanted to do at that moment was get on the

next train back to Vancouver. Driving through the city to the house at 250 Glenrose Avenue in the upper-middle-class Moore Park neighbourhood, she silently grieved the profound homesickness she already felt for Vancouver and the west coast. She took an instant dislike to the house, writing that 'my 1650 furniture looked out of place here. There it all made flowing graceful lines – here it sat bunched up in the conventional little front room.' The kitchen particularly distressed her: 'it is small, dark and inconvenient . . . the electric light has to burn all the time in it, and in Toronto the lights flicker all the time as though troops of moths were flying around them.' As I read though her journal sixty years after the fact, the unhappiness, mourning, and melancholy my mother was shrouded in our first months and years in Toronto are palpable. Her bouts of depression incapacitated her for months at a time. A journal note for 25 May 1947 attempts to explain the long lapse in entries: 'I had an illness which de-spirited me.'

That first day in the fall my mother and I joined him in Toronto my father seemed to my mother to be preoccupied. He had told her that he was having creeping doubts about whether it had been a terrible mistake to leave Vancouver. He was already feeling that his ability to be a challenging and provocative teacher and to develop his own scholarly interests would be much more constrained at the University of Toronto. He also did not particularly like the Glenrose house. 'He feels rather cramped in his physical life in this brick house we got in place of wild and free 1650,' my mother wrote. 'In Toronto he has to walk home down the street of close-packed houses; in Vancouver he seemed to roam in from anywhere.' In the fall of 1945 after coming home from the university my father would often cry at night. He took up smoking. Depression and a despairing mood settled on the house like a cold winter mist and on New Year's Day 1946 my mother admitted in her journal:

Since we have arrived here life seems to have been centred by Jack's [my father] heart-searing debate with himself. He regrets deeply having left UBC, he cannot forget it and what the life there meant to him, he cannot become imbued with the life here. He tried to get back and both wrote to and saw President Mackenzie about it. But they were unable to take him back. There is a job in philosophy going at Winnipeg and J. wonders about that. He finds Toronto [the university] tradition-ridden and unmalleable and the pull of the great name curiously ceases when one is in its very shadow. J. has never before felt himself in serious error regarding a major decision – now he does. His life must somehow return to that sense of eagerness which he used to know so fully. This period has not been happy.

When I first read what Friedrich Nietzsche writes affectingly in *Human, All Too Human,* specifically that the 'undissolved dissonances in the relation of the character and sentiments of the parents survive in the nature of the child and make up the history of its inner sufferings,'[16] I knew that the dark flow tides of despair I have felt so consistently for more than sixty years began before I was a year old. Lord Byron's lines from his poem 'The Lament of Tasso' aptly describe my ever-dissolving emotional state then and now:

> The mind's canker in its savage mood,
> When the impatient thirst of light and air
> Parches the heart; and the abhorred grate,
> Marring the sunbeams with its hideous shade,
> Works through the throbbing eyeball to the brain,
> With a hot sense of heaviness and pain.[17]

Human moods are compelling, contagious, and intensely interpersonal and it is well known that moods not only alter the outlooks of those who have them, but also profoundly affect those close to them. In our first few years in Toronto these dark moods hunted my parents down and dogged their spirits. The emotions, events, intensities, and moods that took up residence at 250 Glenrose Avenue when we moved to Toronto served as the source of my future depression and amounted to a troubled inheritance.

At around age two I became intrigued by the furnace and its interior fire, often requesting to be taken to the basement to marvel at this wonder. I would wait then for the thermostat to be turned up and cry out, 'Furnace roar, hot bubble!' My parents were good friends with Helen and Northrop Frye. Northrop Frye (1912–91) taught in the English Department at Victoria College, University of Toronto, for over fifty years and is one of the twentieth century's most important literary theorists. Frye noticed my curiosity, having something of an interest in furnaces himself (in a different sense) with his just-completed book on William Blake, *Fearful Symmetry.* On 21 May 1950, Frye writes in his diary, 'the Irvings came over for tea with their two kids. Allan is a very nice little boy but just beginning to get into the bratty stage. Allan is still interested in furnaces, so we went down and I showed him how the blower works.'[18] In *Words with Power* Frye informs us that blacksmiths often appear in literature as creative symbols, 'like the forger of the new Jerusalem in Isaiah 54:16. This smith, who creates a new city glowing with gems and gold, represents perhaps the closest Biblical parallel to the symbolism of alchemy, and is the Biblical basis for Blake's conception of his culture-hero, the blacksmith Los working with his furnaces.'

Furnace imagery can revolve, Frye tells us, around notions of a hell possessing heat and fire but not light, or more positively in a purgatorial sense, 'a crucible from which the redeemed emerge purified like metal in a smelting operation.' One of Blake's central themes is captured in the metaphorical figure of Albion standing in for a fallen humanity; Los, with his furnaces and fire, 'whose pounding hammer is also the beating of the human heart,' through the arts and creativity and the imagination redeems a fallen, broken world.[19] Speaking personally I believe it is possible, from my reading of Frye over the years, to experience momentary redemption through an attentive and wakened heart, a heart that contains both love and grief as it beats toward the end and darkness.

Memory, through interpretation, is endlessly rearranging the same bright fragments and shards. My own experience of fallenness and redemption in a metaphorical sense is evident in my early childhood memories of the long summer train trips back to the west coast with my mother (and later, my sister) to stay with her parents in Brentwood Bay. They had retired to a lovely cottage just outside Victoria with a wild tangled garden. My father never came along and summer would pass each year without his presence. These were idyllic summers, although I sense my mother was often quite depressed, even more so when at the end of August we would return to Toronto, back to her winters of private sorrow. So despite our moments of happiness in my grandparents' garden daydreaming, lurking just outside the garden fence there were always disquieting thoughts, shadows, decay, and exhaustion.

Another poem of mine in *Queen's Quarterly* tries to capture these early summer experiences:

**Island Spirit**
Early summer ashes in tidal pools
Her spirit creased the Island;
Rising up and shaking the foundations
Up out of the parched and layered earth

A voice spoke and the trees revealed the truth
As time spun backwards.

Across the luminous, salty bay
Blasting afternoon cement works
Draw tranquil earwigs to pumpside
Through spilling sun in a garden of peace
Sapling red trucks ferry their freight
Oblivious to the encircling metal progress.

Riptides in divided autumn,
Caged rabbits hidden in the blackberries
Cool and stretched garter snakes
Sliding through ancient grass
Under the bent wire fence
Out into a downward running world.[20]

From age five my summers on the west coast to this day appear in my mind as bright memories of rowing with my grandfather on Brentwood Bay. He was the essence of maleness for me: a tall, slim, taciturn Scot who smoked a pipe, drank whiskey in his workshop, and had massive sinewy forearms from physical labour and rowing. He owned a beautiful lapstrake rowboat that he had built himself, along with varnished wooden oars. Every afternoon we would walk together down Peden Lane to the bay where the boat was moored. Setting out, he would row first then let me have the oars until I was tired, my forearms screaming from pulling as hard as I could, wanting to impress this man that I was a male in the ancient and noble art of rowing. Years later when I exercise on rowing machines, if I close my eyes, I am back on Brentwood Bay learning to be a man. For me, rowing is a space where the body and mind meet.

It is the now the end of August 2007 and as summer starts to slip into fall I find the late August light consoling. Today I am listening to Brahms's Symphony no. 4 in E minor and reading Henri Cole poems. Lines from his poem 'Jealousy' circle around me:

I, with numb lips and a tight throat,
believing hope,
is a shallow man's illusion . . .
The imagination, like a milk bucket,

is filled with dung . . . .
Self-esteem, like herringbone pavement,
is breaking up in cartfuls.
Where is the comfort of pears on a window ledge?[21]

In the mid-1960s George Whalley's biography, *The Legend of John Hornby*, had an enormous impact on me and it is a book I often return to. Since reading Whalley's account of the wilderness explorer, Hornby has been another male I wanted to emulate. I still do. Hornby was a mild-mannered Englishman who came to Canada in 1909, and fell in love with the Canadian north and barren lands. He flouted all the rules for survival in the north, quickly becoming a legend, until in the winter of 1928 he starved to death on the Thelon River in the Northwest Territories.

Whalley writes that Hornby's life 'suggested not so much the working of accident or fate, as the process of necessity – as though a man may from the start lay down his life for what he is. His name was woven into some parts of the country as the maps showed, and some said his life was too; but he still exercised his own restraint, eluded inquiry, disclosed only a little of himself, withdrawing finally with a gesture of silence.'

From 1909 to 1928 Hornby lived mostly alone as his mind and body drifted through the isolated north. 'The Barren Ground became for him a Garden of Desire, a Country of the Mind rich with "transparent fruit" and "stones on fire." Later these must have seemed figments of a dream. Enduring by himself, sharing nothing fully with anyone, he had a habit of covering his tracks behind him.' Hornby courted discomfort and disaster, as Whalley writes, and 'hardships and starvation seemed to take on a positive value for him, as though they were the only substantial values left.' Hornby had no fear of death, and for many years 'he survived feats of endurance, and endured miracles of survival.' Hornby's mantra was 'what does it matter?' Either you 'got through or you didn't.' He had a remarkable capacity to ignore pain, hunger, and exhaustion and 'what some men will suffer to make a living or a fortune or a reputation, or to extend the limits of knowledge or to alleviate the human condition. Hornby endured continuously, alone, without encouragement, for no reason that anybody could see, for no reason that he himself could give.'[22] When I imagine Hornby's inner life during those long solitary winters he spent in the desolate north, my life seems neither light nor dark, nor joy, but is, just is. The oblivion of the everyday, only a dark moon edged with fire and blood.

The north, for me, also has always had a strong pull, as it did for Glenn Gould in his celebrated 1967 Canadian Broadcast Corporation broadcast, the musically polyphonic *The Idea of North*. In the summer of 1965, a few months after my father died and after I had finished a disastrous second undergraduate year at Glendon College of York University, I got a summer job with the British Columbia Forest Service. After my father's death I decided I wanted to flee to some remote place, and the west coast seemed as good as any. I wrote to all the provincial government departments in British Columbia and the Forest Service offered me a job related to the development of a massive hydro-electric project as a surveyor in the Peace River country north of Prince George. On 10 May 1965, I took the train west trying to fight my anxiety by imagining that whatever the summer brought would be an adventure. There were many other students travelling west for summer jobs and much of the time on the train was spent doing what students do: drinking beer. One night a lovely young woman I was sitting beside in the bar car began surreptitiously fondling me. We parted a few days later in Vancouver and I never saw or heard from her again. But that experience seemed to foretell a summer spent very much in a manly phase.

The Forest Service had assumed I was an engineering student, and when they found out I was a philosophy major, while disappointed, they decided to go ahead with my summer employment anyway. Before being sent north I was given a crash course on basic surveying, using the grounds around the parliament buildings in Victoria. When I arrived at the Forest Service's summer camp a hundred miles north of Prince George, I was rigorously tested by the thirty or so University of British Columbia engineering students who were working there as well. I already had two huge strikes against me: I was from the east, and I was an arts student. It was hard to tell which was worse in their minds, but those first two weeks were very rough. In the end two things 'saved' me: I could drink beer as well as most of them, and I was a pretty good baseball player. We played baseball two or three evenings a week against workers from the many logging camps in the area. My fleetness as a centre fielder tracking down long fly balls, and the endless beers I drank with them after the games, seemed to impress the engineers, and I was gradually embraced as one of them. I felt very much a male that summer, and toward the end of August when the time was fast approaching for me to return to Toronto I tried to work out a way I might stay on in the north over the winter. Finally I did return to school, several weeks after the term had started.

Recently I wrote a short poem, 'Desolate Garden,' inspired by Hornby:

I took the Ontario Northland to Cochrane
Then went north to where no rivers meet
There with stones on fire
I let my broken heart become the earth.

Over the last few months I have renewed my obsessive desire to wear 'sissy' clothes and have found there are many websites, catering to the cross-dressing, transgender community, that sell frilly, frothy, lacy skirts, dresses, and panties. Wearing these clothes is sexually exciting in ways I had never experienced. To feel so girly is a thrilling experience. The orgasms I have in these clothes are intense, and afterwards I will lie for up to an hour in my lacy attire delighting in these new sensations. From an intellectual perspective that appeals to me greatly my cross-dressing practices rupture all meanings trapped in binary logic, show the limits of Hegelian dialectic, and negate homogeneity. They have become moments in time that cannot always be reduced to language, that, best of all, deny and transgress the ordering, controlling functions of language and conceptual thinking. It is as though I am endlessly annihilating myself through my discontinuity, in liminal moments of ecstatic non-being. Wearing frilly clothing creates a rush, a 'cocaine high' like no other.

It is now February 2008 and for the past two months I have been listening to the intense, relentless music of Edgard Varese, in no particular key, filled with unpitched percussion, dissonant shrieking trumpets, and driving rhythms. I have been reflecting on the idea that, from the beginning, I have always been on the other side of the looking glass, but never crossed over. During the first year of my life I experienced something that has haunted me ever since. Perhaps it was an overwhelming absence? Seldom does a day pass when I have not struggled against a crushing sense of absence. Some days I feel as though I am made of only dust and rain homeless like a stray dog barking. Beckett greatly admired the seventeenth-century Flemish philosopher Arnold Geulincx, particularly his notions of ethical obligation. Geulincx's second ethical obligation is simply 'not to go – not to leave one's station until bidden.' His seventh: 'to accept being here.' It is a necessary quality, as Beckett keenly observed, to endure it all until the end, a kind of patient *outlasting* until we are finally excused by death from the ongoing.[23]

# Notes

**Introduction**

1 Gail Bederman, *Manliness and Civilization: A Cultural History of Gender and Race in the United States, 1880–1917* (Chicago: University of Chicago Press, 1995); R.W. Connell, *Masculinities* (Berkeley: University of California Press, 1995); Michael Kimmel with Amy Aronson, *The Gendered Society Reader* (Oxford: Oxford University Press, 2004).

2 Nicolas Bourriaud, *Altermodern, Tate Triennial* (London: Tate Publishing, 2009), 2.

3 Bourriaud, *Altermodern*.

4 Bourriaud, *Altermodern*.

5 Bourriaud, *Altermodern*; Gamal Abdel-Shehid, *Who Da Man? Black Masculinities and Sporting Cultures* (Toronto: Canadian Scholars Press, 2005).

6 David Harvey, *Spaces of Hope* (Berkeley: University of California Press, 2000); Michael Warner, *Publics and Counterpublics* (Brooklyn: Zone Books, 2009).

7 Bourriaud, *Altermodern*, 3.

8 Connell, *Masculinities*.

9 Bourriaud, *Altermodern*.

10 Bourriaud *Altermodern*, 4.

11 Bourriaud, *Altermodern*, 3.

12 William Schroeder, *Continental Philosophy: A Critical Approach* (Oxford: Blackwell, 2005).

13 Julia Kristeva, *Powers of Horror: An Essay on Abjection*, trans. Leon Roudiez (New York: Columbia University Press, 1982).

14 Kristeva, *Powers of Horror*.

15  Michel Foucault, *Power/Knowledge: Selected Interviews and Other Writings, 1972–1977*, ed. Colin Gordon, trans. Colin Gordon (New York: Pantheon, 1980); Abdel-Shehid, *Who Da Man?*

16  Kimmel, *Gendered Society.*

17  Connell, *Masculinities.*

18  Kimmel, *Gendered Society.*

19  Abdel-Shehid, *Who Da Man?*

20  Connell, *Masculinities.*

21  Connell, *Masculinities.*

22  Máirtín Mac an Ghaill and Chris Haywood, *Gender, Culture and Society: Contemporary Feminities and Masculinities* (New York: Palgrave, 2007).

23  Ken Moffatt, *A Poetics of Social Work: Personal Agency and Social Transformation in Canada, 1920–1939* (Toronto: University of Toronto Press, 2001).

24  Foucault, *Power/Knowledge*, 11.

25  Ken Moffatt, 'Beyond Male Denial and Female Shame: Learning about Gender in a Sociocultural Concepts Class,' *Smith College Studies in Social Work: Special Issue on Teaching* 74, no. 2 (2004): 243–56.

26  Judith Butler, *Gender Trouble, Feminism and the Subversion of Identity* (York: Routledge, 1990); Eve Sedgwick, *Touching Feeling: Affect, Pedagogy, Peformativity* (Durham, NC: Duke University Press, 2003).

27  Jeffrey Allan Tucker, *A Sense of Wonder: Samuel R. Delany, Race, Identity and Difference* (Middletown, CT: Wesleyan University Press, 2004).

28  Bederman, *Manliness.*

29  Connell, *Masculinities*; Moffatt, *Poetics.*

30  Christopher Dummitt, *Manly Modern: Masculinity in Postwar Canada* (Vancouver: University of British Columbia Press, 2007); Moffatt, *Poetics.*

31  Connell, *Masculinities*; Moffatt, *Poetics.*

32  Dummitt, *Manly.*

33  Mac an Ghaill and Haywood, *Gender, Culture.*

34  Maurice Hamington and William Cowling, 'The Phenomenological Challenge: The One and the Many,' in *Revealing Male Bodies*, ed. Nancy Tuana, William Cowling, Maurice Hamington, Greg Johnson, and Terrance MacMullan (Bloomington: Indiana University Press, 2002), 287.

35  Hamington and Cowling, 'The Phenomenological,' 287.

36  Michael Kimmel, 'Global Masculinities: Restoration and Resistance,' in *A Man's World? Changing Men's Practices in a Globalized World*, ed. Bob Pease and Keith Pringle (London: Zed, 2001), 21–37.

37  Judith Butler, *Gender Trouble* (New York: Routledge, 1990), 151.

38  Mac an Ghaill and Haywood, *Gender, Culture.*

39  Diana Fuss, *Essentially Speaking* (New York: Routledge, 1989), xi.

40  Michel Foucault, *The Order of Things: An Archaeology of Human Sciences* (New York: Vintage, 1973); Moffatt, *Poetics.*

41  Butller, *Gender.*

42  Mac an Ghaill and Haywood, *Gender, Culture.*

43  Foucault, *Power/Knowledge.*

44  Foucault, *Power/Knowledge,* 117.

45  Connell, *Masculinities*; Bob Pease and Keith Pringle, 'Introduction: Studying Men's Practices and Gender Relations in a Global Context,' in *A Man's World: Changing Men's Practices in a Globalized World,* ed. Bob Pease and Keith Pringle (London: Zed, 2001), 1–18; Mac an Ghaill and Haywood, *Gender, Culture.*

46  Mac an Ghaill and Haywood, *Gender, Culture.*

47  Mac an Ghaill and Haywood, *Gender, Culture.*

48  Connell, *Masculinities.*

49  Connell, *Masculinities*; Mac an Ghaill and Haywood, *Gender, Culture.*

50  Connell, *Masculinities.*

51  Butler, *Gender Trouble,* 25.

52  Butler, *Gender Trouble,* 142.

53  Judith Butler, *Undoing Gender* (Oxfordshire: Routledge, 2004).

54  Butler, *Undoing Gender,* 214.

55  Butler, *Undoing Gender,* 219.

56  Butler, *Undoing Gender,* 219.

57  Julia Kristeva, *Revolt, She Said, Julia Kristeva: An Interview with Philippe Petit,* ed. Sylvere Lotringer, trans. Brian O'Keefe (New York: Semiotexte, 2002).

58  Claire Colebrook, *Understanding Deleuze* (Crows Nest Australia: Allen & Unwin, 2002).

59  Deborah Yashar, *Contesting Citizenship in Latin America, the Rise of Indigenous Movements and the Postliberal Challenge* (Cambridge: Cambridge University Press, 2005), 13.

60  Tucker, *Sense of Wonder.*

61  Jacques Derrida, 'Limited Inc. a, b, c, . . .' in *Postmodernism: Critical Concepts,* ed. Charles Winquist and Victor Taylor (London: Routledge, 1998), 444.

62  Kristeva, *Powers of Horror.*

63  Derrida, 'Limited Inc.,', 310.

64  Janell Watson, 'Schizo-Performativity? Neurosis and Politics in Judith Butler and Felix Guattari,' *Women, a Cultural Review* 16, no. 3 (2005): 306.

65  Kristeva, *Revolt, She Said.*

66  Yashar, *Contesting Citizenship,* 4.

## 1. The Mestizo Refuses to Confess

1 Ruth Frankenberg, *Displacing Whiteness: Essays in Social and Cultural Criticism* (Durham, NC: Duke University Press, 1997).
2 Shannon Sullivan and Nancy Tuana, 'Introduction,' in *Race and Epistemology of Ignorance*, ed. Shannon Sullivan and Nancy Tuana (Albany: State University of New York Press, 2007), 1–13.
3 Lorraine Code, 'The Power of Ignorance,' in *Race and Epistemology of Ignorance*, ed. Shannon Sullivan and Nancy Tuana (Albany: State University New York Press, 2007), 220–1.
4 Brian Taylor, *Responding to Men in Crisis: Masculinities, Distress and the Postmodern Landscape* (London: Routledge, 2006), 45–78.
5 Michel Foucault, *The Hermeneutics of the Subject: Lectures at the College or France, 1981–1982*, ed. Frederic Gros, trans. Graham Burchell ( New York: Picador, 2005).
6 Foucault, *Hermeneutics.*
7 Dorothy Smith, *The Everyday World as Problematic: A Feminist Sociology* (Toronto: University of Toronto Press, 1987).
8 Fairin Herising, 'Interrupting Positions: Critical Thresholds and Queer Pro/Positions,' in *Research as Resistance: Critical Indigenous and Anti-Oppressive Approaches*, ed. Leslie Brown and Susan Strega (Toronto: Canadian Scholars Press, 2005), 133.
9 Herising, 'Interrupting Positions.'
10 Nicholas Holt, 'Representation, Legitimation and Autoethnography: An Autoethnographic Writing Story,' *International Journal of Qualitative Methods* 2, no. 1 (2003): 2.
11 Lloyd Wong and Vic Satzewich, 'Introduction: The Meaning and Significance of Transnationalism,' in *Transnational Identities and Practices in Canada*, ed. Vic Satzewich and Lloyd Wong (Vancouver: University of British Columbia Press, 2006); Patricia Landolt, 'The Institutional Landscapes of Salvadoran Transnational Migration: Translocal Views from Los Angeles and Toronto,' in *Organizing the Transnational: Labour, Politics, and Social Change*, ed. Luin Goldring and Sailaja Krishnamurti (Vancouver: University of British Columbia Press, 2007).
12 Judith Butler, *Bodies That Matter: On the Discursive Limits of 'Sex'* (New York: Routledge, 1993).
13 Daniel Schugurensky and Jorge Ginieniewicz, ' "Eyes to the North": Latin Americans in Canada,' *Dialogos* 3 (2007).
14 Canadian Census, *Cumulative Profile–Canada Provinces and Territories Table Census Regulations*, E-stat, http://estat.statcan.gc.ca.

15  Andrew Duffy, 'Class Struggles: Public Education and the New Canadian,' *The Atkinson Fellowship in Public Policy, A Special Report* (2003), 1–20.

16  Luisa Veronis, 'Immigrant participation in the Transnational Era: Latin Americans' Experiences with Collective Organizing in Toronto,' *International Migration and Integration* 11 (2010).

17  M. Silva, Otra Vision de la Coyuntura Economica, *Elfaro* (18 September 2010), http://www.elfaro.net/es/201003/opinion/1274/.

18  Veronis, 'Immigrant participation.'

19  M. Huezo, *Migracion, Cultura y Cuidadania en El Salvador: Cuadernos sobre el Desarrollo Humana, No 7* (San Salvador: PNUD, 2007).

20  Daniel Hiebert and David Ley, 'Characteristics of Immigrant Transnationalism in Vancouver,' in *Transnational Identities and Practices in Canada*, ed. Lloyd Wong and Vic Satzewich (Vancouver: University of British Columbia Press, 2006); Landolt, 'The Institutional Landscapes of Salvadoran'; Catherine Nolin, 'Spatializing the Immobility of Guatemalan Transnationalism,' *Canadian Journal of Latin American and Caribbean Studies* 29, no. 57–8 (2004).

21  Luin Goldring, 'Latin American Transnationalism in Canada: Does It Exist, What Forms Does It Take, and Where Is It Going?,' in *Transnational Identities and Practices in Canada*, ed. Vic. Satzewich and Lloyd Wong (Vancouver: University of British Columbia Press, 2006).

22  Judith Bernhard and Marlinda Freire, 'Latin Americans in a Canadian Primary School: Perspectives of Parents, Teachers, and Children on Cultural Identity and Academic Achievement,' *Journal of Regional Studies* 19, no. 3 (1998); Judith Bernhard, Marlinda Freire, and Veronica Pacini-Ketchabaw, 'Apoyo a La Participacion De Padres En Las Escuelas Primarias: Un Estudio Etnografico de un Grupo Latino Americano en Canada,' *Educational Policy Analysis Archive* 8, no. 52 (2000); Mirna Carranza, 'Salvadorian Mothers and Their Daughters: Navigating the Hazards of Acculturation in Canadian Context,' (Unpublished doctoral dissertation, University of Guelph, 2007); Mirna Carranza, 'Salvadorian Women Speak: Coping with Past Trauma and Loss in Canada,' *Canadian Social Work Review* 25, no. 1 (2008).

23  Carranza, 'Salvadorian Mothers.'

24  Mirna Carranza, 'Salvadorians: Their Wounded Souls–Historical Oppression and Resilience,' *International Journal of the Humanities* 5, no. 6, (2007); Mirna Carranza, 'Building Resilience and Resistance among Female Salvadorian Youth,' *Child & Family Social Work* 12, no. 4 (2007); Carranza, 'Salvadorian Women Speak'; Mirna Carranza and Ana Rivera, 'Salvadorian Women's Diaspora: Ana Rivera's Story,' *Canadian Women Studies* 27,

no. 1 (2009); Judith Bernhard, Luin Goldring, and Patricia Landolt, *Modelling the Transnational Family: Multi-Local Practices, Relationships and Authority Figures*, in Congress of the Canadian Association for Latin American and Caribbean Studies, Guelph, ON, 2007; Judith Bernhard, Patricia Landolt, and Luin Goldring, 'Transnational, Multi-Local Motherhood: Experiences of Separation and Reunification among Latin American Families in Canada,' CERIS Working papers, no. 40 (2005); Patricia Landolt, Lillian Autler, and Sonia Baires (1999), 'From hermano lejano to hermano major: The Dialectics of Salvadorian Transnationalism,' *Ethnic and Racial Studies* 22, no. 2 (2005); Patricia Landolt and Wei Wei Da, 'The Spatially Ruptured Practices of Migrant Families: A Comparison of Immigrants from El Salvador and the People's Republic of China,' *Current Sociology* 53, no. 4 (2005); Patricia Landolt, 'The Institutional Landscape of the Salvadoran Refugees Migration: Transnational and Local Views from Los Angeles and Toronto,' in *Organizing the Transnational: Labour, Politics, and Social Change*, ed. Luin Goldring and S. Krishnamurti (Vancouver: University of British Columbia Press, 2007).

25  Richard Connell, *Masculinities* (Berkeley: University of California Press, 2005).

26  Connell, *Masculinities*; Máirtín Mac an Ghaill and Chris Haywood, *Gender, Culture and Society: Contemporary Femininities and Masculinities* (New York: Palgrave Macmillan, 2007).

27  Deborah Yasher, *Contesting Citizenship in Latin America* (New York: Cambridge University Press, 2005).

28  Joshua Lund, *The Impure Imagination: Toward a Critical Hybridity in Latin America* (Minneapolis: University of Minnesota Press, 2006).

29  Yasher, *Contesting Citizenship*, 281–308

30  Stuart Hall, 'Cultural Identity and Diaspora,' in *Identity, Community, Culture, Difference*, ed. Jonathon Rutherford (London: Lawrence and Wishart, 1990), 220–6.

31  Hall, 'Cultural Identity,' 220–6.

32  Homi Bhabha, 'The Third Space: Interviews with Homi Bhabha,' in *Identity, Community, Culture, Difference*, ed. Jonathon Rutherford (London: Lawrence and Wishart, 1990), 210–12.

33  Connell, *Masculinities*, 77.

34  Sherene Razack, *Looking White People in the Eye: Gender, Race, and Culture in Courtrooms and Classrooms* (Toronto: University of Toronto Press, 1998).

35  Anthony Gidden, *Modernity and Self-Identity: Self and Society in the Late Modern Age* (Cambridge: Polity Press, 1991).

36  Connell, *Masculinities*, 61.

37  Moya Lloyd, *Beyond Identity Politics: Feminism, Power and Politics* (London: Sage, 2005), 1.

38  Mac an Ghaill and Haywood, *Gender, Culture.*

39  Butler, *Bodies That Matter*; Judith Butler, *Excitable Speech: A Politics of Performativity* (New York: Routledge, 1997); Judith Butler, *Antigone's Claim: Kinship between Life and Death* (New York: Columbia University Press, 2000); Mac an Ghaill and Haywood, *Gender, Culture.*

40  Butler, *Bodies That Matter*; Judith Butler, *Gender Trouble: Feminism and the Subversion of Identity*, 10th ed. (New York: Routledge, 1999); Eve Kosofsky Sedgwick, *Epistemology of the Closet* (Berkeley: University of California Press, 1990).

41  Butler, *Gender Trouble*; Jonathon Culler, 'Philosophy and Literature: The Fortunes of the Performative,' *Poetics Today* 21, no. 3 (2000); Lovell, 'Resisting with Authority: Historical Specificity, Agency and the Performative Self,' *Theory, Culture and Society* 20, no. 1 (2003).

42  Judith Butler, *The Psychic Life of Power: Theories in Subjection* (Stanford: Stanford University Press, 1997), 36–7.

43  David McInnes, 'Sissy-Boy Melancholy and the Educational Possibilities of Incoherence,' in *Judith Butler in Conversation: Analyzing the Texts and Talk of Everyday Life*, ed. Brownwyn Davies (New York: Routledge, 2008).

44  McInnes, 'Sissy Boy'; Connell, *Masculinities.*

45  Rafael Montesinos, *La Masculinidad en ciernes: Resistencias y conflictos en la construcción social de una presencia urgente*, in Rafael Montesinos, coordinator, Masculinidades Emergentes, Miguel Angel Porrua, 2005.

46  Manuel Salas and Alvaro Campos, *Explotación Sexual Comercial Y Masculinidad: Es Estudio Regional Cualitativo Con Hombres De La Población General* (San Jose: OIT/IPEC, 2004).

47  Martha Ramirez, *Hombres Violentos: Un Estudio Antropologico De La Violencia Masculina* (Mexico City: Plaza y Valdez Editores, 2003).

48  Gary Villereal and Alonzo Cavazos, 'Shifting Identity: Process and Change in Identity of Aging Mexican-American Males,' *Journal of Sociology and Social Welfare* 32, no. 1 (2005).

49  Butler, *Bodies That Matter.*

50  Jonathon Culler, 'Philosophy and Literature: The Fortunes of the Performative'; A.Y. Jackson, 'Performativity Identified,' *Qualitative Inquiry* 10, no. 5 (2004).

51  Butler, *Bodies That Matter*, 244.

52  Mitchell Dean, *Governmentality: Power and Rule in Modern Society* (London: Sage, 1999); Frank Furedi, *Therapy Culture: Cultivating Vulnerability in an Uncertain Age* (London: Routledge, 2004): 40–3.

53  Michel Foucault, *The History of Sexuality: An Introduction, Vol. 1*, trans. Robert Hurley (New York: Random, 1978).

54  Henry Parada, 'Social Work Practices within the Restructured Child Welfare System in Ontario: An Institutional Ethnography,' *Canadian Social Work Review* 21, no. 1 (2004): 67–86; Henry Parada, 'Regional Perspectives from Latin America: Social Work in Latin American History, Challenges and Renewal,' *International Social Work* 50, no. 4 (July 2007): 560–9; Henry Parada, Lisa Barnoff, and Bree Coleman, 'Negotiating Professional Agency: Social Work and Decision Making within Child Welfare,' *Journal of Sociology and Social Welfare* 4 (December 2007): 35–56.

55  Bob Pease, *Recreating Men: Postmodern Masculinity Politics* (London: Sage, 2000); Bob Pease and Keith Pringle, *A Man's World: Changing Men's Practices in a Globalized World* (New York: Zed Books, 2001).

56  Carranza, 'Salvadorian Mothers'; Carranza, 'Salvadorian Women Speak.'

57  Carranza, 'Salvadorian Mothers,' 46–8.

58  Carranza, 'Salvadorian Mothers.'

59  Dean, *Governmentality*.

60  Furedi, *Therapy Culture*, 35

61  Furedi, *Therapy Culture*.

62  Janell Watson, 'Schizo-Performativity? Neurosis and Politics in Judith Butler and Felix Guattari,' *Women* 16, no. 3 (2005): 305–20.

63  Butler, *Excitable Speech*, 100.

64  Watson, 'Schizo-Performativity?,' 309.

65  Foucault, *Hermeneutics*.

## 2. Yearning to Break Silence

1  Michel Foucault, 'Technologies of the Self,' in *Ethics: Subjectivity and Truth*, ed. Paul Rabinow, *Essential works of Foucault* (New York: New Press, 1997), 225–51.

2  Ken Moffatt, Wudneh Baileyegu, Sean Martin, Ravi Saravanamuttu, Steven Ruhinda, Frank Sirotich, Lyle Stockwell, and Joseph Vaz, 'Reflecting on Masculinity in a Multicultural Classroom,' Paper presented at the Joint Conference of the International Federation of Social Workers and International Association of Schools of Social Work, Montreal, May 2000.

3 Kenneth Gergen, 'Psychological Science in a Postmodern Context,' *American Psychologist* 56, no. 10 (2001): 803–13; Doug Risner, 'Motion and Marking in Reflective Practice: Artifacts, Autobiographical Narrative and Sexuality,' *Reflective Practice* 3, no. 1 (2002): 5–19.

4 Bob Pease, 'Developing Profeminist Practice with Men in Social Work,' *Critical Social Work* 2, no. 1 (2001): 1–19.

5 Stanley Witkin, 'Writing Social Work,' *Social Work* 45, no. 5 (2000): 389–95.

6 Kathleen M. Tangenberg and Susan Kemp, 'Embodied Practice: Claiming the Body's Experience, Agency, and Knowledge for Social Work,' *Social Work* 47, no. 1 (2002): 9–19.

7 Robert W. Connell, 'Masculinities and Globalization,' *Men and Masculinities* 1, no. 1 (1998): 3–23; Robert W. Connell, *Masculinities* (Berkeley: University of California Press, 1995); Stephen Whitehead, *Men and Masculinities* (Cambridge: Polity, 2002); Witkin, 'Writing Social Work,' 392; For an example of the use of auto-ethnography to challenge assumptions about the expressions of masculinity see Jack Sternbach, 'Lessons Learned about Working with Men: "A Prison Memoir,"' *Social Work* 45, no. 5 (2000): 413–23.

8 Gergen, 'Psychological Science,' 810.

9 Witkin, 'Writing Social Work,' 392.

10 Madeleine Grumet, 'Autobiography and Reconceptualization,' in *Contemporary Curriculum Discourses: Twenty Years of JCT*, ed. William F. Pinar (New York: Peter Lang, 1999), 24–9.

11 Janice Ristock and Joan Pennell, *Community Research as Empowerment: Feminist Links and Postmodern Interruptions* (Toronto: Oxford University Press, 1996).

12 Grumet, 'Autobiography,' 29.

13 Adrienne Chambon, 'A Foucauldian Approach Making the Familiar Visible,' in *Reading Foucault for Social Work*, ed. Adrienne Chambon, Allan Irving, and Laura Epstein (New York: Columbia University Press, 1999), 51–81; Bob Smart, *Michel Foucault* (New York: Routledge, 1985).

14 Michel Foucault, 'The Subject and Power,' in *Michel Foucault: Beyond Structuralism and Hermeneutics*, ed. Hubert Dreyfus and Paul Rabinow (Chicago: University of Chicago Press, 1983), 208.

15 Chambon, 'Foucauldian Approach,' 67–8.

16 Foucault, 'Technologies,' 225.

17 Chambon, 'Foucauldian Approach,' 57.

18 Michel Foucault, *The Archaeology of Knowledge*, trans. A.M. Sheridan Smith (New York: Pantheon, 1972).

19 Robin Clair, *Organizing Silence: A World of Possibilities* (Albany: State University of New York Press, 1998).

20 Eva Alberby and Jorunn Elidottir, 'The Sounds of Silence: Some Remarks on the Value of Silence in the Process of Reflection to Teaching and Learning,' *Reflective Practice* 4, no. 1 (2003): 41–51.

21 Chambon, 'Foucauldian Approach,' 58–9; Ernesto Laclau and Chantel Mouffee, *Hegemony and Social Strategy: Towards a Radical Democratic Politics* (London: Verso, 1985); Bob Pease 'Deconstructing Masculinity: Reconstructing Men,' in *Transforming Social Work Practice: Postmodern Critical Perspective,* ed. Bob Pease and Jan Fook (New York: Routledge, 1997), 97–112.

22 Pease, 'Deconstructing Masculinity,' 103–4.

23 Pease, 'Deconstructing Masculinity,' 103.

24 Clair, *Organizing Silence,* 51; Laclau and Mouffee, *Hegemony and Social Strategy,* 115; Pease, 'Deconstructing Masculinity,' 103–4.

25 Judith Butler, 'Imitation and Gender Insubordination,' in *Inside/Out: Lesbian Theories, Gay Theories,* ed. Diane Fuss (New York: Routledge, 1991); Robert Connell, *Masculinities* (Cambridge: Polity, 1995).

26 Butler, 'Imitation and Gender Insubordination,' 28–9.

27 Ursula Franklin, *The Real World of Technology,* Canadian Broadcasting Corporation Massey Lecture Series (Toronto: Canadian Broadcasting Corporation Enterprises, 1990); Julia Kristeva, *Powers of Horror: An Essay on Abjection* (New York: Columbia University Press, 1982).

28 Clair, *Organizing Silence,* 15.

29 Stephen Riggins, 'An Interview with Michel Foucault,' in *Ethics, Subjectivity and Truth,* ed. Paul Rabinow; *Essential Works of Foucault 1954–1984* (New York: New Press, 1997), 121–34.

30 Anne Gere, 'Revealing Silence: Rethinking Personal Thinking,' *Composition and Communication* 53, no. 2 (2001): 208.

31 Gere, 'Revealing Silence.'

32 Connell, *Masculinities,* 186–203

33 Kristeva, *Powers of Horror.*

34 Gilles Deleuze and Felix Guattari, *Anti-Oedipus: Capitalism and Schizophrenia,* trans. Robert Hurley, Mark Seem, and Helen Lane (London: Athlone Press, 1984); Julia Kristeva, *Intimate Revolt: The Powers and Limits of Psychoanalysis,* trans. Jeannie Herman, vol. 2 (New York: Columbia University Press, 2002); Julia Kristeva, *Revolt She Said,* trans. Brian O'Keefe, ed. Sylvere Lotringer (New York: Semiotext(e), 2002).

## 3. Instruction in the Art of the Masculine

1 Daryl Vocat, in discussion with the author, Ryerson University, 30 November 2005.
2 Daryl Vocat, 'Infestant Propaganda,' publisher Daryl Vocat, http://darylvocat.com/propaganda.htm.
3 Vocat, 'Infestant Propaganda.'
4 Vocat, discussion, 7 December 2005.
5 Vocat, discussion, 21 December 2005.
6 Vocat, discussion, 7 December 2005.
7 William F. Pinar, 'Regimes of Reason and the Male Narrative Voice,' in *Representation and the Text: Reframing the Narrative Voice,* ed. William G. Tierney and Yvonna Lincoln (Albany: State University of New York Press, 1997).
8 Gilles Deleuze and Felix Guattari, *Anti-Oedipus, Capitalism and Schizophrenia,* trans. Robert Hurley, Mark Seem, and Helen R. Lane (Minneapolis: University of Minnesota Press, 1983); Gilles Deleuze and Felix Guattari, *A Thousand Plateaus: Capitalism and Schizophrenia,* trans. Brian Massumi (Minneapolis: University of Minnesota Press, 1987).
9 Deleuze and Guattari, *Anti-Oedipus*; Henry A. Giroux, 'Postmodern Education and Disposable Youth,' in *Revolutionary Pedagogies, Cultural Politics, Instituting Education, and the Discourse of Theory,* ed. P. Pericles Tifonas (New York: Routledge, 2000); Julia Kristeva, *'Revolt, She Said': An Interview by Philippe Petit,* trans. Sylvere Lotringer, ed. Brian O'keefe (New York: Semiotext(e) Foreign Agents Series, 2002).
10 Vocat, ' Infestant Propaganda.'
11 Vocat, 'Infestant Propaganda.'
12 Deleuze and Guattari, *Anti-Oedipus.*
13 Vocat, 'Infestant Propaganda.'
14 Vocat, 'Infestant Propaganda.'
15 Vocat, 'Infestant Propaganda.'
16 Vocat, 'Infestant Propaganda.'
17 Judith Butler, *Bodies That Matter: On the Discursive Limits of 'Sex'* (New York: Routledge, 1993); Jonathan Culler, 'Philosophy and Literature: The Fortunes of the Performative,' *Poetics Today* 21, no. 3 (2000): 503–19; Terry Lovell, 'Resisting with Authority: Historical Specificity, Agency and the Performative Self,' *Theory, Culture and Society* 20, no. 1 (2003): 1–17.
18 Culler, 'Philosophy and Literature.'
19 Vocat, discussion, 30 November 2005.
20 Vocat, discussion, 30 November 2005.

21  Daryl Vocat, 'What My Parents Want Me to Be When I Grow Up, A-Z,' publisher, Daryl Vocat, http://darylvocat.com/a-z%20small.html.
22  Vocat, 'What My Parents Want.'
23  Vocat, discussion, 30 November 2005.
24  Vocat, discussion, 7 December 2005.
25  Daryl Vocat, 'Daryl Vocat's Home Page,' publisher, Daryl Vocat, http://darylvocat.com.
26  Vocat, discussion, 30 November 2005.
27  R.M. Vaughan, 'The Big Picture,' *National Post*, 8 October 2005.
28  Vocat, discussion, 30 November 2005.
29  Vocat, discussion, 30 November 2005.
30  Deleuze and Guattari, *Anti-Oedipus*.
31  Ken Moffatt, *A Poetics of Social Work: Personal Agency and Social Transformation in Canada, 1920–1939* (Toronto: University of Toronto Press, 2001).
32  Vocat, discussion, 30 November 2005.
33  Vocat, discussion, 30 November 2005.
34  Vocat, discussion, 30 November 2005.
35  Alecia Youngblood Jackson, 'Performativity Identitified,' *Qualitative Inquiry* 10, no. 5 (2004): 673–90.
36  National Council of Boy Scouts of Canada, *The Cub Book: A Book of Things for Boys 8 to 10* (Ottawa: National Council of Boy Scouts of Canada, 1970), 96.
37  Boy Scouts of Canada, *The Cub Book*, 8.
38  Boy Scouts of Canada, *The Cub Book*.
39  Vocat, discussion, 30 November 2005.
40  Vocat, discussion, 30 November 2005.
41  Vocat, discussion, 30 November 2005
42  Vocat, discussion, 30 November 2005
43  Vocat, discussion, 21 December 2005.
44  Todd May, *Gilles Deleuze: An Introduction* (Cambridge: Cambridge University Press, 2005), 17.
45  Vocat, discussion, 21 December 2005.
46  Deleuze and Guattari, *Anti-Oedipus*.
47  Vocat, discussion, 30 November 2005.
48  Culler, 'Philosophy and Literature.'
49  Michel Foucault, *The Order of Things: An Archaeology of Human Sciences* (New York: Vintage, 1973).
50  Butler, *Bodies*.
51  Derek Conrad Murray and Soraya Murray, 'Uneasy Bedfellows: Canonical Art Theory and Politics of Identity,' *Art Journal* 65, no. 1 (2006): 23–39.

52 Deleuze and Guattari, *Anti-Oedipus.*
53 Butler, *Bodies That Matter*, 145.
54 Gilles Deleuze, *Repetition and Difference.*
55 Vocat, discussion, 21 December 2005.
56 Deleuze and Guattari, *Anti-Oedipus.*
57 May, *Gilles Deleuze.*
58 Deleuze and Guattari, *Thousand Plateaus.*
59 Deleuze and Guattari, *Anti-Oedipus.*
60 Deleuze and Guattari, *Thousand Plateaus.*

## 4. Troubling Role Models

1 I capitalize Black throughout the chapter to represent the fact that like all racial and ethnic groups (e.g. Asians, British, South Asians), Black constitutes a specific ethnic, racial, or cultural group and 'as such requires denotation as a proper noun' (1710); Cheryl I. Harris, 'Whiteness as Property,' *Harvard Law Review* 106, no. 8 (June 1993): 1707–91.
2 Patrick Shannon, *Reading Poverty* (Portsmouth, NH: Heinemann, 1998).
3 Carl E. James, '"You're Doing It for the Students': On the Question of Role Models,' in *Experiencing Difference*, ed. Carl E. James (Halifax: Fernwood Publishing, 2001), 89–93.
4 *Invisible City*, DVD, prod. Mehernaz Lentin and Gerry Flahive, dir. Hubert Davis, 2 hrs. 23 min., National Film Board of Canada, 2009.
5 John Macfarlane, 'We Used to Think of Guns as an American Problem,' *Toronto Life*, February 2006, 17.
6 'The Many Fatherless Boys in Black Families,' *Globe and Mail*, 16 November 2005.
7 Linda Diebel, 'Where Are the Men?' *Toronto Star*, 19 August 2007.
8 Diebel, 'Where Are the Men?'
9 Charles Johnson, 'Shall We Overcome? The Black American Condition Today,' *Society* 43 (2006): 13.
10 Christopher M. Spence, *On Time! On Task! On a Mission! A Year in the Life of a Middle School Principal* (Halifax: Fernwood Publishing, 2002).
11 Louise Brown and Kristin Rushowy, 'Schools Plan Calls for Boys-Only Classes,' *Toronto Star*, 21 October 2009.
12 Eduardo Bonilla-Silva, *Racism without Racists: Color-Blind Racism and the Persistence of Racial Inequality in the United States* (Oxford: Rowman & Littlefield, 2003); Abby Ferber, 'The Construction of Black Masculinity: White Supremacy Now and Then,' *Journal of Sport and Social Issues* 31 (2007):

11–24; Frances Henry and Carol Tator, *The Colour of Democracy: Racism in Canadian Society* (Toronto: Thomson Canada, 2004).

13  Ferber, 'Construction of Black Masculinity,' 15.

14  Colin Wayne Leach, 'Against the Notion of a "New Racism,"' *Journal of Community and Applied Social Psychology* 15 (2005): 432–45; Teun A. van Dijk, 'New(s) Racism: A Discourse Analytical Approach,' in *Ethnic Minorities and the Media*, ed. Simon Cottle (Milton Keynes: Open University Press, 2000), 33–49.

15  Etienne Balibar, 'Is There a "Neo-Racism?"' in *Race and Racialization: Essential Readings*, ed. Tania Das Gupta et al. (Toronto: Canadian Scholars Press, 2007), 83–8.

16  Balibar, 'Neo-Racism?," 85.

17  Vala Jorge, 'Expressions of "New" Racism,' *International Journal of Psychology* 44 (2009): 1–3.

18  Bonilla-Silva, *Racism without Racists*; Patricia Hill Collins, *Black Sexual Politics* (New York: Routledge, 2004); Ferber, *The Construction of Black Masculinity*; Henry and Tator, *The Colour of Democracy*.

19  Bonilla-Silva, *Racism without Racists*, 3.

20  Henry and Tator, *Colour of Democracy*, 19.

21  Henry and Tator, *Colour of Democracy*, 19.

22  Bonilla-Silva, *Racism without Racists*, 3–4.

23  Bonilla-Silva, *Racism without Racists*; Carl E. James, *Seeing Ourselves: Exploring Race, Ethnicity and Culture* (Toronto: Thompson Educational Publishing, 2010).

24  Martha Augoustinos, Keith Tuffin, and Danielle Every, 'New Racism, Meritocracy and Individualism: Constraining Affirmative Action in Education,' *Discourse and Society* 16 (2005): 317.

25  Collins, *Black Sexual Politics*, 178.

26  Bonilla-Silva, *Racism without Racists*; Henry and Tator, *Colour of Democracy*.

27  Bonilla-Silva, *Racism without Racists*, 26.

28  Asians are often referenced here for their educational accomplishments, especially noting that they might have been immigrants, or have language differences and still succeed better than long-time residents or those of many generations. See Gordon Pon, 'Importing the Asian Model Minority Discourse into Canada: Implications for Social Work and Education,' *Canadian Social Work Review* 17 (2000): 227–91; Stacy Lee, *Up against Whiteness: Race, School and Immigrant Youth* (New York: Teachers College Press, 2005).

29  Bonilla-Silva, *Racism without Racists*; Ferber, 'The Construction of Black Masculinity'; Henry and Tator, *Colour of Democracy*; Eileen Walsh,

'Representations of Race and Gender in Mainstream Media Coverage of the 2008 Democratic Primary,' *Journal of African American Studies* 13 (2009): 121–30.

30 Henry and Tator, *Colour of Democracy*, 2004.

31 Augoustinos, Tuffin, and Every, 'New Racism, Meritocracy and Individualism,' 317; Patricia Hincey, *Finding Freedom in the Classroom: A Practical Introduction to Critical Theory* (New York: Peter Lang, 2008).

32 Paul Gordon and Francesca Klug, *New Right, New Racism* (London: Searchlight Publication, 1986), 22.

33 Gordon and Klug, *New Right, New Racism*, 22.

34 Augoustinos, Tuffin, and Every, 'New Racism, Meritocracy and Individualism,' 317.

35 Ferber, 'Construction of Black Masculinity,' 11.

36 Indeed, Canadians admire and support their athletes who are Canadian-born, like Jamal Maglorie, and teams such as the Raptors and Argonauts with their many black players.

37 Carl E. James, *Race in Play: Understanding the Socio-Cultural Worlds of Student Athletes* (Toronto: Canadian Scholars Press, 2005).

38 Ferber, 'Construction of Black Masculinity'; James, *Race in Play*.

39 Ferber, 'Construction of Black Masculinity,' 20.

40 Ferber, 'Construction of Black Masculinity,' 20.

41 Ferber references Collins as saying that 'there is a traditional family script in place in sports that works to minimize the threat of Black masculinity. The coach is similar to the White male father figure, whereas Black male athletes are like the children, under the father's control and subject to his rule. It is only when they accept and play this role that they are fully embraced and accepted and seen as nonthreatening' (Ferber, 'Construction of Black Masculinity,' 20).

42 Ferber, 'Construction of Black Masculinity'; Carol Schick and Verna St Denis, 'What Makes Anti-Racist Pedagogy in Teacher Education Difficult? Three Popular Ideological Assumptions,' *Alberta Journal of Education Research* 49 (2003).

43 Moira Welsh, 'Why Kids Join Gangs,' *Toronto Star*, 29 April 2006.

44 CBC transcripts, February 2007, http://www.cbc.ca/toronto/features/withoutmen/patterson.html#feature.

45 CBC transcripts, February 2007, http://www.cbc.ca/toronto/features/withoutmen/rivers.html. It seems that what Reverend Rivers had to say impressed the Ontario Conservative party enough that they invited him to speak at a convention the following year.

46 Wendell Adjetey, 'Inner-City Youth Need Positive Role Models,' *National Post*, 19 August 2009.

47 Spence, *On Time! On Task! On a Mission!*, 71.

48 Spence was sure to say that attendance at such school would be based on 'choice' and it would not be 'segregation' (*Toronto Star*, 21 October 2009).

49 Carl E. James, 'Schooling and the University Plans of Black Students from an Urban Neighborhood,' in *Culture, Curriculum, and Identity in Education*, ed. H. Richard Milner (New York: Palgrave Macmillan, 2010), 117–39.

50 Louise Brown and Kristin Rushowy, 'Schools Plan Calls for Boys-Only Classes,' *Toronto Star*, 21 October 2009.

51 Kimberley Tavares-Carter, 'The Dearth of Black Male Educators in the Secondary Panel' (master's thesis, York University, 2009), 51.

52 Tavares-Carter, 'Dearth of Black Male Educators,' 51.

53 Tavares-Carter, 'Dearth of Black Male Educators,' 50.

54 Tavares-Carter, 'Dearth of Black Male Educators,' 54.

55 One respondent even went further to talk of his admiration for his older sister and how he did 'things to make her proud' of him, like spending more time on his school work. Tavares-Carter, 'Dearth of Black Male Educators,' 73.

56 James, *Seeing Ourselves*; like Morgan, Conrad joined his mother from Jamaica at age twelve.

57 Lawson Bush V, 'How Black Mothers Participate in the Development of Manhood and Masculinity: What Do We Know about Black Mothers and Their Sons?' *Journal of Negro Education* 73 (2004): 384.

58 Shannon, *Reading Poverty*, 1998.

59 Tavares-Carter, 'Dearth of Black Male Educators,' 54.

60 Verna St Denis, Rita Bouvier, and Marie Battiste, *Okiskinahamakewak-Aboriginal Teachers in Saskatchewan's Publicly Funded Schools: Responding to the Flux. Final Report–October 31, 1998* (Regina: Saskatchewan Education Research Networking Project, 1998), vii.

61 Carl E. James, 'Masculinity, Racialization and Schooling: The Making of Marginalized Men,' in *The 'Boy Problem': Interrogating Issues of Masculinity and Schooling*, ed. Wayne Martino, Michael Kehler, and Marcus B. Weaver-Hightower (New York: Haworth Press, 2009), 113.

## 5. Queering Asian Masculinities and Transnationalism

1 See Gordon Pon, 'Becoming Lost and Found: Peace, Christianity, and Anti-Oppression' (electronic version), *Critical Social Work* 8, no. 1 (2007) for a

critical discussion of Christianity, oppression and implications for anti-oppression.

2 Donna Baines, ed., *Doing Anti-Oppressive Practice.* (Halifax: Fernwood, 2006); Lisa Barnoff and Ken Moffatt, 'Contradictory Tensions in Anti-Oppressive Practice in Feminist Social Services,' *Affilia: Journal of Women and Social Services* 22, no. 1 (2007): 56–70; Narda Razack, *Transforming the Field.* (Halifax: Fernwood, 2002).

3 Kenneth McLaughlin, 'From Ridicule to Institutionalization: Anti-Oppression, the State and Social Work,' *Critical Social Policy* 25, no. 3 (2006): 283–305.

4 McLaughlin, 'Ridicule.'

5 Izumi Sakamoto and R.O. Pitner, 'Critical Consciousness in Anti-Oppressive Social Work Practice: Disentangling Power Dynamics at Personal and Structural Levels,' *British Journal of Social Work* 35 (2005): 435–52.

6 Barbara Heron, 'Self-Reflection in Critical Social Work Practice: Subjectivity and the Possibilities of Resistance,' *Reflective Practice* 6, no. 3 (2005): 341–51; Dennis Miehls and Ken Moffatt, 'Constructing Social Work Identity Based on the Reflexive Self,' *British Journal of Social Work* 30 (2000): 339–48; Gordon Pon, 'Becoming Lost'; Narda Razack, *Unsettling the Field* (Halifax: Fernwood, 2002); Izumi Sakamoto and R.O. Pitner, 'Use of Critical Consciousness in Anti-Oppressive Social Work Practice: Disentangling Power Dynamics at Personal and Structural Levels,' *British Journal of Social Work* 35 (2005): 435–52; Renita Wong, 'Knowing through Discomfort: A Mindfulness-Based Critical Social Work Pedagogy' (electronic version), *Critical Social Work* 5, no. 1 (2004); June Yee and Gary Dumbrill, 'Whiteout: Looking for Race in Canadian Social Work Practice,' in *Multicultural Social Work in Canada*, ed. John Graham and Ali Al-Krenawi (Don Mills: Oxford University Press, 2003), 98–121.

7 Wong, 'Knowing through Discomfort.'

8 Donna Baines, 'Bridging the Practice-Activism Divide in Mainstream Social Work,' in *Doing Anti-Oppressive Practice*, ed. D. Baines (Halifax: Fernwood, 2007), 50–66; Carolyn Campbell, 'The Search for Congruency: Developing Strategies for Anti-Oppressive Social Work Pedagogy,' *Canadian Social Work Review* 19, no. 1 (2002): 25–42; Robert Mullaly, *The New Structural Social Work* (Don Mills: Oxford University Press, 2007).

9 Paulo Friere, *Pedagogy of the Oppressed* (New York: Seabury Press, 1974).

10 Elizabeth Ellsworth, 'Why Doesn't This Feel Empowering? Working through the Repressive Myths of Critical Pedagogy,' *Harvard Educational Review* 5 (1987): 297–324; Jan Fook, *Social Work: Critical Theory and Practice* (Thousand Oaks: Sage, 2002).

11  Deborah Britzman and Jen Gilbert, 'What Would Have Been Said about Gayness in Teacher Education?' *Teaching Journal* 15, no. 1 (2004): 81–96.

12  Britzman and Gilbert, 'What Would.'

13  Ellsworth, 'Why Doesn't.'

14  Deborah Britzman, 'That Lonely Discovery: Anne Frank, Anna Freud, and the Question of Pedagogy,' in *Lost Subjects, Contested Objects: Toward a Psychoanalytical Inquiry of Learning* (Albany: State University of New York Press, 1998), 113–35.

15  David Eng, 'Out Here and Over There: Queerness and Diaspora in Asian American Studies,' *Social Text* 15, no. 3/4 (1997): 31–52.

16  Celia Haig-Brown, *Resistance and Renewal: Surviving the Indian Residential School* (Vancouver: Tillacum Library, 1988).

17  Terry Woo, *Banana Boys* (Toronto: Riverbank Press, 2000).

18  Woo, *Banana Boys.*

19  Daniel Yon, *Elusive Culture: Schooling, Race, and Identity in Global Times.* (New York: State University of New York Press, 2000).

20  Blye Frank, 'Queer/Selves/Queer Schools: Young Men and Sexualities,' in *Sex in Schools: Canadian Education and Sexual Regulation*, ed. Susan Prentice (Halifax: Our Schools/Our Selves, 1994), 44–59.

21  Edward Said, *Orientalism* (London: Penguin, 1978); Wah-Shan Chou, *Tongzhi: Politics of Same Sex Eroticism in Chinese Societies* (New York: Haworth, 2000).

22  Greg Leong, 'Internalised Racism and the Work of Chinese Australian Artists: Making Visible the Invisible World of William Yang,' *Journal of Australian Studies* (2002): 79–88; Chou, *Tongzhi.*

23  Chou, *Tongzhi.*

24  Judith Butler, *Gender Trouble: Feminism and the Subversion of Identity* (New York: Routledge, 1990).

25  Tania Das Gupta, *Racism and Paid Work* (Toronto: Garamond Press, 1996); R. Leong, 'Foreword: Unfurling Pleasure, Embracing Race,' in *On a Bed of Rice: An Asian American Erotic Feast*, ed. Geraldine Kudaka (New York: Bantam Doubleday, 1995), xi–xxx.

26  Das Gupta, *Racism and Paid Work*, 27.

27  Rana Kabbani, *Europe's Myths of the Orient* (Bloomington: Indiana University Press, 1986).

28  Anthony Chan, *Gold Mountain* (Vancouver: Gold Star, 1983); Guida Mann, 'Racialization of Gender, Work, and Transnational Migration: The Experience of Chinese Immigrant Women in Canada,' in *Race and Racism in 21st Century Canada: Continuity, Complexity, and Change*, ed. Sean Hier and B. Singh Bolaria (Peterborough: Broadview Press), 235–52; Gordon Pon, 'The

Art of War or the Wedding Banquet? Asian Canadians, Masculinity, and Anti-Racism Education,' *Canadian Journal of Education* 25, no. 2 (2000): 139–51.

29  Chan, *Gold Mountain*.

30  Mona Pon, 'The Social Construction of Chinese Masculinity in *Jack Canuck*,' in *Gender and History in Canada*, ed. Joy Parr (Toronto: Copp Clark, 1996), 68–88.

31  David Palumbo-Liu, *Asian/American: Historical Crossings of a Racial Frontier* (Stanford: Stanford University Press, 1999); Gordon Pon, 'Importing the Asian "Model Minority" Discourse into Canada. Implications for Social Work and Education,' *Canadian Social Work Review* 17, no. 2 (2000): 227–91.

32  Eng, 'Out Here and Over There,' 31–52.

33  Richard Fung, 'Looking for My Penis: The Eroticized Asian in Gay Porn Video,' in Bad Object Choices, ed., *How Do I Look?* (Seattle: Bay Press, 1991), 145–168.

34  Eng, 'Out Here and Over There.'

35  Jigna Desai, 'Homo on the Range: Mobile and Global Sexualities,' *Social Text* 73, no. 4 (2002): 65–89; David Eng, *Racial Castration: Managing Masculinity in Asian America* (Durham, NC: Duke University Press, 2001).

36  Eng, *Racial Castration*.

37  Benedict Anderson, *Imagined Communities: Reflections on the Origin and Spread of Nationalism* (New York: Verso, 1991).

38  Gayatri Spivak, *The Post-Colonial Critic: Interviews, Strategies, Dialogue* (New York: Routledge, 1990).

39  Frank Chin, Jeffery Chan, Lawson Inada, and Shawn Wong, eds., *Aiiieeee! An Anthology of Asian-American Writers* (New York: Meridian, 1974).

40  Frank Chin, Jeffery Chan, Lawson Inada, and Shawn Wong, eds., *The Big Aiiieeee! An Anthology of Chinese American and Japanese American Literature* (New York: Meridian, 1991).

41  King-Kok Cheung, 'Art, Spirituality, and the Ethic of Care: Alternative Masculinities in Chinese American Literature,' in *Masculinity Studies and Feminist Theory: New Directions*, ed. Judith Gardiner (New York: Columbia University Press, 2002), 261–89; David Eng, 'Out Here and Over There'; Palumbo-Liu, *Asian/American*.

42  Britzman and Gilbert, 'What Would.'

43  Chin, Chan, Inada, and Wong, *Aiieee!*.

44  Eng, 'Out Here and Over There.'

45  Eng, 'Out Here and Over There,' 35.

46  Frank Chin and Jeffery Chan, 'Racist Love,' in *Seeing Through Shuck*, ed. Richard Kostelanetz (New York: Ballantine, 1972), 68.

47  Eng, 'Out Here and Over There,' 35.

48  Michael Omi and Dana Takagi, 'Thinking Theory in Asian American Studies,' *Amerasia Journal* 21, no. 1 (1995): 21–2.

49  Eng, 'Out Here and Over There,' 41.

50  Richard Fung, dir., *Sea in the Blood* (2000); *Dirty Laundry* (1996).

51  Maurice Poon and Peter Ho, 'A Qualitative Analysis of Cultural and Social Vulnerabilities to HIV Infection among Gay, Lesbian, and Bisexual Asian Youth,' *Journal of Gay and Lesbian Social Services* 14, no. 3 (2002): 43–78; Maurice Poon, Peter Ho, and J.P. Wong, 'Developing a Comprehensive AIDS Prevention Outreach Program,' *Canadian Journal of Human Sexuality* 10, no. 1–2 (2001): 25–39.

52  Eng, 'Out Here and Over There.'

53  Maurice Poon, 'The Discourse of Oppression in Contemporary Gay Asian Diasporal Literature: Liberation or Limitation?' *Sexuality and Culture* 10, no. 3 (2006): 29–58.

54  Ang Lee, dir., *The Wedding Banquet* (Samuel Goldwyn Company, 1993).

55  Mark Chiang, 'Coming Out into the Global System: Postmodern Patriarchies and Transnational Sexualities in *The Wedding Banquet*,' in *Q & A: Queer in Asian America*, ed. David Eng and Alice Y. Hom (Philadelphia: Temple University Press, 1998).

56  Eng, 'Out Here and Over There.'

57  Heron, 'Self-reflection.'

58  Heron, 'Self-reflection.'

59  Eng, 'Out Here and Over There.'

60  Personal communication, 8 October 2010.

61  Paul Gilroy, *The Black Atlantic* (Cambridge: Harvard University Press, 1993); K. Gosine, 'Essentialism versus Complexity: Conceptions of Racial Identity Construction in Education Scholarship,' *Canadian Journal of Education* 27, no. 1 (2002): 81–99; Stuart Hall, 'Old and New Identities, Old and New Ethnicities,' in *Globalization, and the World System: Contemporary Conditions for the Representation of Identity*, ed. D. King (London: Macmillan, 1991), 41–68; Carl James, *Seeing Ourselves* (Toronto: Thompson, 2000).

62  W.E.B. Du Bois, *The Souls of Black Folk* (New York: Dover Publications, 1994).

63  Cheung, 'Art, Spirituality, and the Ethic of Care,' 284.

64  Baines, 'Bridging the Practice-Activism Divide.'

## 6. 'Keeping It Real'

1  Daniel Yon, *Elusive Culture: Schooling, Race, and Identity in Global Times* (New York: State University of New York Press, 2000).

2 Yon, *Elusive*, 123.

3 Yon, *Elusive*, 131.

4 Erving Goffman, *The Presentation of Self in Everyday Life* (New York: Doubleday, 1959).

5 Victor Turner, *The Ritual Process: Structure and Anti-Structure* (New York: Aldine de Gruyter, 1969).

6 Richard Schechner, *Performance Theory* (London/New York: Routledge, 1988), 186–7.

7 Clifford Geertz, *Works and Lives: The Anthropologist as Author* (Stanford: Stanford University Press, 1988), 173.

8 Judith Butler, *Undoing Gender* (New York/London: Routledge, 2004).

9 Butler, *Undoing Gender*, 142.

10 Butler, *Undoing Gender*, 148.

11 Butler, *Undoing Gender*, 1.

12 Ronald Berger and Richard Quinney, eds., *Storytelling Sociology: Narrative as Social Inquiry* (Boulder/London: Lynne Rienner Publishers, 2005), 9, quoting Sara Lawrence-Lightfoot and Jessica Hoffmann-Davis, *The Art and Science of Portraiture* (1997).

13 Judith Butler, *Gender Trouble: Feminism and the Subversion of Identity* (New York: Routledge, 1990), 3.

14 Robert W. Connell, *Masculinities* (Berkeley/Los Angeles: University of California Press, 1995).

15 Máirtín Mac an Ghaill, *The Making of Men: Masculinities, Sexualities, and Schooling* (Milton Keynes/Philadelphia: Open University Press, 1994), 56.

16 Nancy Lesko, introduction to *Masculinities at School: Research on Men and Masculinities*, ed. Lesko (Thousand Oaks, CA/London/New Delhi: Sage, 2000).

17 Michael Kimmel, 'Masculinity as Homophobia: Fear, Shame and Silence in the Construction of Gender Identity,' in *Theorizing Masculinities*, ed. Harry Brod and Michael Kaufman (Thousand Oaks, CA: Sage, 1994).

18 Mac an Ghaill, *The Making of Men*; Wayne Martino and Deborah Berrill, 'Boys, Schooling, and Masculinities: Interrogating the "Right" Way to Educate Boys,' *Educational Review* 55, no. 2 (1999): 99–117.

19 William Shakespeare, *The Tragedy of King Richard the Third*, in *The Complete Works of Shakespeare*, ed. David Bevington, 3rd ed. (Glenview, IL: Scott, Foresman and Company, 1980), I, i, 154–7.

20 Robert W. Connell, 'Cool Guys, Swots and Wimps: The Interplay of Masculinity and Education,' *Oxford Review of Education* 15, no. 3 (1989): 291–303.

21 Fiona Leach, 'Learning to Be Violent: The Role of the School in Developing Adolescent Gendered Behaviour,' *Compare* 33, no. 3 (2003): 385–400.

22 *Education as Enforcement: The Militarization and Corporatization of Schools*, ed. Kenneth Saltman and David A. Gabbard (New York: RoutledgeFarmer, 2003); Henry A. Giroux, *The Giroux Reader*, ed. Christopher G. Robbins (Boulder: Paradigm Publishers, 2006).

23 Kathleen Gallagher and Philip Lortie, '"How Does Knowin' My Business Make You Any Safer?": Critical Pedagogy in Dangerous Times,' *Review of Education, Pedagogy, and Critical Studies* 27, no. 2 (2005): 141–58.

24 Peter McLaren, *Schooling as a Ritual Performance: Towards a Political Economy of Educational Symbols and Gestures* (London/Boston: Routledge & Kegan Paul, 1986).

25 Wayne Martino, 'Masculinities: The Implications and Uses of Foucauldian Analyses in Undertaking Ethnographic Investigations into Adolescent Boys' Lives at School,' in *Dangerous Encounters: Genealogy and Ethnography*, ed. Maria Tamboukou and Stephen Ball (New York: Peter Lang, 2002), 156.

26 Gunilla Halldén, '"To Be or Not to Be": Absurd and Humoristic Descriptions as a Strategy to Avoid Idyllic Life Stories–Boys Write about Family Life,' *Gender and Education* 11, no. 4 (1999): 469–79, quoting Mary-Jane Kehily and Anoop Nayak, 'Lads and Laughter: Humour and the Production of Heterosexual Hierarchies,' *Gender and Education* 9, no. 1 (1997).

27 Deborah Chambers, Estella Tincknell, and Joost Van Loon, 'Peer Regulations of Teenage Sexual Identities,' *Gender and Education* 16, no. 3 (2004): 411.

28 Robert W. Connell, *Gender and Power* (Cambridge: Polity Press, 1987).

29 Kenneth Clatterbaugh, 'What Is Problematic about Masculinities?' *Men and Masculinities* 1, no. 1 (1998): 24–45.

30 Fiona Leach, 'Learning to Be Violent: The Role of the School in Developing Adolescent Gendered Behaviour,' *Compare* 33, no. 3 (2003): 386.

31 Jennifer McCormick, '"Drag Me to the Asylum": Disguising and Asserting Identities in an Urban School,' *Urban Review* 35, no. 2 (2003): 111–28.

32 Louise Archer and Hiromi Yamashita, 'Theorizing Inner-city Masculinities: "Race," Class, Gender and Education,' in *Gender and Education* 15, no. 2 (2003): 122.

33 Archer and Yamashita, 'Theorizing,' 129.

34 Archer and Yamashita, 'Theorizing,' 129.

35 Rebecca P. Coulter, 'Boys Doing Good: Young Men and Gender Equity,' *Educational Review* 55, no. 2 (2003): 135–45; Wesley D. Imms, 'Multiple Masculinities and the Schooling of Boys,' *Canadian Journal of Education* 25, no. 2 (2000): 152–65.

36  Lesko, introduction to *Masculinities at School.*

37  Michael Peterson, *Straight White Male: Performance Art Monologues* (Jackson: University Press of Mississippi, 1997).

38  Chambers, Tincknell, and Van Loon, "Peer Regulations'; Victoria Foster, Michael Kimmel, and Christine Skelton, ' "What about the Boys?": An Overview of the Debates,' in *What about the Boys?: Issues of Masculinity in Schools,* ed. Wayne Martino and Bob Meyenn (Milton Keynes/Philadelphia: Open University Press, 2001); Michael Kimmel, *Gendered Society,* 2nd ed. (New York: Oxford University Press, 2004); Martino and Berrill, 'Boys, Schooling, and Masculinities.'

39  James Messerschmidt, 'Becoming "Real Men": Adolescent Masculinity Challenges and Sexual Violence,' *Men and Masculinities* 2, no. 3 (2000): 286–307.

40  Chambers, Tincknell, and Van Loon, 'Peer Regulations.'

41  Butler, *Gender Trouble,* 139.

42  Martino and Berrill, 'Boys, Schooling, and Masculinities,' 114.

43  Anoop Nayak, ' "Boyz to Men": Masculinities, Schooling and Labour Transitions in De-industrial Times,' *Educational Review* 55, no. 2 (2003): 147–59.

## 7. Dancing without a Floor

1  Gary Kinsman, *The Regulation of Desire, Homo and Hetero Sexualities* (Montreal: Black Rose Books, 1996); Tom Warner, *Never Going Back: A History of Queer Activism in Canada* (Toronto: University of Toronto Press, 2002).

2  Samuel A. Delany, *Times Square Red, Times Square Blue* (New York: New York University Press, 1999).

3  Thomas Hirschmann, 'The Munro Doctrine, the Art Fag,' *Now,* 26 June–2 July 2003: 37; Will Munro, in discussion with the author, Toronto, Ontario, 25 March 2003.

4  Julia Kristeva, *Powers of Horror: An Essay on Abjection* (New York: Columbia University Press, 1982).

5  Kristeva, *Powers of Horror,* 65.

6  Hirschmann, 'The Munro Doctrine.'

7  Mikhail Bakhtin, *Rabelais and His World,* trans. Helene Iswolsky (Bloomington: Indiana University Press, 1984).

8  Kristeva, *Powers of Horror.*

9  Munro, discussion, 28 January 2003.

10  Munro, discussion, 28 January 2003.

11 Munro, discussion, 28 January 2003.

12 Munro, discussion, 28 January 2003.

13 David Hart, 'Queer as Punk: An Interview with Scott Trevealen and Will Munro,' *Lesbian and Gay Archivist* 20 (Spring 2004): 8–9.

14 Hart, 'Queer as Punk,' 9.

15 Munro, discussion, 25 March 2003.

16 Munro, discussion, 25 March 2003.

17 Sarah Liss, 'The Munro Doctrine, the Shit Disturber,' *Now*, 26 June– 2 July 2003: 37–9; Munro, discussion, 10 September 2003.

18 Munro, discussion, 25 March 2003.

19 Munro, discussion, 28 January 2003.

20 Munro, discussion, 28 January 2003.

21 Michael Comeau, discussion, 18 January 2008.

22 Rene Ricard, 'The Radiant Child,' *Artforum* 20 (1981): 35–43.

23 David Bowman, *This Must Be the Place: The Adventures of Talking Heads in the 20th Century* (New York: HarperCollins, 2001); Bob Colacello, *Holy Terror: Andy Warhol Close Up* (New York: HarperPerennial, 1990); Jayne County, Performance, Shame Event, Vazaleen, Lee's Palace, Toronto, Ontario, 27 June 2003; Phoebe Hoban, *Basquait: A Quick Killing in Art* (New York: Penguin, 1998); Dee Dee Ramone, with V. Kofman, *Lobotomy: Surviving the Ramones* (New York: Thunder Mouth's Press, 2000); Ricard, 'The Radiant Child.'

24 Hoban, 'Basquait.'

25 Warner, *Never Going Back.*

26 John Grube, ' "No More Shit": The Struggle for Democratic Gay Space in Toronto,' in *Queers in Space, Communities, Public Places, Sites of Resistance,* ed. Gordon Brent Ingram, Anne-Marie Bouthillette, and Yolanda Rette (Seattle: Bay Press, 1997), 127–46.

27 Grube, ' No More Shit.'

28 Warner, *Never Going Back.*

29 Warner, *Never Going Back.*

30 Warner, *Never Going Back.*

31 Grube, 'No More Shit,' 145.

32 Delany, *Times Square Red.*

33 Mikhail Bakhtin, *Problems of Dostoyevsky's Poetics,* trans. and ed. Caryl Emerson (Minneapolis: University of Minnesota Press, 1984).

34 Benjamin Boles, 'The Munro Doctrine, the Party Animal,' *Now*, 26 June– 2 July 2003: 37; Bruce La Bruce, 'Bath Time in Berlin,' *Eye Weekly*, 22 May 2003): 18; Shannon Mitchell, 'Too Queer for Punks, Too Punk for Queers, Skinjobs Burn Rainbows,' *Trade, Queer Things* (Summer 2003): 21–3.

35  Hart, 'Queer as Punk.'
36  La Bruce, 'Bath Time in Berlin,' 18.
37  Munro, discussion, 28 January 2003.
38  Delany, *Times Square Red*, 111.
39  John Rajchman, *The Deleuze Connections* (Cambridge, MA: MIT Press, 2001).
40  Munro, cited in Liss, 'Shit Disturber.'
41  Liss, 'Shit Disturber.'
42  Rajchman, *Deleuze Connections*.
43  William Haver, 'Queer Research; or How to Practise Invention to the Brink of Intelligibility,' in *The Eight Technologies of Otherness*, ed. Sue Golding (New York: Routledge, 1997), 277–92.
44  Jayne County, performance, Vazaleen, Shame Event, 27 June 2003.
45  Jayne County, performance, 27 June 2003.
46  Jayne County, performance, 27 June 2003.
47  Gilles Deleuze and Felix Guattari, *Anti-Oedipus: Capitalism and Schizophrenia* (Minneapolis: University of Minneapolis Press, 2000).
48  Munro, discussion, 28 January 2003.
49  Deleuze and Guattari, *Anti-Oedipus*.
50  Michel Foucault, 'Truth and Power,' in *Power/Knowledge: Selected Interviews and Other Writings, 1972–1977*, ed. Colin Gordon (New York: Pantheon, 1980), 109–33; Ken Moffatt, *A Poetics of Social Work: Personal Agency and Social Transformation in Canada, 1920–1939* (Toronto: University of Toronto Press, 2001).
51  Haver, 'Queer Research,' 291.
52  Munro, discussion, 10 September 2003.
53  Ramone, *Lobotomy*.
54  Munro, discussion, 25 March 2003.
55  Moffatt, *Poetics of Social Work*.
56  Munro, discussion, 25 March 2003.
57  Munro, discussion, 25 March 2003.
58  Munro, discussion, 25 March 2003.
59  Bakhtin, *Rabelais*; Robert Stam, *Subversive Pleasures: Bakhtin, Cultural Criticism, and Film* (Baltimore: Johns Hopkins University Press, 1989).
60  Bakhtin, *Rabelais*, 7.
61  Zygmunt Bauman, *Liquid Modernity* (Cambridge: Polity Press, 2000); David Harvey, *Spaces of Hope* (Berkeley: University of California Press, 2000).
62  Bakhtin, *Rabelais*; Allan Irving and Ken Moffatt, 'Intoxicated Midnight and Carnival Classrooms: The Professor as Poet,' *Radical Pedagogy* 4, no. 1, http://radicalpedagogy.icaap.org/content/issue4_1/05_irving-moffatt.html.

63 John Rajchman, 'Unhappy Returns: The Po-Mo Decade,' *Artforum, 40th Anniversary Issue, the 1980s Part 2* (2003): 61–72.

64 Rajchman, 'Unhappy Returns'; Eve K. Sedgwick, 'Introduction,' in Eve K. Sedgwick, *Touching, Feeling, Affect, Pedagogy, Performativity* (Durham, NC: Duke University Press, 2003), 1–36.

65 Sedgwick, 'Introduction,' 8.

66 Sedgwick, 'Introduction.'

67 Sedgwick, 'Introduction.'

68 Munro, discussion, 28 January 2003.

69 R.M. Vaughan, 'Generation V,' *Toronto Life*, (September 2007): 33–41.

70 Michel Foucault, 'Friendship as a Way of Life,' in *Michel Foucault, Ethics, Subjectivity and Truth: The Essential Works of Foucault, 1954–1984, Volume 1*, ed. Paul Rabinow (New York: New Press, 1997), 135–40.

71 Michel Foucault, *The Order of Things: An Archaeology of the Human Sciences* (New York: Random House, 1973).

72 Bakhtin, *Problems of Dostoyevsky's Poetics*, 166.

73 Haver, 'Queer Research.'

74 Michael Bronski, *The Pleasure Principle: Sex Backlash, and the Struggle for Gay Freedom* (New York: St Martin's Press, 1998); Delany, *Times Square Red*; Kinsman, *Regulation of Desire*; Munro, discussion, 10 September 2003; Urvashi Vaid, *Virtual Equality, The Mainstreaming of Gay and Lesbian Liberation* (New York: Doubleday, 1995).

75 Haver, 'Queer Research,' 283.

76 Bakhtin, *Problems of Dostoyevsky's Poetics*, 166.

77 Haver, 'Queer Research.'

78 Julia Kristeva, *Revolt, She Said: An Interview by Philippe Petit*, trans. Brian O'Keefe, in *Semiotext(e)*, ed. Sylvère Lotringer (New York: Foreign Agents Series, 2002).

79 Munro, discussion, 28 January 2003.

80 Rajchman, 'Unhappy Returns.'

81 Kristeva, *Revolt, She Said*, 25.

82 Kristeva, *Revolt, She Said*, 42.

83 Kristeva, *Revolt, She Said*.

84 Munro, discussion, 25 March 2003.

85 Munro, discussion, 25 March 2003.

86 Kristeva, *Revolt, She Said*, 42.

87 Deleuze and Guattari, *Anti-Oedipus*.

88 Rajchman, 'Unhappy Returns,' 62.

89 Will Munro, 'Pride Terrorism,' *Fab*, 5 June 2003: 30–1.

90 Munro, 'Pride,' 31.

91 Munro, 'Pride.'
92 Munro, discussion, 28 January 2003.
93 Mitchell, 'Too Queer for Punks,'
94 Mitchell, 'Too Queer for Punks,' 23.
95 Bakhtin, *Rabelais*, 95.
96 Haver, 'Queer Research,' 282.
97 Munro, discussion, 28 January 2003.
98 Munro, discussion, 28 January 2003.

## 8. Boy to the Power of Three

1 Jill Dolan, 'The Discourse of Feminisms: The Spectator and Representation,' in *The Feminist Spectator as Critic*, ed. Jill Dolan (Ann Arbor: UMI Research Press, 1988), 1–18.
2 Kate Davy, 'Fe/Male Impersonation: The Discourse of Camp,' *Discourse* 11, no. 1 (Fall–Winter 1988–9): 55–73.
3 Sue Ellen Case, 'Toward a Butch-Femme Aesthetic,' in *The Lesbian and Gay Studies Reader*, ed. Henry Abelove, Michèle Aina Barale, and David M. Halperin (New York: Routledge, 1993).
4 Judith Butler, *Gender Trouble: Feminism and the Subversion of Identity* (New York: Routledge, Chapman & Hall, 1990), 123.
5 Homi Bhabha, 'Are You a Man or a Mouse?' in *Constructing Masculinity*, ed. Maurice Berger, Brian Wallis, and Simon Waterson (New York, Routledge, 1995), 116–23.
6 Andrew Parker and Eve Kosofsky Sedgwick, eds, *Performativity and Performance* (New York: Routledge, 1995), 1.
7 Kathleen Martindale, *The Making of an Un/popular Culture: From Lesbian Feminism to Lesbian Postmodernism* (New York: State University of New York Press, 1996), 32.
8 Martindale, *Making*, 30.
9 Davy, 'Fe/Male Impersonation,' 145.
10 Davy, 'Fe/Male Impersonation,' 145.
11 Jill Dolan, ' "Lesbian" Subjectivity in Realism: Dragging at the Margins of Structure and Ideology,' in *Performing Feminisms: Feminist Critical Theory and Theatre*, ed. Sue Ellen-Case (Baltimore: Johns Hopkins University Press, 1990), 42.
12 Dolan, 'Lesbian,' 49.
13 Dolan, 'The Discourse,' 116.
14 Case, 'Toward a Butch-Femme.'

15 Teresa De Lauretis, 'The Technology of Gender,' in *Technologies of Gender: Essays on Theory, Film and Fiction* (Bloomington: Indiana University Press, 1987), 26.

16 Case, 'Toward a Butch-Femme,' 305.

17 Robert Wallace, 'Performance Anxiety: "Identity," "Community," and Tim Miller's *My Queer Body*,' *Modern Drama* 39 (1996): 98.

18 Butler, *Gender Trouble*, 6.

19 Judith Butler, *Bodies That Matter: On the Discursive Limits of 'Sex'* (New York: Routledge, 1993), 15.

20 Butler, *Bodies That Matter*, 5.

21 Peggy Phelan, 'Reciting the Citation of Others; Or, A Second Introduction,' in *Acting Out: Feminist Performances*, ed. Lynda Hart and Peggy Phelan (Ann Arbor: University of Michigan Press, 1993), 19–22.

22 Christine Gledhill, *Stardom: Industry of Desire* (New York: Routledge, 1991), xiv.

23 Diana Fuss, *Identification Papers* (New York: Routledge, 1995), 146

24 Butler *Bodies That Matter*, 235.

25 Butler, *Bodies That Matter*, 231.

26 Eve Kosofsky Sedgwick, *Epistemology of the Closet* (Berkeley: University of California Press, 1990), 89.

27 Sedgwick, *Epistemology*, 89.

28 Elspeth Probyn, 'Lesbians in Space: Gender, Sex and the Structure of Missing,' *Gender, Place and Culture* 2, no. 1 (1995): 81.

29 Wallace, 'Performance Anxiety,' 102.

30 Lynda Hart, 'Identity and Seduction: Lesbians in the Mainstream,' in *Acting Out: Feminist Performances*, ed. Lynda Hart and Peggy Phelan (Ann Arbor: University of Michigan Press, 1993), 131.

31 Hart, 'Identity and Seduction,' 134; Judith Butler, ' Imitation and Gender Insubordination,' in *Inside/Out: Lesbian Theories, Gay Theories*, ed. Diana Fuss (New York: Routledge, 1991), 29.

32 Butler, *Bodies That Matter*, 233.

33 Names are a curious thing with drag kings. Many have at least two, their birth names and at least one character name. Given that drag kings are part of a queer community, not all drag kings are comfortable using their full legal names. For clarity, I will identify kings primarily through their character names, although I will often use full names if I have received permission to do that. Some names mark a character or persona performed by a king while others might mark a trans-identity taken on by the king and then, by extension, performed on stage. Character names, of course, are far more interesting, given the way in which irony is built into them. Some

names are spins on popular characters from Hollywood movies (for instance, Dirk Diggler is from the movie *Boogie Nights*; Man Murray references the Canadian singer Anne Murray) while others are ironic spins either on a birth name or character trait or popular identity. Names are an important feature of the performance long before a single king steps onto a stage. Moreover, many kings do identify as trans – but many do not, identifying as butch, queer, gay, or, in some cases, femme or feminine.

34 Judith Halberstam, *Female Masculinity* (Durham, NC: Duke University Press, 1998), 260.
35 Sedgwick, *Epistemology*, 89.
36 Barbara Johnson, *A World of Difference* (Baltimore: Johns Hopkins University Press, 1987), 16.
37 Stuart Hall, 'For Allon White: Metaphors of Transformation,' In *Stuart Hall: Critical Dialogues in Cultural Studies,* ed. David Morley and Kuan Hsing Chen (London: Routledge, 1996), 143.
38 Mikhail Bakhtin, *The Dialogic Imagination* (London: University of Texas Press), 91.
39 Ann Cvetkovich, *An Archive of Feelings: Trauma, Sexuality and Lesbian Public Cultures* (Durham, NC: Duke University Press, 2003).
40 Cvetkovich, *Archive*, 8.
41 Cvetkovich, *Archive*, 7–8.
42 Cvetkovich, *Archive*, 18.
43 Cvetkovich, *Archive*, 20.
44 Phelan, 'Reciting the Citation of Others.'

**9. Eyes of Excess**

1 Friedrich Nietzsche, *Ecce Homo*, trans. Walter Kaufmann (New York: Vintage Books, 1969), 223.
2 Samuel Beckett, *The Complete Short Prose: 1929–1989*, ed. S.E Gontarski (New York: Grove Press, 1995).
3 Beckett, *Complete Short Prose.*
4 Friedrich Nietzsche, *Thus Spoke Zarathustra*, trans. R.J. Hollingdale (Baltimore: Penguin Books, 1961), 144, 177.
5 Franz Kafka, *The Castle*, trans. Willa Muir and Edwin Muir (New York: Alfred A. Knopf, 1965), 272, 198.
6 Heinz Politzer, *Franz Kafka: Parable and Paradox* (Ithaca: Cornell University Press, 1962), 280.
7 http://www.crossdresserheaven.com

8  Andrew Hussey, ed., *The Beast at Heaven's Gate: Georges Bataille and the Art of Transgression* (New York: Rodopi, 2006), 83.

9  Michel Foucault, *Language, Counter-Memory, Practice*, ed. Donald Bouchard (Ithaca: Cornell University Press, 1977), 185.

10  Foucault, *Language*, 45.

11  Gilles Deleuze, *Francis Bacon: The Logic of Sensation* (Minneapolis: University of Minnesota Press, 2002).

12  Kay Redfield Jamison, *Touched with Fire: Manic-Depressive Illness and the Artistic Temperament* (New York: Simon and Schuster, 1993), 132.

13  Michael Ondaatje, *Divisadero* (New York: Alfred A. Knopf, 2007), 136.

14  Robert Lowell, *Collected Poems*, ed. Frank Bidart and David Gewanter (New York: Farrar, Straus and Giroux, 2003), 191–2.

15  Allan Irving, *Queen's Quarterly* 101, no. 2 (Summer 1994): 507.

16  Friedrich Nietzsche, *Human, All Too Human*, trans. Helen Zimmern (New York: Russell & Russell, 1964), 295.

17  Lord Byron, *The Poetical Works of Lord Byron* (London: Oxford University Press, 1926), 356.

18  Northrop Frye, *The Diaries of Northrop Frye, 1942–1955*, ed. Robert D. Denham (Toronto: University of Toronto Press, 2001), 355.

19  Northrop Frye, *Words with Power: Being a Second Study of the Bible and Literature* (San Diego: Harcourt Brace Jovanovich, 1990), 296, 301.

20  Irving, *Queen's Quarterly*: 506.

21  Henri Cole, *The Visible Man* (New York: Alfred A. Knopf, 1998), 48.

22  George Whalley, *The Legend of John Hornby* (Toronto: Macmillan of Canada, 1962), 3, 4, 131.

23  Robert Scanlan, 'Indeflectible Courtesy,' in *Beckett Remembering, Remembering Beckett*, ed. James and Elizabeth Knowlson (New York: Arcade Publishing, 2006), 295, 299.